Morning and Noon is Dean Acheson's warm, modest, and charming account of his youth and early career.

Born in Middletown, Connecticut, in 1893, the future Secretary of State grew up in a golden time and a golden place. With grace and humor he brings back to us the American Age of Innocence in a New England country town: the sound of horses' hoofs on shaded streets; the roaring forge in the blacksmith's shop where men talk freely and listening boys learn much; the quiet of a New England Sunday morning under the elms. In this setting childhood meant something that lasted all a man's life. That meaning is seldom so nostalgically captured as it is in these pages.

After college and the Law School, Dean Acheson, as Law Clerk to Justice Brandeis, lived in the midst of great affairs in Washington. Yet the capital in the twenties still had much of the charm of a small town where "everyone" knows everyone else. His new job threw young Acheson into close association with the Justices of the Supreme Court — that "Old Court" whose members, differing radically in temperament, learning, and political views, were nonetheless men of stature and dignity. Strong convictions led

continued on back flap

Acheson rejoined the administration as Assistant Secretary of State. It is here that the present story ends. It is not carried on through the author's most famous years, for, as he points out, "As involvement and responsibility grew, as the criticism for the outcome of events began to focus upon oneself, detachment and objectivity became suspect. The element of self-justification could not be excluded." What we have is the very personal story of the formation of a man.

MORNING AND NOON

MORNING
and NOON

DEAN ACHESON

ILLUSTRATED WITH PHOTOGRAPHS

HOUGHTON MIFFLIN COMPANY BOSTON

The Riverside Press Cambridge

1965

Chapter 1 was published in part in the December 15, 1962, issue of the *Saturday Evening Post.* © 1962 by The Curtis Publishing Company.

The quotations in Chapter 2 from the Adams-Jefferson letters are from *Correspondence of John Adams and Thomas Jefferson, 1812–1826,* edited by Paul Wilstach. Copyright 1925 by The Bobbs-Merrill Company. Copyright renewed 1953 by Arthur Hellen. Reprinted by permission of the publishers.

Portions of Chapter 8 are from an article first published in *Esquire* Magazine for July 1961. © 1961 by Esquire, Inc.

The remarks made at the funeral services for Mr. Justice Brandeis were first published by the *Harvard Law Review.* Copyright 1941 by The Harvard Law Review Association.

The quotations from Alexander M. Bickel, *The Unpublished Opinions of Mr. Justice Brandeis,* published by The Belknap Press of Harvard University Press, are copyright © 1957 by the President and Fellows of Harvard College.

The passages from the *New York Times* quoted in Chapters 8 and 9 are reprinted by permission. © 1933 by The New York Times Company.

The quotations in Chapter 9 from Vol. II of *The Public Papers and Addresses of Franklin D. Roosevelt,* compiled by Samuel I. Rosenman, are quoted by permission of Random House, Inc. Copyright 1938 by Franklin Delano Roosevelt.

E
7 4 8
. A 15
A 3

First Printing w

To FF

Can two walk together,
except they be agreed?

Amos 3:3

ACKNOWLEDGMENTS

I WISH TO ACKNOWLEDGE with gratitude the permission to use in this book the material which has previously appeared in the *Saturday Evening Post, Esquire* Magazine, *Harvard Law Review, The Sun* of Baltimore, and the *Groton School Quarterly*.

Words are quite inadequate to express my indebtedness and gratitude to Miss Barbara Evans, my collaborator and editor in now the fifth book we have lived through together. In the words of the spiritual, nobody knows the trouble she's seen, and, more than that, the improvements she has wrought.

CONTENTS

INTRODUCTION

A MUTUAL FRIEND quotes Thornton Wilder as insisting that preferably before beginning, but certainly before finishing, a book the writer should ask himself, "Why am I writing this book?" If he is uncertain about the answer, the reader is likely to be confused about the book, about the sort of a book it is. The first answer to this question which popped into my mind was not helpful — that writing gives me pleasure, a sort of masochistic pleasure, to be sure, achieved each day by subduing a healthy disinclination to get to work. Writing is hard; pleasant, but hard. I have been used to hard work for a good part of my life. There seemed to be no alternative. But the alternative to writing a book is very clear. It is not writing a book; and either doing nothing or something easier. Upon reflection the mild pleasure in besting the old Adam appeared to be a by-product, not an explanatory reason.

The explanatory reason has to do with pleasure also, but of a different sort. Parts of my life were lived in times, amid surroundings, and with people which and who have completely vanished, leaving no trace — at least, no trace that can bring to those who never knew those times, those surroundings, those people living pictures of them. To see this whole ensemble alive, if only briefly, is to become aware of our past, or part of it. And out of our past we come, with our hopes, our fears, our beliefs, our limitations. A good many of the people who appear in this book may seem, at first, mere shadows cast by a name. I have tried to make them live as parts of the vanished time in which they were once so much alive. Some of the people will bear familiar names; but time and biography will have made them mythical characters, figures modeled out of virtues or faults. I have tried to bring back something of the living persons who once inhabited these shadows, to help us see their times as they saw them, breathe the air they breathed, share their passions, their hopes, their follies, their disappointments.

This book is autobiographical, but not an autobiography. My life is the thread on which are strung beads of experience, each of which — to be sure — contains some part of me. But their significance to others does not come from this. To them I am the reporter who has wormed his way into the very heart of these events. So it will not be surprising, I hope, that there are gaps in my own life story, which is only indirectly the story of this book. Some parts of my experience, pleasant enough, had little interest for me when they occurred, or since. Some of it was unpleasant at the time and equally so to recall. Still other parts were too personal to share. These I have passed by, centering on those portions of the thread which carry revealing beads of the past.

Why, I have been asked, do I stop when I do? Why just the experiences of Morning and Noon? Why not go on to Afternoon, the time of larger events? Duff Cooper wrote that he counted life by decades. "The first covers childhood, the second boyhood, the third youth. Then for thirty years a man is middle-aged, until he hears the clock strike sixty and knows that old age has begun." Why stop with the experiences of the middle of middle age?

The answer, at least for me, is that about at this time occurred a sea change in my relations to events happening around me. Up to this time involvement gave the zest of participation, but left enough detachment for objective observation, report, and cogitation. But by forty the balance began to shift and the relationship to change. As involvement and responsibility grew, as the criticism for the outcome of events began to focus upon oneself, detachment and objectivity became suspect. The element of self-justification could not be excluded. One must watch one's words. They were likely to become, in lawyers' jargon, part of the *res gestae*, essential circumstances surrounding the subject.

General George C. Marshall felt this deeply and often observed that to act and to record required wholly different gifts, abilities, and disciplines. The attempt to do both is apt to produce a confusion of roles which only exceptional performers in both can resolve. Sir Winston Churchill comes to mind. The failures in this attempt who over the years have amused me most have been the writers of memoranda of conversation. Never yet have I seen a writer of one of these appear to disadvantage. These memoranda always contain the crushing riposte which one wishes, after the conversation, one had thought of.

So I have stopped this book before the confusion of roles became too great.

Finally, I have kept in mind, in writing, the exasperated question of a perceptive young lady. "What is the use of a book," thought Alice, "without pictures or conversation?"

MORNING AND NOON

I

THE RADIANT MORN

THE GOLDEN AGE of childhood can be quite accurately fixed in time and place. It reached its apex in the last decade of the nineteenth century and the first few years of the twentieth, before the plunge into a motor age and city life swept away the freedom of children and dogs, put them both on leashes and made them the organized prisoners of an adult world. As for the Athens of this golden age, it lay, of course, in the Connecticut Valley, just where the river leaves white fields of shade-grown tobacco, and enters the gorge channeling it past Haddam and Hadlyme, to broaden again at Essex, before its journey's end in the Sound. Here a town, in the exact center of the state and appropriately called Middletown, once the head of navigation on the Connecticut and an entrepôt for trade to the northern frontier, flowered briefly when clipper ships dropped anchor there, home round the Horn from China. This boom left imposing houses on High Street at the top of the hill, with its four rows of great elms. Now Wesleyan University owns them all; but in the golden age the last of the barons still lived there —the Russells, the Hubbards, the Alsops, Governor Weeks, Mr. Richard De Zeng with his gray derby, who put a plate-glass window between his horse and cow to permit companionship.

In the eighteen-nineties Middletown was a market town with a few small factories — textile, silver, marine hardware, and some years later, a venture which soon failed, the Eisenhuth

Horseless Vehicle Company. Nothing presented a visible hazard to children. No one was run over. No one was kidnaped. No one had teeth straightened. No one worried about children, except occasionally my mother, when she saw us riding on the back step of the ice wagon and believed, fleetingly, that one of the great blocks of Pamecha Pond ice would fall on us. But none ever did. Unharmed, in hot weather we sucked gallons of ice chips from what was doubtless polluted ice.

We lived near the bottom of the hill in the rectory on Broad Street arched by elms. Farther down ran Main Street, on which the church faced, and then Water Street with the railroad, the docks, warehouses, and the river. Main Street — wide, treeless, dusty, trolley-car tracks down the center, on either side low shop-fronted buildings, and wide sidewalks edged with iron pipe running through stout posts, to which every sort of carriage, wagon, and dray was hitched — teemed with life. Down its dusty length came parades: the circus heralded by distant tooting of a steam calliope; the Civil War Veterans with blue frockcoats and wide blue felt hats, often escorted by the Governor's Foot Guards and band from Hartford in colonial uniforms; Masonic parades; religious parades; Fourth of July parades with floats; visiting fire department parades; and sometimes from Water Street one could see river parades with a fireboat from New London making a moving cascade. Then, too, Main Street was the place for unscheduled but expectable events of great dramatic content — the runaway team, a resisting drunk being put into the police wagon, a prisoner being taken out of it in front of the Court House, an occasional fistfight.

Each fair morning in the summer brought its opportunity to observe life on Main Street. The walk with my father to the Post Office, unless forfeited by misdemeanor or rain, led down the boardwalk behind the house, past the church, and along Main Street to the old brownstone building. The second store from the driveway by the church was Mr. Walsh's harness store. He would be in the doorway, Jove-like with his gray beard covering the top of his working apron, standing beside the great wooden horse which, over the years, became identified in my mind with the one Ulysses made.

There would begin a review of the state of man. Customers and passersby would join in. Every subject was taken to pieces, sometimes put together again, and sometimes just left lying around. Wars, politics, the Irish question, the tariff, Queen Victoria's Diamond Jubilee, and the sad propensity of mankind for strong liquors. Everyone had opinions on nearly every subject. To stand there and listen would be dull and end in aching legs. To pull at my father's coat would involve hazards not to be lightly risked. The solution was to sit on the platform of the wooden horse and absorb the kaleidoscopic life of Main Street.

But the center of the golden age was just short of Main Street Between the back of the church and adjoining Divinity School on one side, and three houses, of which ours was one, on the other, stretched an open field of perhaps three acres; an Elysian Field where heroes met for converse, council, and the games of heroes. Most of the battles of the Boer and Spanish-American wars were fought here. TR's Rough Riders, dismounted for the purpose since our pony had no martial spirit, stormed San Juan Hill, the terrace rising from the field to where our washing was hung out, only to be repulsed with heavy loss by an infuriated laundress. And many a beleaguered fort in the apple trees along our side of the field was saved from howling Indians below by the arrival of the U.S. cavalry led by Buffalo Bill.

On the other side of the field adventure lurked in another form. Here Dr. Watrous, our neighbor and courtly dentist — who for years, with his trim white mustache and pince-nez on a black cord, seemed to me as mysterious and faintly sinister a worldling as Cardinal Richelieu in *The Three Musketeers* — had a large, round bed of luxuriant canna plants. These had unexpected potentialities. For one thing, like a magnet they pulled every ball thrown or kicked on the field straight for the center of the bed. Then, again, the cannas became a jungle in which hostile natives lay in ambush for unsuspecting explorers on safari. But a second ambush awaited the ambushers or the fielder racing for the high fly. The Doctor's cook, armed with broom and possessed of astonishing speed in a sprint, peered through the cellar door. Once her prey entered the jungle, she shot out on a course laid to cut him off from home. Warning shouts gave a chance, but no more; decoys could go in but at a risk. For her the prize, of course, was a ball confiscated, but a broom thump on a fleeing backside gave sound satisfaction, too. The last thing desired was to stop the fun; so when her collection of balls became too great, some were cautiously returned to circulation. Deflation had gone too far.

On the south side of the Elysian Field a row of apple trees roofed the boardwalk from the house to the church, brushing the brick wall of the Judge's stable. Its small, wooden-shuttered windows stood open in the summer, offering a temptation, sometimes too great for resistance, to feed the horses inside the green apples outside. The Judge, a silent and ominous man, took an unsympathetic view of this practice and had some disconcerting and apparently infallible method of knowing when it had occurred, and his representations to the highest quarters had unpleasant consequences in the lowest.

The rough justice of this was plain even to partisans. After all, the horses were the Judge's and the pleasure of feeding them green apples was minor and ephemeral. But his opposition to another practice had no such justification. Fortunately, it was less effective. The game of "cops and robbers" required not only that the "robbers" should get a good start on their pursuers, but that its direction should be unknown. Hence the importance of fast disappearance; and hence, also, the importance of the route via the apple trees to the stable roof down to the carriage yard and into the maze of backyards and alleys where the "cops" would flounder endlessly. The Judge set his face as strongly against this overhead route as a slaveowner against the underground before the Civil War. The hired man was set to enforce the prohibition of its use. But his heart was not in it. The race went usually to the swift, and identification was hard. His shouts, to be sure, gave away the direction of flight, but his presence inhibited direct pursuit. Opinion was pretty well united against the Judge in this controversy. "Cops" and "robbers" were as one; and even our parents, who often had a subversive weakness for an enemy point of view, paid only lip service to his. This time it was not his horses but we climbers who ran the risks.

A prime source of bliss was a livery stable equipped with a blacksmith's shop, on the north side of the field and opening onto Washington Street. There lived the family horse and our pony. At least, the pony slept there. His headquarters on summer days were under our veranda, a latticed and spacious enough place for small creatures. There, too, were his harness and express wagon, which served as fire engine with the addition of the garden hose and reel, and as stagecoach when made precariously topheavy by a sizable packing box. The wagon was infinitely better adapted to these roles than the pony, who never wanted to do anything thought of by anyone else. Mean, as well as lazy, and uncooperative, he knew who was afraid and who would fight back. The timid did well to feed him sugar on a tennis racquet; but he was as gentle as a lamb if one had one's fist cocked for a fast punch in the nose. And what a master he was of the painful nip in the back of an incautious handler! My mother maintained that he would respond to love; but she was wrong about this. He was absorbed solely in his own grand design of how to live in idleness.

Worthless as he was, the pony was our passport to the livery stable; and, strangely enough, my mother, who rarely made trouble for anyone, was the chief opponent of our going there. The men's talk, she said, was not nice. Here she was quite right; but, with so much to see, one could not be bothered to listen. So we went and said nothing about it.

The blacksmith's shop held first place. Around the bright, wide entrance horses waited their turn, stamping and whisking flies lazily. In the dim and smoky interior the current customer stood rump to the light. Beyond him were the raised coal fire with overhanging hood, the bellows, which one would sometimes be allowed to pump, driving the dull fire into incandescence, and horseshoes of every size ranged on rods projecting from the wall. Against this Rembrandt background, the glow from the fire picked out the blacksmith's streaked face, arms, and undershirt, and the tawny richness of his leather apron.

We knew every step in the ritual. Off came the old shoe with a quick wrench from curved, long-handled pliers. Then a wicked knife trimmed the hoof. We shivered, but the horse seemed asleep. A shoe was selected, tried for size, and thrust with tongs into the fierce fire, followed by a squirt of tobacco juice. Time now for pause and banter with men leaning and squatting around the entrance. This doubtless was the talk my mother had in mind. But we were mesmerized by the horseshoe as it turned from black to brightest scarlet. The climax approached. Out came the shoe sparkling and incandescent. With a few preliminary taps on the anvil, like an orchestra tuning up, the blacksmith began a crescendo of hammer blows, turning the shoe from one side to the other and on edge. Sparks flew against the apron and around the shop; the noise was very satisfying. Then he shaped a prow on the front of the shoe to keep it from being knocked off by a stumble, opened the nail holes, heated it again and put it with a sizzle and acrid smell against the hoof to make a perfect fit. Finally came a hissing plunge into the water barrel and the almost anticlimactic nailing and clinching on.

The stable housed far more rats than horses, and colonies grew up in all the neighboring houses, not least in ours. Protests mounted; so much so that, after the historic night when the stable burned, it was never rebuilt. But before that, the war on the rats mounted, with the blacksmith in the middle of it. The stable and surrounding houses set good-sized wire traps, built on the principle of a lobster pot. Once the traps were full, the scene shifted to the stable yard, where the blacksmith shook the rats out one by one for his terrier, almost mad with excitement. The rat reached the ground running; but the terrier had him within a yard, gave one lightning shake, and was back crouching and barking under the trap. Doubtless this was all very bad and little better than bear-baiting, although no one seemed to think so, and we were never forbidden to attend these Roman holidays.

Those whose memories go back to the golden age speak of the "old" rectory and the "new" rectory. The old one was torn down a few years after the turn of the century; and the new one wasn't finished until the eve of my long exile to school and beyond, forever. Built just too late to have any architectural merit, the old rectory antedated the era of comfort. The architect's idea — if there had been either architect or idea — appeared to have been to exclude light. Colored or frosted glass lent itself well to this purpose. In the cellar not only had light been almost wholly excluded, which apparently the rats liked, but water had not been excluded at all, which the rats apparently did not like. In our periodic states of flood, hip-booted men continually waded in the cellar trying to stop water coming in or induce it to go out, and creating the atmosphere of a sinking ship which the rats were leaving by coming upstairs. My mother after ten years in the old house moved out of it into a rented one, telling the astonished vestry that they had the choice of a new rectory or a new rector.

One ceremony went out of my life when we left the old rectory — the nightly lighting of the gas lights, performed by Maggie as celebrant, with me as her acolyte. She carried a small stepladder for the high hall lights and an instrument which has followed the bed warmer into extinction. A wooden handle, a yard or so long, had along its side, and curving away from it toward the end, a slotted tube to hold a wax taper, and at its end a brass socket for turning the valve handles of the gas fixtures. Each evening at dusk the little procession made its tour with lighted taper, leaving a trail of light behind it.

Within the rectory the foreign element topped the American two to one; in influence, the disparity was far greater. My sister and I were by constitutional right citizens of the United States, while the other five were subjects of the Queen-Empress, Victoria, Defender of the Faith, though Cazzie, the cook, and her niece Maggie, the maid, would have hotly denied allegiance to either Queen or Faith. They were Irish, direct from the Auld Sod, and their opinion of the British was unfavorable.

To say that Cazzie was the cook would be putting it the wrong way around. Cazzie did the cooking, but she was herself, a powerful and endearing self. Mrs. Jane Corell was her proper name, a widow, with two boys about our age who were often around the kitchen or playing with us. Cazzie was ample, articulate, affectionate, and quick-tempered. She also suffered from "nerves." "Nervous?" she replied to a solicitous inquiry of my mother's. "I'm that nervous I could jump up on them swill barrels and scream."

The descriptive word for Maggie was one much in use then, "green," just out from Ireland. My mother used to tell of a dinner to which she had invited some of the town notables. It progressed well enough until dessert failed to appear. Much ringing of the hand bell produced a distraught Maggie, who announced, "Please, mum, the puddin' has fell on Aunt Jane." From our point of view Maggie was perfect. Infinitely good-natured, she could easily be distracted from putting out our light and induced to go on reading. In this way we got to know many unique words. Any word of more than two syllables Maggie took with imaginative rush. The result was quite unlikely to resemble the text, which, if it was not one we knew by heart, did not bother us. We simply learned a new and quite unusual word, with which even our elders were unfamiliar.

"Himself," as Cazzie called my father, was the son of an Ulster-born, Scotch-Irish, professional British soldier, who had served in the Crimea, and a south-Irish mother from Cork, descendant of English settlers brought there by Henry II to live "within the pale." Coming to Canada in his teens after his mother's death and his father's second marriage, he put himself through school and the University of Toronto, at first by working and sleeping in a millinery warehouse. During his university years, the Queen's Own Rifles, a militia regiment to which he belonged, was sent to Saskatchewan with the force raised to subdue an Indian uprising in 1885, under one Louis Riel, subsequently hanged. At Cut Knife Creek the Indians surprised the Queen's Own in a sharp engagement. My father became a national hero overnight by being "mentioned in dispatches" for rescuing a wounded comrade under fire. Not unnaturally, then, the dominant influence in the rectory was a British subject with deep affection for Ireland, where he had spent long periods with his mother's people.

My mother's loyalties were clear, too. Her grandfather, a prosperous miller of Norfolk, England, with a strong urge to adventure, had, in 1832, brought out his family and relatives, fifty-four strong, to Upper Canada and settled in Toronto. There on the shore of Lake Ontario they built the "Old Mill," a famous landmark with its great sail arms, milling the grain from the new lands then being opened, and developing a profitable sideline from the waste, in the form of Canadian whisky. A bank and real estate investments raised the family's social position. One of my mother's brothers became Mayor of Toronto;

another took the Queen's Own, of which he became colonel, to the coronation of King George V, and returned a knight. My mother's enthusiasm for the Empire and the Monarch was not diluted by any corrupting contact with Canadian nationalism. On the contrary, it was renewed from the very headwaters when she went to boarding school in England.

Miss Wilson, her headmistress, became a major influence and lifelong friend. Nearly fifty years later my mother brought this elderly lady, on her only visit to our wild country, to see us in Washington. We suggested a visit to Mount Vernon, to which our guest demurred on the ground that she did not think a log cabin would be interesting. Explanations failed to convince her, but politeness led her to agree. Her surprise was immense, but most impressive of all to her were the gifts which the Father of Our Country received from the monarchs of Europe. On the way back to Washington she was silent for a long time, and then said to my mother, "Ella, what I can't understand is how a gentleman of that quality could have risen up against his king." Mother was a monarchist of the same stripe. Later on, both she and my father became American citizens, and, while the old allegiance was sincerely renounced, old affections were not.

The seventh dweller in the rectory held a place in our lives unique and important. Her name was Sin, short for gay, petite, rattlebrained, endlessly kind and good-natured, Marie Sinclair, a Toronto girlhood friend of my mother, whose family had met reverses which were not discussed. After my sister and I were born, our mother's health was not good, and we were soon quite too much for her. My father at a very early date took the view that his jurisdiction was limited. He would read to us, teach us verse, occasionally discipline us (on reference from lower authority), but there he stopped.

Then it was that Sin came to live with us, a friend to my mother, executive officer of the house, elder sister to us, and

English nanny rolled into one. A small, delicate creature, she always hurried along with staccato and slightly tremulous walk, as though shaken by the intensity of her own energy. Her Canadian-English inflection was an endless source of amusement to our contemporaries; our speech she simply deplored. Sin was our beloved companion, the sharer of our sorrows and our hopes, who would play with us, read to us, comfort us when we got into trouble with headquarters, but who could never get us to go to bed without Cazzie's threats to lay us across her knee. Perhaps she came to us as a stopgap, or in the hope of finding a husband where her family's troubles would not be a handicap. She had plenty of friends and admirers, but the years went by without matrimony, and, when we went off to school, she joined her brother in Montreal and became a librarian. Sin, too, was a loyal British subject.

To the American minority in the rectory in those days, nationality was not a divisive notion. Our country, of course, was the best. But England, as my mother and Sin described it, and Canada, where sometimes we went for Christmas, were very good, too. And the Ireland, half idyl and half myth, of Cazzie's tales, was so entrancing that no wonder she always cried over having left it.

In the course of the year we joyfully celebrated each national festival. Cazzie's came first on the seventeenth of March. My father hung on the flagpole over our front door a great green flag with a golden harp on it, and all the local Irishmen would go by the house to take off their hats to it. My sister and I stood on the front steps and shouted, *"Erin go bragh!"* which was well received. Whatever our hearers thought it meant, it was to us the end of an incantation which we had to recite in unison before my father would produce from behind his back presents which he had brought us from some journey. The whole mystic utterance (as delivered) went: *"E pluribus unum! Sic semper McGuiness! Erin go bragh!* Whoop!" The "Whoop!" produced the presents. At dinner on St. Patrick's Day we had green ice cream and green peppermint shamrocks.

The Queen's birthday, the twenty-fourth of May, was a very quiet affair. The Union Jack flew from the flagpole, and at dinner we were given a few drops of diluted claret, with which we stood solemnly while my father said, "The Queen," at which we all said, "The Queen," too, and drank our claret, which was not very good.

This innocent and eclectic enjoyment of nationalism was shattered by the Boer War. We should have been forewarned by dissent in the kitchen that our warm espousal of the British cause was heading us for trouble. But we had had no experience of public disapproval, the loneliness of a small minority, or how fierce nationalism could be when aroused. Middletown was solidly pro-Boer, not with the detached choosing up of sides as in our games, but with the attribution of moral opprobrium to our admirations. Our Tommies, Kipling's "absent-minded beggars" ordered South, so appealing in the *Illustrated London News*, so gallant besieged in Ladysmith, were to our erstwhile friends bullies bent on crushing the sacred flame of liberty, as in Ireland, and starving women and children in "concentration" camps. In our reenactment of the battles, the British always lost — as, indeed, they did in South Africa — but from failure of recruits, and Ladysmith, despite historic fact, was never relieved.

Only Christmas rivaled the Fourth of July on our calendars, a day by which preceding days were numbered ("Only two more days before the Fourth," etc.), a fitting climax to weeks of purchases, comparisons, and harassments of parents ("Why can't I have cannon crackers? I'm older'n Joe, and he can," etc.). Dawn came early in July, and everyone took oath that first-up would fire salutes under the windows of sleeping friends. Broad Street was soon an embattled front, steady artillery fire interspersed with machine-gun fire — the word then was Gatling gun, out of Kipling — as one of us, with reckless extravagance, put off a whole package of firecrackers at once.

At noon, brief peace and sanity returned, as my father performed his one child-chore of the year, and a noble one it was. The eight children of our block on Broad Street climbed into an express wagon, with the rest of their explosive equipment and a picnic lunch, to be carried off by him to a pond on the edge of town, too muddy and choked for bathing and appropriately called by us "Polliwog Pool." It lent itself, however, to such absorbing spectacles as blowing up the battleship *Maine*, an ancient toy boat wound up and started across the pond with a lethal cargo of a cannon cracker. At lunch my father told Indian stories, of which he was a master. Finally, tired, hot, and replete we jogged home ready to review the parade from the church steps, and, after bath, bread, jam, and milk, and the briefest pinwheels and Roman candles — bed.

The Fourth lacked only one joy. It was not Bob's day. With the first firecracker he retired to the farthest corner under the veranda. No inducement would coax him out. This was distressing, since he was my closest companion of these years; in fact, had been brought into our lives to perform just this role. At the time a contagious child's disease had me quarantined. When the prisoner was most sorry for himself, my father came upon a litter of collie puppies tumbling about in a hardware-store window, and had one of his best (as they affected me) ideas. Thereafter Bob and I were never separated, not even in bed, until education, for much of the year, put asunder those whom surely God had joined together.

Bob, named for the famous Son of Battle, belonged to the pre-Albert-Payson-Terhune species of collie. Indeed his ancestry was not above suspicion. His strong points were character and an inexhaustible capacity for love. "Bob," my father used to say, "is a gentleman." Undoubtedly a sorcerer had changed him from human into canine form; for, while enjoying fetching balls or tug-of-war, conducted with great vigor and fierce growls, his main interests were ours. No dog food for him; he wanted our food; and our plan for the day was his also. He had no peer as a snow-house builder. One needed only a pile of snow, say from a slide off the church roof or a path shoveled through a drift, and Bob. When the spot chosen for the door was shown and the magic word "dig" uttered, he was out of sight in no time, with snow flying out behind him. Then too, he was adjustable, digging on his side or back for wall and ceiling work. But his moments of ecstatic joy were brought on by preparations for an expedition. He would jump, bark, dash from house to pony cart, get in everyone's way, and, finally, when threatened with being left behind, would lie panting by the pony, tensely waiting.

The usual expedition was to spend a night in the hills west of the town, where little valleys ran parallel to the main rise of ground, each with its clear stream and a cave or more in its steep sides. The wagon train which hit this Oregon Trail contained two or three pony carts to carry the gear and a dozen boys, some on ponies, some on bicycles, with Bob in the lead. As soon as streets ended and the open road wound uphill, Bob covered three times the distance we did, always at his tireless canter, investigating everything for a quarter of a mile on either side of the road, flushing birds, chasing anything that ran except chickens, walking stiff-legged and bristling up to dogs who did not. Occasionally, some of the outriders pushed ahead to set an ambush. Then Bob had to be tied in the pony cart much against his will, or taken with the ambushers and held. Otherwise he gave the show away every time.

The moment one knew Bob's true worth came later on when, with food cooked and eaten, a few final games over, and talk exhausted, we crawled between blankets on the hard cave floor. Whispering died away; the fire at the cave mouth sank, consumed by the blackness beyond. An owl hooted; something rustled in the bushes. Then with Bob beside one, under the same blanket, firmly locked by an arm, one could doze off in dreamless security.

For a month in the summer the whole family went farther afield — first to the Montowese House at Indian Neck on the Sound near Branford. Preparations for this expedition, a twenty-five-mile, all-day affair, rivaled those of the Children of Israel getting ready to leave Egypt, and nearly drove Bob crazy. Trunks, bags, and impedimenta went off in a two-horse express wagon the day before we did. Bob had to be forcibly restrained from accompanying it. Early next morning the pony cart, with Bob and my next-door friend as company for me, was given a two-hour start. My sister went with the family and the lunch, since we were not trusted to spend a whole day together in amity; and, furthermore, every form of conveyance after the baby carriage made her carsick. We had a rendezvous about halfway for lunch and inspection. Twenty-five miles was nothing to Bob, but the pony and his passengers had had enough by the end of that day.

The memory of those seaside visits has dimmed to an eventless repetition of putting our bathing suits on and off in dark little cupboards built above high tide, below the bluff, hours playing on the beach with an occasional coerced dip in the Sound, and meals in the large dining room, where Sin with her unimaginative ideas of a diet suitable for the young vetoed more venturesome exploration of the hotel menu.

Except for the journey itself, the seaside was for us a tame affair. One event only stands out; for a time it seemed to threaten disaster. Bob started to follow us to a children's party up the row of cottages and was told peremptorily to "go home." As usual he watched for a few minutes with infinite sadness, then turned back. But on our return he was not at the hotel, nor at bedtime, nor in the morning. Tears and wails of self-reproach were stopped only by a message from Middletown that evening that Bob was on the doorstep, safe but hungry. Joy reigned when the lost sheep was regained, but we minded our words and manners more carefully.

There was nothing tame, however, about summers that followed at Round Mountain Lake. They began with the ecstasy
of lying in one's berth on the night train, the rhythm of the
clicking wheels beneath, the window curtain raised a cautious
inch on the kaleidoscope of dark shapes outside punctuated by
a flash of platform lights, the shiver at the lonely, lost-soul wail
of the engine ahead. Can an airplane, with pretty stewardesses
checking seat belts, or the family station wagon, spinning off
the miles on crowded turnpikes, bring to any child nowadays
the mystery of migration from one world into another — a
migration accomplished between falling asleep and waking,
into a world unfamiliar on first experience, familiar yet unfamiliar and retaining much of its mystery on each return; into a
world wholly fair and desirable that transforms the traveler until he is returned to his own world, forgetting much but retaining deep within him an unexplainable joy to be released by some
sound or smell, like the smell of wood smoke?

So it was with us. We had been on trains overnight before,
going to Toronto, but those journeys began and ended sedately
in stations. This one ended in a new world. Round Mountain
is in west-central Maine, near the Rangeley Lakes. A car
dropped off the Bar Harbor Express took us to the town of
Farmington; there we got our first long breath of Maine mountain air and breakfast. A short ride to the end of a narrow-gauge
logging railroad left us on a platform in the woods, where buckboards waited for the last excruciating trek to camp. The mere
thought of it was too much for my sister. For a few miles one
could ride without danger of a major dislocation; but, when the
forest really closed in and the mountains began in earnest, only
the luggage rode.

A clearing edged by log cabins sloped down to an oval lake.
A mile across it Round Mountain rose steeply; to the right the
lake stretched off four or five miles to dark hills of spruce and
hemlock rolling away without a break. Ducks bobbed on the

bright water and a pair of loons farther off. On either side of the clearing, and at a half-dozen points along the shore, trails led into woods — silent woods, damp and cool, where an occasional bird flitted along a parallel course and a startled red squirrel dashed up a tree to scold angrily overhead. The movement of a leaf betrayed creatures seldom seen. Underfoot the trail's deep, damp brownness cushioned and gave spring to our steps. Shafts of sunlight, piercing the evergreen roof, highlighted a fallen and rotting tree covered by moss, a patch of ferns and bunchberries, a lichened rock. On wet days mosquitoes and blackflies reminded us that, even in Paradise, all was not perfect. Icy ambrosia waited to be dipped from a spring half hidden in the roots of a great pine. On these occasions my father would quote the Lord to Gideon: "Every one that lappeth of the water with his tongue, as a dog lappeth, him shalt thou set by himself . . . By the three hundred men that lapped will I save you, and deliver the Midianites into thine hand . . ." Lapping may have worked for them, but it left us very dry. We sucked or rolled birchbark cups.

At Round Mountain it is my father who stands out. In the woods or on a stream there was no better performer or more knowledgeable teacher, though his methods were incisive and his patience not without end. We began with the canoe — what not to do, first of all, not to fool in one; then how to handle it, including an upset, inevitable in the long run. Fly casting came next, an agonizing ordeal unless one understands the basic propositions of physics involved, that a slack line suddenly jerked back will be aimed for the caster's face, a poor target for a fishhook, and that, unless the caster pauses on the back-cast for the line to straighten, the fly will be snapped off.

His patience was surprising when it came to imparting the art of fly fishing itself — to let the fish take the fly before striking, to keep the tip of the rod up so that fish pull against the bend of it and not straight against the leader, to let the fish tire by running and being reeled in, always keeping a taut line and away from snags and the canoe itself. This can be exasperating work for a teacher, almost unbearable when a trout neatly disengages from a blunderer's hook. Sometimes, too, events seem to disprove precepts. Years later, having taken my father's place as a teacher, I had just finished a biting harangue to my son for dreaming off while his fly idly sank to sure disaster on the stream's weedy bottom, when the reel roared out and he nearly lost the rod. Twenty minutes later, weak from excitement, we netted his catch, a two-pound trout, the prize of the trip. When we took the hook out, there was a fingerling which had taken the fly first, and, unknown to the fisherman, assumed the forbidden role of live bait. It took some time to straighten out the moral of that lesson.

After we moved through the novitiate of the woods to serious business, my father came to deeper and more lasting lessons. As a prelate he was a baffling man, widely read in theology and Christian doctrine, yet rarely speaking of either, privately or in his sermons, which so far as I can remember dealt more with ethics and conduct. But no conviction could have been deeper than his in a code of conduct, based on perceptions of what was decent and civilized for man inextricably caught up in social relationships. If his goal was the salvation of his soul, it was a salvation by works, performed with charity and humor as well as zeal. Through this mixture of belief ran a strong strain of stoicism. Much in life could not be affected or mitigated, and, hence, must be borne. Borne without complaint, because complaints were a bore and nuisance to others and undermined the serenity essential to endurance.

These impressions came much later, of course, but his code was instilled on the trails of our camping trips. There one learned that everyone else was tired, thirsty, and wondered how much farther we had to go; that everyone else's pack was heavy, too. A tendency to whine or grouse resulted in ignominious dismissal to the end of the line. This was good medicine. So was the drill, on making camp, in finding a job to do and doing it, not flopping down and waiting to be told. So was the next lesson that, just as there was an obligation to do one's share of the work, there was an obligation to do one's share of the entertaining.

Around the campfire after supper he told endless stories, but the favorites were of the Northwest Rebellion — the herds of buffalo on the prairie, the Indians, friendly and unfriendly, the sergeant-major who sounded his own reveille by walking along the rows of sleeping men, hitting the soles of their feet with a blackthorn stick and calling, "Up, Up, Up, and hear the little birdies sing! There ain't no little birds, but the principle's all the same!" This became our camp reveille also. The storyteller was master of ceremonies, too, drawing all, campers and guides alike, into making their contributions. My most successful one was

"A capital ship for an ocean trip
Was the Walloping Window-Blind."

Home from these summers in the woods, my father resumed, as he appeared to the children at least, his Olympian detachment. So, when the revised story of the night of the great commotion began to be whispered about in the kitchen, with much giggling, it seemed quite incredible. That memorable adventure began after we had gone to bed; but, like everyone else in the house and the neighborhood, we were thoroughly alerted participants before the excitement was over.

Some women's group, coming to the rented house on Pearl Street to meet with my mother, had driven my father out, leaving behind urgent exhortation to get it over early. Reconnaissance on his return showed the meeting still in session. He worked his way through shrubs to a window through which my mother alone could see him and began making faces of disapproval and gestures of dismissal. My mother's response to this apparition was to shriek, "There's a face at the window!" Considerable hubbub ensued, in which some of the bolder spirits rushed out of the house, calling for help. My father, beating a hasty retreat, found himself cut off from the street by this sortie and by the emergence from his front door of our neighbor, the senior vestryman of the church, Mr. J. Peters Pelton, an eminently respectable druggist with impressive gray Burnside whiskers. So he doubled back to escape through the clothes yard, over the back fence and, thence, through other yards to the next street. This maneuver was succeeding when a clothesline caught him under the chin, throwing him heavily.

The fugitive, shaken, but still mobile, vaulted the fence and escaped in the darkness through an awakening neighborhood. His return by indirect route brought him home in time to join in the search, play Watson to Mr. Pelton's Holmes in the discovery of the escape route, and satisfy the alarmed neighborhood that the rascal had gotten clean away. My mother's suspicions were aroused by her husband's unwonted cooperativeness and by a welt under his chin. As she thought of it, that face at the window became more familiar. When confronted by the charge direct, he confessed with assurance of immunity. But my mother's security was not adequate to the temptation, and the story leaked.

Some golden hours of those far-off days came toward their close. For a time, our supper proved an agonizing interlude between afternoon and evening. In one of his infrequent interventions in our affairs, my father, who had gotten the idea that rice was good for us, decreed that we should have boiled rice for supper. Not rice pudding with raisins, a very different story; but plain, nauseous, boiled rice eaten with milk and sugar. It took some time to get the stuff down, except on those happy evenings when Cazzie's boys came to the house to wait for her. Then, by Tom Sawyer trickery of pretended enjoyment, we often got them to eat it for us.

Once supper was over, we could choose between meeting the night boat from Hartford to New York and watching the evening drill at the firehouse. The fire drill struck with hard, blunt impact. The river boat moved in mystery, quickening the heart, bringing a catch in the breath, as always happens to me when a ship's lines are cast off, a gap widens between ship and dock, and handkerchiefs flutter. A ship sailing does not seem a conveyance going from one place to another, but something going out of one's life to an unknowable bourne.

The boat came like a scene on the stage of the McDonough Opera House. First, one saw the masts and funnel above the trees on the island in the river, and a dull glow through them; then a plume of steam followed by the deep demand for the bridge to open. She came through the draw, a floating island of light and shimmering white. Sounds and movements seemed to merge — bells, shouts, the rattle of winches, people and hand trucks coming off and going on, all in a glare of light. This movement ended with the signal to cast off lines, the widening gap of water, fainter bells, and fading lights.

The river steamer was our spectacle. We had no ballet or music; the theoretically forbidden nickelodeon was a flicker of banalities, silent except for the tinkle of a piano. Occasionally at the "Opera House" a tired road company presented *Uncle Tom's Cabin;* or the college dramatic club, *The Rivals* or *Charlie's Aunt.* But none of these moved the spirit; none excited the imagination. The steamer did, appearing and disappearing like a vision, and a portent of some Cathay far beyond the bend which extinguished its lights.

The drill at the firehouse took place at seven-thirty every evening except Sunday. The wide, two-story brick building on Main Street housed, on the high-ceilinged first floor, a chunky brass pumping-engine and a long hook-and-ladder, each drawn by two heavy horses, with the firemen's quarters above. Through a round hole in the ceiling a brass pole permitted spec-

tacular descent. As seven-thirty approached, high arched doors
were folded back, and firemen kept the inquisitive out of harm's
way.

We held our breath. Then came, on the dot, a deafening roar
from the horn on the roof; bells clanged; the doors of the horses'
stalls behind the engines banged open, and the huge horses clat-
tered out, headed straight for the watchers at the doors. The
more timid spectators, unnerved by all the noise, shrank back.
We old hands knew better. The horses stopped in their tracks
under the harness hanging from ropes above them. Waiting
firemen snapped on bridles, collars, girths, and traces. Drivers
leaned forward in their seats, reins in hand. As the last man
sprang aside, the horses plunged forward, the firemen leaping
for the runningboards and handholds of the machines. With
bells ringing, smoke pouring from the engine's funnel, and the
navigator of the back wheels of the hook-and-ladder making his
broad swing into the street, they dashed past us at full gallop.

A brave show! Some real *aficionados* waited for the return,
the tricky backing-in, the unharnessing and rubbing down.
One of the few rules laid upon us was to be home when taps
sounded and the light was fading fast.

It was fading, too, on the golden age, on what was for me
the morn of creation. The day, set so lightheartedly more than
a decade before, when I should go away to school, was just
ahead. Nothing could have been more casual and unplanned.
A youth living in the old DeKoven-Alsop house on the hill
had come with a parent to felicitate the Rector and his wife on
the birth of a son. My father, inquiring, as an adult inevitably
does of the young, how he liked his school, received an enthusiastic reply and was urged to let the youth, on his return, enroll
me for entrance twelve years thence. My father agreed, but
my mother, as she would recount, burst into tears; I looked, she
said, singularly ill-equipped to be leaving home.

She was right in many ways, especially in her sense of the imminence of that departure. All my life I have tried to hold off

the future by saying to myself that time is a fraud, that weeks, months, years which seem to stretch ahead forever are collapsible. Take your eye off them for a moment and the future is yesterday. The writer of Ecclesiastes understood it well. But I could, and can, never acquire his resignation, not even when I would tell myself on the first day of vacation that it was not even worth-while unpacking my bag, so soon passeth it away and it is gone. Now, when midsummer day dawns, I feel the winter solstice pluck at my sleeve.

Only when one looks back, is the true nature of time's fraud plain. The victim is bemused into the belief that it is standing still, motionless, that the moment of joy is preserved in sunlight like a Renoir picnic, while, in truth, termite jaws are eating everything behind the paint. So time was destroying the very stuff of rural New England which made our lives the way they were. I did not understand that life in the golden age was the very distillation of that place and time, until both place and time were left behind. The fact of change was plain enough; understanding of its nature came more slowly.

Our life in our valley was wholly unorganized, wholly free. Not the freedom of the Celestial City, where saints would sing in unison, and, in unison, cast down their golden crowns before a glassy sea. Not the freedom of citizens of Plato's Republic or of the welfare state. Rather, the freedom of wild things, not knowing unison, whose discipline came from pains and penalties externally and impersonally imposed, not penalties devised and inflicted by one's own kind with connotations of personal disapproval. Even our parents — or parent — in the disciplinary role, appeared as a force of nature. The penalty for falling out of a tree was to get hurt. The penalty for falling out with my father was apt to be the same thing. Result followed cause in a rational, and hence predictable, way but left no spiritual wound. The judgment of nature upon error is harsh and painful, but it is not a lecture or a verdict of moral or social obloquy.

After the golden age, life lost this pristine, unorganized, amoral freedom. The organization of boarding school, like the wolf, in Icelandic saga, which ran up the sky and devoured the sun, devoured my early freedom. School life was organized from the wakening bell to the policed silence which followed lights-out. All was organized — eating, studying, games, so-called free time, the whole thing. One could understand and accept rendering unto Caesar the things which were Caesar's, the control of one's external life. The mind and spirit were not Caesar's; yet these were demanded, too. And I, for one, found it necessary to erect defenses for the last citadel of spiritual freedom.

All of this was still ahead.

On Sunday evening there were no games, night boats, or fire drills. Our parents went early to the church on missions preparatory to evensong. Then I would lie on the terrace in back of the rectory, concentrating on the sky over the Divinity School. There, high up, swallows circled above the chimney. As the evening deepened, the circle thinned; yet one could never see a swallow leave it. Rumor had it that they disappeared down the chimney of the school, but the keenest eye could not see them do it. All at once, while there was still light enough to see, the circle was gone. The mystery remained. A voice from the house called me to bed. Soon the katydids and cicadas took over the night, the rise and fall of their pulsing giving the illusion that the world hummed as it spun like the great wheel in the hardware factory powerhouse. One sank into drowsiness. Faintly from the church, growing a little louder as the choir passed from the church into the vestryroom, came the music of the recessional, probably a favorite of my father's:

> "The radiant morn hath passed away;
> And spent, too soon, her golden store.
> The shadows of departing day
> Creep on once more."

2

"I'VE BEEN WORKIN' ON THE RAILROAD"

THE SUMMER of 1911 began badly. It began with mumps, a sardonic present on my graduation from school. Isolation gave plenty of time for unwelcome reflection. If I had known then that adolescence is more often than not a disturbed time, when unhappiness and joy are most unevenly measured out, it would have brought proportion to my thoughts. For the past six years had been unhappy ones. If I had read then some of the letters between John Adams and Jefferson in their old age, they would have brought consolation of a sort and modest hope.

"Putting to myself your question, would I agree to live my seventy-three years over again forever?" wrote Jefferson. "I hesitate to say. With Chew's limitations from twenty-five to sixty, I would say yes; and I might go farther back, but not come lower down."

Cheer up, I would have thought, even the great Jefferson thought so ill of the time you have been through that under no circumstances would he repeat it. He might venture again into the years ahead of you but not into those behind. On whether the joys of life compensated for the pains, the two old men never quite agreed on the precise issue. Jefferson did "not agree that an age of pleasure is no compensation for a moment of pain." He thought "that life is a fair matter of account, and the balance often, nay generally, in its favor. It is not indeed easy, by calculation of intensity and time, to apply a common measure, or to fix the par between pleasure and pain; yet it exists, and is measurable. On the question, for example, whether to be cut for the stone? The young, with a longer prospect of years, think these overbalance the pain of the operation. Dr. Franklin, at the age of eighty, thought his residuum of life not worth that price. I should have thought with him, even taking the stone out of the scale."

To this Adams fired back: "Let us state a few questions '*sub rosa.*'

"1. Would you accept a life, if offered you, of equal pleasure and pain, *e.g.* one million of moments of pleasure and one million moments of pain? 1,000,000 pleasure = 1,000,000 pain. Suppose the pleasure as exquisite as any in life, and the pain as exquisite as any, *e.g.* stone, gravel, gout, headache, earache, toothache, colic, &c. I would not. I would rather be blotted out.

"2. Would you accept a life of one year of incessant gout, headache, &c., for seventy-two years of such life as you have enjoyed? I would not. 1 year of colic = 72 of *boule de savon.* Pretty, but unsubstantial. I would rather be extinguished."

As I contemplated my Holbein jowls, my thoughts were not as complicated as these, but along these lines and as somber. The last chapter suggests that the transition from the wild freedom of my boyhood to the organized discipline of adolescence at boarding school was not a change for the happier. The authoritarianism of the English "public" school of the last century, with its austere and muscular Christianity, upon which ours was modeled, was not for all temperaments. To adapt oneself to so sudden and considerable a change required what is now called a "well-adjusted" personality. Mine apparently was not. At first, through surprise, ignorance, and awkwardness, later on and increasingly through wilfulness, I bucked the Establishment and the system. One who does this fights the odds. The result was predictable, painful, and clear.

As Lord Melbourne might have said, there was no damned nonsense about merit connected with the experiment on either side; little blame, but certainly folly, on mine. But how could one know all this? What had occurred was enough, despite the confidence of youth, to induce a measure of self-doubt and doubt about the next step. Buoyant embarkation upon the next conventional course hardly seemed self-evident. Perhaps something novel, even adventurous, was indicated. Tennyson had Ulysses declare, "I am a part of all that I have met." If one changed what one met, it might work beneficially the other way around on oneself. At any rate it would produce new tests. So adventure it was to be, when once those jowls subsided.

At this time, a new transcontinental railway was being pushed across northern Canada, the Grand Trunk Pacific, now the Canadian National. A senior construction engineer was a brother of my mother's friend, our beloved governess of years past, Marie Sinclair. A letter to her, and in a short time I was off to a new world.

From North Bay, almost in the center of Ontario, the Temiscaming & Northern Ontario Railroad ran northwest to an obscure end in the wilderness about a hundred and sixty miles south of the southern tip of Hudson Bay, called James Bay. From Cochrane, a railroad camp and supply depot established at the end of the line, the transcontinental line was being built east and west. On a June day in 1911 I set out from North Bay for this outpost beyond the frontier, but did not arrive quite on schedule. Our combination passenger and freight train did not boast many facilities. Among its innumerable stops was one at a platform in the woods to let off prospectors for the Porcupine gold rush and allow others to stretch their legs and get some food. The lunchroom was in a tent about two hundred feet from the platform. The engineer promised to signal departure in ample time — unfortunately it was not ample enough. The train had gathered speed by the time I gained the platform; piled-up equipment forbade a run; I grabbed at a car handrailing and was thrown. An unknown rescuer pulled me back from the platform's edge and the turning wheels. We fell off its end onto the hard earth. When my mind cleared, I saw women uncovering their eyes.

No "western set" at Hollywood ever approached Cochrane. A very few months before it had been forest. Two-foot stumps filled the one and only street and were almost impossible hazards to teams and buckboards. On either side of the street, board-walks had been built over the stumps, and back of them the houses — of logs to shoulder height, with canvas roofs. Signs proclaimed the "Four Macs Hotel," eating places, outfitters, hardware stores, clothiers; but no firearms, no liquor stores, no saloons. This was Indian country and the "Mounties" (the Royal North West Mounted Police) permitted no nonsense. In-dian men in corduroy and buckskin strolled along the board-walks, followed by squaws, some with papooses on their backs. On either side of the street a pair of Mounties in Stetson hats, scarlet jackets, blue riding breeches with a yellow stripe, and rid-ing boots patrolled day and night. But the center of life was the railroad, the yards, seen through a mist of escaping steam and coal smoke, the offices and warehouses, also built of logs and can-vas, and the dumps of supplies — coal, rails, ties, equipment of every sort.

After a night in the "Four Macs," a long, hot, and malodorous barrack full of snoring men, the railroad construction office gave me orders to proceed the next day by construction freight train one hundred and twenty miles west to the end of steel at the Missinaibi River, and report to the Resident Engineer-in-Charge for the lowest job at the residency, axeman. The rest of the day was spent in collecting my working clothes — knee-length elk-skin boots, woolen socks, thin woolen underclothes, although the days were already hot, flannel shirts, rubber coat, Stetson hat, blackfly netting and several pairs of gauntlet gloves, for work and blackfly protection, and a pack to carry all my stuff. City clothes went into the suitcase, checked at the construction office.

My new clothes looked to me very new and stagey, but to my surprise attracted less attention then the ones put off had.

The work train was off early, a string of freight cars, two ancient wooden passenger cars, and a caboose. The cars were jammed with laborers, chiefly southeastern Europeans, going to take up their contracted sections of the right-of-way farther west. When the conductor came around looking at passes, he left me in no doubt that I had made a *faux pas* by getting into the car with the workmen. Residency types, even axemen, did not travel with common laborers. I had let down the barrier of caste, albeit through ignorance, and with it our side — a minute group, as I learned later, for whom prestige was a major factor in handling large numbers of illiterate laborers. I was brusquely ordered back to ride in the caboose, a childhood ambition, thought unattainable, now suddenly realized. Modest behavior in this Valhalla was rewarded by careless acceptance.

All day a sense of joy possessed me, sometimes riding like a prince in the lookout of the caboose, where one could see all the way to the engine's cab; sometimes watching while we dropped off a freight car and shunted it into the desired position; sometimes consuming the endless tea and snacks which the crew would cook up on the wood-burning stove. At dusk we pulled off on a siding, losing our engine, which went off for coal, water, and a better night than the caboose offered. The laborers piled out of the coaches and lit cooking fires along the right-of-way. In the caboose we cooked a more substantial meal. The night brought problems of its own. Clouds of mosquitoes and blackflies took over the caboose. Attempts to rig up netting proved futile. Grass and moss were then put on top of the coals in the stove. The billows of smoke which resulted drove out the enemy and most of the company as well. But we soon learned from the old hands to roll up in blankets on the floor, where a few inches of breathable air could be found until the smudge had to be renewed. It was magnificent. Smoke, crying eyes, and ravenous insects were as nothing compared to the intoxication of knowing that this was "life."

The next day I reported for work. The "Chief" did not bother with trifles; but his executive officer, the instrument man (he operated the surveying instruments, transit and level) asked me wearily whether I had ever seen an axe, and raised an eyebrow when a required demonstration showed that summers in the Maine woods had not been wasted. A word about life on the Missinaibi is useful, for, although after ten days I was sent on west to a more rugged setting to replace an ailing axeman, those ten days made me a veteran — at least, I thought so.

From a high bluff we looked out on a bend in a broad and beautiful river. Until the railroad came, no one but Indians had navigated the river or landed on its bank. To go overland through the forest, through swampy muskeg, centuries' deposit of dead flora into which one could sink to the knee, was impossible. No habitations existed two hundred miles north or south of the right-of-way. From time to time Indians passed up or down the river in their canoes. Occasionally one of them would sell a sturgeon at the cookhouse, to the vast improvement of the menu. On the bluff, beside the group of four or five log cabins which constituted the residency, a second group made up a Hudson's Bay Company Trading Post, and a third housed men working on the bridge. All in all a budding community, not destined to blossom, in the silent forest.

The bridge, a temporary wooden structure of complicated jackstraw arrangement, had collapsed — not utterly — under a too heavily loaded train. Attempts were being made to repair and strengthen the bridge, to push on with laying the steel, that is, the tracks, pending the erection of a steel bridge. The work of the residency, in fact, was winding up. The right-of-way and roadbed were finished, except for final ballasting, steel laid, tunnels and cuts excavated. What remained was checking out the off-take drainage, the culverts, spots where the roadbed might be sinking, and so on. This sent us up and down our ten miles of track on our handcar, keeping out of the way of locomotives, and lifting-off to run surveys.

These journeys soon revealed the rugged humor of my fellow workers in breaking in a neophyte. If we had neither surveying instruments nor the Chief or his Vice aboard, the stage was set. The handcar picked up speed. Then, at a signal hard to detect, those on the front pump handle pulled up hard and threw their weight to one side. The result was almost certain derailment, with bodies flying about in a most hazardous manner. The game bore certain resemblances to Russian roulette, but the casualties were remarkably low, perhaps due to the scarcity of crushed stone ballast and the softness of the ditches. My colleagues were noisily delighted at each denouement; my own merriment was somewhat forced. Fortunately, while all were still sound in limb, we tired of the sport.

It was soon apparent to me that to attain man's estate I must either chew tobacco or smoke a pipe. The former seemed wholly beyond my capacity for adventure. Cigarettes meant Bull Durham and rolling one's own, which would mark me for what I was. So the choice went to a plug of Hudson's Bay smoking tobacco and a bulldog pipe from the same source. Sitting around the bunkhouse after supper, careful watching of the others got me through slicing the plug, rolling the cuttings in my palm, filling and lighting the pipe. I puffed in a sophisticated way. Then intimations of approaching death crept over me, more and more lethally; doubt grew that I could move a limb. Laughter penetrated the roaring in my ears. When finally I staggered into the night air, the whole company of the bunkhouse came along to assist.

My days on the Missinaibi were ended by a call over our primitive hand-cranked telephone from a resident engineer over a hundred miles farther west asking for a replacement at the lowest level. The rule of last-in first-out pointed to me. The handcar took me and my pack across the still fragile bridge and over the few miles of track on the other side. No sense of adventure raised my spirits as the car started back, leaving me to shoulder my pack, alone as far as eye could reach along the narrowing cut through an endless forest. Every ten miles, so my departed friends had said, a resident engineer's camp would give me food and bunk; after a day or so laborers' huts would appear between them.

In that empty country travelers were under the protection of the gods, as heralds in Homer. At any residency they might move into the bunkhouse and up to the table, unquestioned, until the spirit pushed them on. Mine did not push me that first day farther than the nearest camp. Next day about noon my feet gave out, happily near the hut of two laborers. Language difficulties proved insurmountable to conversation, but no bar to understanding and hospitality. My hosts shared soup, hardtack, and the floor with me, and introduced me to the therapy of soaking blistered feet in strong tea. A day's rest brought an end to my troubles and sent me cheerfully off, eating and sleeping usually at residencies but sometimes at laborers' huts. In about a week I was looking with sinking heart at my home to be, Residency 25.

In a swampy clearing along the right-of-way four or five structures stood on piles with military precision, joined together by a boardwalk and connected with the right-of-way by another. Three or four feet of the walls were log; the rest and the ceiling, canvas. To have been told that I would become fond of this dreary spot would have been unbelievable. But so it was to be.

Seven men and a cat inhabited these log-tents. The Chief Engineer, young, handsome, and brooding, even morose, lived alone, as a captain should. Exuding authority, he commanded almost without words; a frown, raised eyebrow, movement of a hand, each was eloquent. His entrance into the cookhouse would quiet even the cook. It was hinted that he was brilliant but destroying himself by liquor. Of his ten miles of line, he was the czar of construction from virgin forest to completed railroad bed. His lieutenant, the instrument man, a former vaudeville actor who was trying to qualify as a civil engineer, reversed the temperament of his superior — a gay, hearty, good-natured man, a perfect extrovert, with an excellent voice.

The rodman and force accountant have faded from my mind, undoubtedly because they soon departed from our lives. The other axeman, a competent French-Indian lad, and I took over their jobs as well as our own without strain — he handling the measurement rod in running elevations, and I walking over our ten miles every day, checking off those of our thousand or more men at work, injured, or ill, and doing whatever could be done for them. This was usually nothing; and very effective it was, too.

Regardless of hierarchy, life at the residency centered about our French-Canadian cook, Lorin, cast in the great Falstaffian tradition. With all Falstaff's gusto, his vitality, wit, not a moment of dullness could exist around him. Even when alone, he sang and talked, partly soliloquy, partly recitation, partly addressed to the cat or the stove or anything about the kitchen. Songs and talk were noisy, bawdy, often vulgar in the extreme. Among them were constantly replenished dialogues between a coarse old father and his dainty daughter in pursuit of refinement. Many involved her dog, Ping-Pong, as, for instance:

Daughter (rendered in falsetto): "Oh, Father, I just love Ping-Pong."

Father (with a roar): "Ping-Pong be damned. We'll have no bloody Chinaman around here!"

For men marooned together on a desert island, as it were, he was both a lifesaver and an alternative to manslaughter. Months later, when I had gotten to college, Lorin's recitations and stories put me in the novel role of ribald wag.

In a more material way Lorin's genius performed miracles

with most unpromising culinary resources, all brought in by dog sled before the snow melted, and all canned, dried, or salted. That mainstay of diet, the potato, for example, emerged from tin drums in dried, shrunken particles a little larger than rice, but of a grayish hue, and had to be soaked in boiling water. Nevertheless, out of such gruesome materials and salted meat Lorin kept us not only far from mutinous but even contented. Of course, it would have been a gross breach of the rules to have admitted this. His riposte to ritualistic criticism was to write out menus so revolting that a truce became mandatory. His art soared on those days when a surveying party came out of the bush with a bag full of "fool grouse" which could be knocked off a limb with a long stick. The most welcome of sounds was the call to meals, struck on a triangle outside the cookhouse; and, of sights, Lorin in chef's white hat and white robe — for he had style — carrying platters for the Chief to serve.

In northern Ontario summer daylight comes early and fades late, fulfilling the prophecy in Revelations — "And there shall be no night there." And we breakfasted before sunrise. Once our little company had found its stride, I was off immediately with my notebook for one end of our fief, and back again from a ten-mile walk, before civilized folk had started for work. Even this allowed time for a mug or two of coffee with special friends, rechristened "Mike" or "Shorty" or "Bill," however they had been known in Bulgaria. We were ready then for hard work, usually surveying a route for a drainage ditch off the right-of-way. The terrain was wet and flat; the bush, thick; the muskeg, deep and hiding exasperating traps for a foot among the tree roots.

Then there were the blackflies, ferocious as tigers. Once off the right-of-way, they enveloped us in clouds. To escape some of their torture, we equipped ourselves like beekeepers. Netting, fitted over the brims of our Stetsons and tucked into the necks of our shirts, furnished protection except where it touched the neck. Gauntlets kept the furies off our hands and out of our sleeves.

The Chief, with maps and field glasses, stood like Napoleon on the mound of the roadbed, with his lieutenant sighting through the level below him, while the Indian and I stumbled about in the bush trying to find a noticeable fall of ground. The Indian carried the white rod with its red and black figures and movable target, while I removed obscuring trees on orders shouted from the command post. Usually, after several false starts, we found a practicable fall and marked the course and width of the proposed ditch. This was when the sweat ran. The thermometer of a midsummer morning would climb to the nineties. Not a breath of air penetrated the bush. (Yet we often struck frozen earth at four or five feet.) Only a madman took off his hat and netting to wipe his brow. As the Chief would observe solemnly on the walk back to camp, a morning in the bush was a good way to work up an appetite. It was, indeed, for both food and for that ingenious device which let cold water from an elevated barrel into a perforated oil can, thence onto an appreciative recipient.

After "dinner" we girded ourselves for the afternoon, a repetition of the morning. The sun was still high when that was over and off I went to cover the other end of our line while the men were still working. Back again, camp chores — splitting the wood, filling the water barrel, digging a latrine, teasing the cat, prepared us for the last substantial meal of the day. The evening in the bunkhouse belonged to Lorin and the ex-vaudevillian, but the small audience often slept before the final act.

Later in the summer came what was called "measuring up." This determined the men's payments under their contracts. Groups of from two to six would subcontract from the roadbed contractor for a number of "stations" — each hundred feet of right-of-way. The stations had been surveyed, numbered, and marked off. They felled the trees (building huts with the logs), removed the stumps (at day-labor rates), and excavated from either side of the future roadbed the fill to build it to a specified height, at rates depending on what they struck from muskeg to solid rock. These contracts were chancy; the men, simple, illiterate, and already in debt to the contractor for their grubstake at high prices.

They were also our friends. It would be misleading to overstress their simple virtue. They were hot-tempered and on occasion violent. The knife wounds for which they begged antiseptics and bandages did not appear to be self-inflicted or accidental. The few deaths that occurred in our small domain were not always as mysterious as our bland report — "from causes unknown" — would suggest. We had, however, devised enough of a common language to learn the main outlines of their lives and hopes. The latter were simple and likely to be disappointed when their accounts were totted up. We were not contractors' men, but government men, and anticipated some of the objectives of the welfare state by methods which can only be defended by observing that no others seemed available. My colleague sharpened the point of his rod so that leaning on it would sink it a foot or two in the soft earth. I wound up on my hand three feet of the "chain" — which was not a chain at all, but a steel measuring tape. These simple aids had a beneficial effect on the computation of the cubic excavation and its conversion into a cash credit.

Perhaps our efforts were unnecessary; because, as our party appeared for the measuring up, each group, with sound Balkan instinct, presented to the Chief a bottle of murderous-looking whisky. It must have been hard to get, and risky for the transporters, probably the peddlers who kept coming through and putting up in our bunkhouse. Perhaps these bottles might have had their effect upon the figures without our intervention; perhaps they heightened its effect. However that may be, their effect on the Chief was unmistakable, if not disastrous. When enough of them had been carried to his quarters, he took several days off and went on a roaring drunk. Only the instrument man ventured into the tent, sometimes bearing food, sometimes getting a drink. When, in his judgment, the time had come, an assault on the tent was mounted — a ticklish operation, since the Chief had the only firearm. He was tied up on his bed to await return to consciousness and a magnificent hangover. What liquor remained was removed and locked up. After a few tense days, the process of measuring up was begun again, and the cycle resumed. Surely I was seeing the world, even though the area was restricted.

By early September the last of our workmen had left us. The Chief's sobriety seemed more somber than ever. The steel-laying gang had reached the residency to the east of us. One day I walked beyond our boundary to see the mechanical monsters at work. The end for our small company was close. A sense of sadness was not dispelled even by my new eagerness for experience ahead. These men had done more for me than they would ever know and, in doing it, had become a part of me. They had given me new eagerness for experience. The simple, extroverted pattern of their lives had revived a sense of freedom amidst uncoerced order, extinguishing the memory of "pain as exquisite as any," in John Adams's words, from suffocating discipline and arbitrary values.

They had restored to me a priceless possession, joy in life. Never again was I to lose it or doubt it. Decades later I was to hear a President of the United States expound the doctrine that the joy of life lay in work. He did not, I hope, mean it literally. Perhaps he was reaching for the concept behind the Greek definition of happiness as the use of all one's powers toward the achievement of excellence in an environment affording them scope. His idea was too colored by Puritanism. Work is part, an important part, of life, but only a part. Joy in life encompasses far more. Justice Holmes was thinking of that "more," not of another opinion, when, approaching ninety, he said to me, "If that ceiling should open, and through the opening should come the voice of God saying, 'Wendell, you have five minutes to live,' I should reply, 'Very well, Boss, but I wish it were ten.' "

Since there was nothing to be done until the steel gang reached us, the Chief agreed to release the three of us who had educational duties to meet, and to hold the fort with Lorin until replacements arrived. We took off for the last time down the well-beaten path with very tangled feelings. From the middle of the next residency to where the newly laid steel was safe for a train, handcars were an improvement on walking. A couple of days brought us to Cochrane — but what a changed Cochrane! A month before, the great Porcupine forest fire had gone through there destroying the whole town, railroad offices, and warehouses — but most important for me, my bag with all my city clothes.

The paymaster's office wrote us checks for what seemed like small fortunes and advised us not to cash them until we got home. Since my pass would take me to Toronto and I had enough money on me to eat until then, it seemed a good suggestion.

When we three parted at North Bay, it came to me with a shock that what the well-dressed man wore on a railroad survey in the northern Ontario bush was not *de rigueur* on the Canadian Pacific Railway express. It became more and more important to find my uncle's bank in Toronto, turn my check into legal tender of the realm, and shed those outlandish clothes.

At the bank door I was repulsed by a uniformed popinjay, who ushered in the respectable and kept out bums, of whom I was the prototype. The claim that I was the president's nephew was a joke good enough to be shared with passersby. But the check, a government check, shook him. He sent in for help, as the curious gaped. I was brought inside for more private interrogation, tentatively identified by the great man's secretary, and finally admitted to his presence.

Word of me had obviously preceded me, for I was met by a tirade about making a spectacle of myself and a laughingstock of the family. My uncle had a dictatorial manner heightened by a striking resemblance to King George V and Czar Nicholas II, including mustache and pointed beard. It occurred to me that Prince Edward might, also, have had to struggle to maintain a straight face while receiving a wigging from the Monarch. At length explanations prevailed and more avuncular sentiments were expressed. The check did not impress the president of the bank as much as the doorman, but doubtless restrained him from contributing to my re-outfitting. He did, however, try to restrain me from taking all of the check in cash; but on this I was adamant. A bank clerk was detailed to guide me through my purchases and return me to my uncle's house.

Once possessed of civilized clothes, shoes, and suitcase and having bequeathed the skin I had shed and my old knapsack to him who desired them, we went in search of a more important purchase. A long cherished plan had been to devote the first substantial sum which came my way to eliminating a frustration. My mother liked things associated with those close to her. A gift conveying what I wished might now be possible. At length we found a small gold-filigree brooch studded with pearls. She wore it until her death.

I got back to my uncle's house with just enough money to buy my ticket home. So ended one of the most important few months of my life.

3

THE OLD ORDER CHANGETH

WE CAME to Washington that September (of 1919) when Woodrow Wilson fell "like Lucifer, never to hope again." He had gone to the people with his "solemn referendum" on the League of Nations against the Senate "Irreconcilables" and the reservations of Senator Lodge. The blow fell in Colorado. In silence and mystery the special train sped back to the capital. There mystery grew as the weeks passed, the bland medical bulletins continued, but no word came from the President. Not even the faithful Joe Tumulty saw him. He had simply disappeared. Rumors flew. More weeks passed. The government and the Senate Democrats wallowed rudderless. In Congress wolves tore at the carcass of the Covenant and howled for the blood of the Administration. From the White House, only silence; but for an occasional Sibylline utterance from the High Priestess.

In the circle in which we moved depression and bewilderment deepened. Justice Brandeis, whose law clerk I was, brushed aside attempts to draw him out, giving the impression that things were so much worse than could be imagined as to be beyond discussion. We went on with our work and our lives, as I imagine people did in Rome in the fifth century with the defenses of the frontiers crumbling. A year passed; the depression grew; the forthcoming election, a bad prospect, turned into a horror in fact. A sack of the city by the victorious barbarians appeared a certainty. It was.

In the fall of 1920 we moved from a small apartment on Vermont Avenue above Thomas Circle, between the Georgian Wylie house, now gone, and Mr. Theodore Noyes's house, also gone, to a minute house on Corcoran Street. The Washington of 1920 was a small, gangling southern city. I remember with nostalgic affection the old Shoreham Hotel at 15th and H Streets, a period piece of southern hostelry, with a most serene dining room decorated in white with mirrors and chandeliers. There Joe Tumulty and a group of friends lunched daily and Joe recited his favorite Shakespearean passages.

The Justice's apartment and also his office were on Connecticut Avenue in Stoneleigh Court, built by and named after John Hay's father-in-law. Every morning at ten o'clock the Justice and Mrs. Brandeis took the air in a smart runabout behind a handsome and spirited hackney. The Justice, a Kentuckian, himself handled Sir Gareth, as Mrs. Brandeis had romantically named their horse. Later on, when automobile traffic made the drives too dangerous, Sir Gareth grew old on our farm in Maryland, mildly pulling a less distinguished buggy.

Poindexter, the messenger, and I constituted the whole office staff; and Poindexter, half the household staff as well. Out of the office window we could see Senator Elkins's mansion on K Street, and Poindexter would talk of the glamorous parties given there when the Duce d'Abruzzi was thought to be courting Miss Katherine Elkins, and of earning nickels as a boy by holding restless horses in the torchlight while footmen handed ladies from their broughams.

Across Connecticut Avenue from Stoneleigh Court the fashionable Magruder grocery furnished the ladies' morning meeting place, while farther up the Avenue they danced in the evening at Rauscher's, the caterer's ballroom. In the basement of Stoneleigh Court Charlie Laudano had his barbershop. For forty years we were to be friends. In those days he was barber to the diplomatic corps. Later I insinuated him into the State Department, where he outstayed me. One day, after I had gone, I said to him, "Charlie, how's my friend Foster?"

"Not so good, not so good," he replied. "I think he's got hold of that damned initiative and can't let go of it." In the old days, the Justice patronized his shop twice a week. Mrs. Brandeis did not like him to have his hair cut. He solved the problem by these frequent visits and his admonition, "Charlie, the invisible haircut!"

North from our office, Connecticut Avenue, its broad sidewalks shaded by double rows of sycamore trees, passed first the Convent and Academy of the Visitation, whose brick wall enclosed the whole block where the Mayflower Hotel is today; then St. Matthew's Cathedral and Chief Justice White's house on Rhode Island Avenue, and on past the British Embassy at N Street, to join Massachusetts Avenue in a traffic and social jumble at Dupont Circle.

While commerce was moving up Connecticut Avenue, society was leaving K Street to settle on Massachusetts Avenue from Scott Circle west. A massive enclave grouped around Dupont Circle — Miss Mabel Boardman's large and somber brick house, the marble palaces of the Countess Gizycka, née Eleanor (Cissy) Patterson, and of the Leiters across the street. On the other side of the Circle came the Henry Spencers, Speaker Longworth, Mrs. Walsh, Mrs. Townsend, and the Misses Patten. At Sheridan Circle, where the General in bronze perpetually rallies his troops from defeat at Winchester, another wave of mansions and embassies moved — and still moves — westward.

Hidden away above Dupont Circle is a more modest street. Quite properly, Admiral Du Pont on his granite pedestal, himself soon to be replaced by Daniel Chester French's marble fountain, turned his back on it. Corcoran Street runs east from a dead end at 19th to be lost, temporarily in the broad confluence of 18th

Street and New Hampshire Avenue, before again briefly taking up its way, to peter out at 13th Street. On the south side of the street at its west end we lived in one of a row of small identical houses, each with an overhanging bay window on the second floor, giving a slightly Walt Disney impression of a twelfth-century Normandy village. In this area existed what might be called a ghetto of near respectability and intelligence in the midst of high position, wealth, and fashion.

I say "near" respectability because of one of our neighbors whose conduct was unpredictable. One evening we had dining with us a most proper Bostonian, who was a law clerk to Justice Holmes. Not long afterward, distaste for America of the twenties drove our guest to England and British citizenship. On the evening I mention, just as dinner ended, our unpredictable neighbor in fez, false beard, and his conception of the probable clothes of an Armenian rug peddler, and with some of his own unimpressive rugs over his arm, pushed past a bewildered cook and stamped muttering up the stairs, the cook protesting behind him. Surprise, embarrassment, and the torrent of his speech as he laid out his wares and pressed a sale on our guest and my wife, as the householders, carried all before him. The performance was first class, but soon ended as the disguise was penetrated and the peddler revealed as our entertaining and then obscure friend, Sinclair Lewis. Our guest was definitely not amused.

Within a few doors of the Lewises lived the Stuart Chases. All three of us vied with one another for obscurity and in describing the parlous state of the country, our fellow citizens, and the world in general.

Lewis, called "Red" or "Hal" (his full name was Harry Sinclair Lewis), wrote stories for magazines and story plots, including mysteries, for other writers. One novel, *Free Air*, had misfired; and he was currently working on another. All of his friends had read parts of it; and part of them, all. We were unanimous that it, too, was doomed to failure. The book-buying

American public, we pointed out sagaciously, would not pay to be made fun of, particularly, in its earnest and self-conscious pursuit of culture. We were so overwhelmingly wrong that some tried to change their votes retroactively when *Main Street* became a literary prodigy and added new words to the language.

The Lewises immediately skyrocketed into orbit among the notorious and the great, his own gift for the outrageous adding to his and the book's publicity. In an era which also witnessed the Scopes "monkey" trial in Tennessee, Lewis would thunder from church pulpits against the "fundamentalists" and other literal interpreters, defying God to strike him dead. This was worth columns in a press which had little else to report except scandals in Washington and disintegration in Europe.

Grace Hegger Lewis was entranced by this meteoric change in their fortunes. A gay and attractive woman, she now had the clothes to set her off. Over the length of years, I see a saucy black hat — not one of those bucket affairs — set rakishly on the side of her head with an artistic feather curling down below her ear. She still declared her birthplace to have been Brooklyn; but now added wistfully, "However, I was conceived in Vienna." Her excitement was contagious when a White House messenger came with an invitation to tea with Mrs. Harding. We waited for the report. "Before the usher could announce me," said Grace, "I rushed up to Mrs. Harding and said, 'I'm Mrs. Main Street!'"

It was all great fun, but it was sad, too. Success was not good for that marriage, or for either of the parties to it, or for Lewis's work. Soon all of the small ghetto company had left Corcoran Street, but the Lewises came back to Washington twice during the twenties; each time the atmosphere seemed more strained, more frenetic. Only their son, Wells, named for H. G. Wells, a handsome boy, full of promise, seemed to improve. Unhappily he was destined never to fulfill his promise. He was killed in the Second World War.

Lewis was restless, seemingly seeking some refuge from himself in which to work. He fled first from his study at home to a secret office downtown; but soon found — or said he found — an even more secret one, while still keeping the first one as defensive cover. Books continued to flow from him in the Daumierlike style and pattern of *Main Street*, directed at various sectors of American life — business, the church, medicine, and so on. They won him a Nobel prize. Sales continued; so did the photographic memory, the quick release. But insight seemed to have gone, though I had no chance to learn at first hand, for the Lewises were divorced and we drifted apart.

In 1920, Stuart Chase did not write books; he audited them, and did so for the Federal Trade Commission in hot pursuit of those seeking in the classic split infinitive of the Clayton Act, "to substantially lessen competition" in any line of commerce. Stuart believed in competition. With William James and my boss, he was "against bigness and greatness in all their forms"; but the tide was running against them. Already he had been marked out for special notice by that Republican stalwart, Senator James Watson of Indiana. After charging that the Commission's staff which had investigated the meatpackers were themselves "packed with men who are avowed socialists, anarchists, reds and radicals," he added that Chase "beside being a wellknown exponent of socialistic doctrines . . . was president and organizer of the Fabian Club of Chicago, 'a society founded for the express purpose of furthering the doctrines of socialism.'" The New Freedom was even nearer its end than its unhappy originator in the White House. Not long after the change of administration, Chase left the government. Before long he, too, blossomed into a new and highly successful career as a literary philosopher.

The new President paraded down Pennsylvania Avenue on March 4, 1921. The most "striking feature of the parade," the *Washington Post* reported, was "the biggest broom ever made," gilded of handle, topped by an American flag, given to the President by an Oklahoma delegation to typify the "possibilities of change of administration from Democratic to Republican." The day was a rarely auspicious golden one, and the crowds shouted and jumped up and down with frantic enthusiasm at being rid of high endeavor and being led back to normalcy. We and our friends stood with a small group on S Street, bareheaded while a cripple, helped from his car, hobbled laboriously to the door of his new house. At the threshold he turned, took off his top hat to us and disappeared. Again, three years later, we stood there while his coffin was carried out.

Meanwhile, the new Administration developed its own curious blend of piety, vulgarity, and corruption. At first, attention centered on the piety. "I met the President, today," said Justice Brandeis after the Court's official call. "He has a fine face. I have hope of him." This was significant, coming from the Justice, one of whose maxims, adopted from Lincoln, was, "At forty every man is responsible for his face." Justice Clarke, an enthusiast for the League of Nations, found hope in another quarter — "Hughes is our best hope for finding a way into the League."

Soon the gilded broom had swept the White House clean of any lingering taint of professional intellectuality. Poker parties with senatorial pals provided relaxation. There were rumors of a scene at the house on McPherson Square of the publisher of the *Washington Post*, Ned McLean, when Secretary Hughes found that a party for the Cabinet was to be entertained by movies of a Dempsey championship fight, illegally transported in interstate commerce. A young woman of doubtful reputation had her skull bashed in — it was said by a bottle — in an equally doubtful hotel, after a riotous party allegedly attended by some who might more profitably have spent the night gathering strength for official duties.

"The little green house on K Street" was whispered to be the scene of deals, appointments, and payoffs. The word "oil" began to be bruited about. About this time, Mrs. Brandeis being ill and attended by nurses, the Justice for a while slept on a couch in his office. I was no longer his law clerk, and it was then that our former relationship subtly changed. Being lonely, he would send word that, if convenient, he would welcome an evening call on him in the office. There, with no work to stand between us, and all alone, he would say conspiratorially, "Dean, what is the latest dirt?"

The Justice was an arresting figure; his head of Lincolnian cast and grandeur, the same boldness and ruggedness of features, the same untamed hair, the eyes of infinite depth under bushy eyebrows, which in moments of emotion seemed to jut out. As he grew older, he carried a prophetic, if not intimidating aura. It was not in jest that later law clerks referred to him as Isaiah. But it would be wrong to leave the impression here. For more than twenty years I had the great privilege of his friendship and learned much of his mind and spirit at once worldly and austere, severe and loving; of his affections, detached and yet wholly committed. During that time I became assured of his affection and I believe that he never doubted my devotion. One of the greatest honors and hardest tasks which has come to me was to speak at his funeral service.

I started with the advantage of working for him when he had been only three years away from active practice and of knowing two close friends of the old days, Herbert White of the Plimpton Press in Boston, and Norman Hapgood, once the sensational muckraking editor of *Collier's Weekly*, the destroyer with Brandeis of Taft's Secretary of the Interior, Richard Ballinger. These two men and the Justice's sisters-in-law were the only people whom I ever heard call him "Louis." Mrs. Brandeis's name for him, as nearly as I can render it, sounded like "Leurps."

I shall never forget my first meeting with Herbert White. Answering a ring of the office doorbell, I found a genial and rumpled stranger who asked me whether "Louis" was in. He was not, and I said so, adding that he could be seen only by appointment. If he would give me his name, etc.

"Don't give me that stuff," he said good-naturedly. "I'll come in and wait for him. I see he has you hypnotized, too. Come on in with me and tell me who you are." With that he led casually into the study, with me tagging along. He pulled a chair up to the desk, to my horror swept onto the floor a stack of carefully place-marked U. S. Reports, and put his feet up. Surely, I thought, surely a bolt direct from the hand of Jove will strike this impious profaner of the shrine itself.

Instead, he went on imperturbably, "I'm Herbert White. Louis and I used to do a lot of sailing and trout fishing together. I never went along with that fox hunting of his. He was a great guy in those days. Still is. But not much use to his friends since he got sight of the Holy Grail." I was beginning to come out of shock, but he saw me glancing nervously at the doors. "Sit down," he said. "For God's sake, relax! He doesn't eat children."

I took a semiseat facing the door, ready to spring to attention, in no way convinced by the last observation. "I remember the day and hour of the conversion," he went on. "We were sitting around a campfire in Maine after a great day's fishing. I wanted to plan for tomorrow. But he started off on the damnedest bellyache you ever heard. The tie-up between government and money; the way the banks used other people's money against their interest; the way big corporations skinned the public and pushed the laboring man around; insurance companies fought savings bank insurance, and railroad management didn't know its own business or interest. On and on it went."

"Finally," he ended, "I'd had enough. 'Louis Brandeis,' I said, 'you've had the best day ever on the river, a wonderful dinner, and your pants are dry. What the hell's the matter with you?' "

I heard the key in the lock and was already on my feet when

the Justice came in. "Ah, Herbert," he said, "I see that you are already giving my new law clerk his first lesson."

"Good morning, sir," I murmured and faded through the doorway into my own room.

Norman Hapgood's devotion to the Justice was no less intense than Herbert White's, but more discerning, combining as he did both sympathy and skepticism. He was even skeptical — and this shocked me deeply — of Justice Holmes. Passages from the latter's writings which seemed to me close to holy writ, Norman would airily dismiss as commonplaces of agnosticism gilded by a romantic turn of prose. His rare gift for controversy and ridicule was a useful astringent at a *fin de siècle* institution still observed in Washington in the nineteen-twenties. This was the "at home" day of ranking ladies of our officialdom, when the rest of us paid respectful homage. Monday was always Supreme Court day. Cabinet wives, senatorial wives, high-ranking military wives at Fort Meyer and the Naval Observatory, each group had its day when cards were left — two of a husband's and one of a wife's, with the corners turned down — and ceremonial tea consumed. Most of these occasions were as tepid as the tea. But on one afternoon in Mrs. Holmes's drawing room, without a word of warning and at a moment of perfect peace, General Pershing and his staff appeared in overpowering military array and brilliance, leaving even indomitable Mrs. Holmes limp.

The Brandeises' "at home" was purposeful and austere. The hostess, erect on a black horsehair sofa, presided at the tea table. Above her, an engraved tiger couchant, gazing off over pretty dreary country, evoked depressing memories of our dentist's waiting room. Two female acolytes, often my wife and another conscripted pupil of Mrs. Brandeis's weekly seminar on child education, assisted her. The current law clerk presented newcomers. This done, disciples gathered in a semicircle around the Justice. For the most part they were young and with spouses — lawyers in government and out, writers, conservationists from

Agriculture and Interior, frustrated regulators of utilities or monopolies, and, often, pilgrims to this shrine. Occasionally older friends came in. These, though admirers, were definitely not disciples: Adolph Miller of the Federal Reserve Board and his wife, whom Franklin K. Lane (Secretary of the Interior) hailed as the "fair ship, *Mary Miller* . . . the gayest thing on the sea, and when her sails were all set from jib to spanker she made a gladsome sight, and some speed"; Robert Woolley, who had been Publicity Director for the Democratic National Committee and the First Liberty Loan and who looked like a kewpie doll, and his daughter; Joseph Eastman, Chairman of the Interstate Commerce Commission, and his sister, much admired by the Justice; sometimes, Mrs. Robert (Belle) LaFollette and Mrs. Brandeis's delightful sisters, Pauline and Josephine Goldmark. Except for Eastman, these and other elders were inclined to create a rival center around Mrs. Brandeis. Though she gave signs of pleasure when this occurred, she kept it under strict control.

Looking back over forty years, two interacting themes seem to have dominated the Justice's talk — the Greek Genius (he was an admirer of Alfred Zimmern's *The Greek Commonwealth*) and the Curse of Bigness. These themes crossed like the lines on a telescopic sight on any unfortunate who was reported to be going, not back to his home town, but to New York or Chicago or Philadelphia (Boston rarely provoked the same reaction, perhaps because the Justice himself forsook Louisville for Boston) to seek fame or riches, or both, in some large firm or business. Then the great eyebrows would jut menacingly forward. Short forward jabs with the back of the right hand would underline each sentence; and he would be off on the curse of these metropolitan maws which, having first corrupted with promise of money and power, sucked in and devoured the youth and promise of the country. He spoke of the impotence of an individual really to affect the course of any big community or organization. They ran themselves by a mechanics ungovernable by man. To govern and shape a community no larger than New Jersey would stretch the capacities of a Pericles. It could be done; but better still in smaller communities. Those who would spend their lives there could achieve not the preeminence (and distorted development) of specialists, but a rounded and full understanding of life, the only wisdom which could be trusted with leadership.

Fortunately, memory can be amplified by contemporaneous appraisal of the mind and convictions so hidden by his reserve. In the autumn of 1920, as I began my second year with the Justice, Felix Frankfurter prodded me into trying my hand at analysis. This is what I wrote:

Dear Frankfurter,

When you spur me with both heels, the challenge and the delicate flattery, I must have a go at the hurdle that might bring a better man a cropper. Talking about greatness in men is always an unsatisfactory business. The inarticulate judgments and intuitions have the field all to themselves; they are the court of last resort. And observations of courts make me realize how much of their own philosophy they read into the facts which they state.

The accepted opinion of the Justice is that he is one of the faithful, a "friend of the people," an enthusiast. He is supposed to be burning with the true social faith which on its emotional side calls on the disenfranchised to

> "Loose the chains that fall on you
> Ye are many, they are few."

and on its intellectual side is filled with the excitement of the possibilities which might come from the application of an intelligent plan to human institutions. It sees how easily the oppressors could be routed by a general staff of humanity and it comes from the vision burning with the new religion. The Justice is the "Plumed Knight" of these people. His silence and reserve and impersonalness have let the traditions grow and grow.

Now if he were this sort of a person he would be a very considerable man. He would be the kind of person who is moved to great things by what other people call fanatical faith. His ability would be open to the same admiration. But the motive force, the courage, the character which makes the man would in my opinion be drawn to some extent from outside the man. He would be acting under the influence of a spiritual stimulant when "following the gleam." He might have the keenest appreciation of the value of life and all the joys and sorrows which go with it and yet believe it worth turning upside down or throwing away altogether for the realization of the vision which transcends anything he ever imagined. That this sort of thing is not the "greatest" is of course, only my pre-judgment of life.

But I am quite convinced that the Justice is not this sort of a person at all. On the emotional side he has, of course, human sympathy. But it is a sympathy with people who are suffering, not with potential gods who are being held back in their development. He doesn't believe much in chains, and that sort of thing. And he isn't more than wistfully moved by the possibility of applying intelligence to life on a large scale because he knows that there isn't that much intelligence to apply. Instead — as I see him — he thinks that the great end in life lies with the individual mind, in its building up its own worlds, in its explorations and darings and triumphs over weaknesses and fears and laziness, and, perhaps, something more — but that I don't even guess at. But he sees that for most the road to this is quite shut off and for the rest it is getting more and more impassable as great stupid institutions, growing larger and larger fall across the way and crowd into the little space which the individual has.

As I said, I don't think that the Justice puts the slightest faith in mass salvation through universal Plumb Plans. People haven't the intelligence for that sort of thing. They have only the intelligence to operate in small personal groups which deal with the things with which they are intimately acquainted. New "functional" governments, "social discipline" and all that sort of thing leaves him cold. But he can believe that all through this mass of blubber, society, there are individual minds which are working and which may be able to guide a handful of followers out of the wilderness, if they are let alone. But that "if" is a very big one. No one is ever let alone. The capacity for stupid, wasteful, ruinous interference seems to be infinite in these masses of blubber. His goal seems to be by the use of intellect to gain a purely negative freedom from interference for people who want to use their intellects.

The Justice told me once that when they asked him what title should be put on his Oregon brief, he said "What Any Fool Knows." A good part of his life has been spent in telling stupid people what any idiot ought to have been able to see at a glance. And he did it and still does it without the slightest idea that it is hastening the Kingdom of Heaven. But it may give some fellow a chance to run. And that he considers worth a lot. He is not one of those who believes, as Justice Holmes says, that if you sit on the world long enough it will hatch. Neither does he believe that there isn't any hatching going to be done. But it will be done by an individual here, a little group there, or a community or perhaps, a state if it is small and homogeneous enough. And the Justice has considered it eminently worth while to point out exhaustively and thoroughly and patiently that these efforts should not be stupidly interfered with.

The reason I said "not 'the greatest' " — which was not a good expression — was because it seems to me greater to be able with full knowledge of the facts to put a lifetime of the same energy and courage into gaining half an inch, or even into preventing a loss, which other people put into a vision of world salvation.

And I thought that if some of his admirers knew him better they would like him less because they might discover that the Justice thought that they were damn fools. The ranters and the boys who carefully tag every one of a man's acts with its appropriate epithet in the language of political theory, the person who proceeds with more warmth than knowledge — none of these people would like the Justice as well if they checked up their vague impressions of him and discovered his of them.

By the date you see that this was started a month ago. I put it away as wholly inadequate. But I shall never do much better. So along it goes.

Best wishes for the holidays.

D. G. A.

Herbert White, like so many of Justice Brandeis's friends and admirers, was misled about him. What the Justice caught sight of and what moved him deeply was not the Holy Grail in the sense of a symbol of mass salvation, but the blocks which the human establishment, callous, cumbersome, and crass put in the way of the individual search for fulfillment.

Among the friends of the Brandeises whom we knew and saw at this time were the La Follettes, the whole gifted family. The old Senator and Mrs. La Follette were the very embodiment of the Progressive Era, now guttering out. Belle La Follette was said to be the first woman to be graduated in law in Wisconsin, though she never practiced. The Senator, born before the Civil War, founder and leader of Wisconsin progressivism, as a last gallant gesture carried the Progressive banner into the presidential election of 1924 in protest against the choice offered by the major parties, Calvin Coolidge or John W. Davis. The next year he died, and "Young Bob," who for some years had been the head of his Senate office, succeeded him. Bob was no less able than his father and a man of strong convictions, but the times were against him. Although an even more adventurous progressivism was soon reborn, Bob La Follette did not rise with it. His life ended in illness and tragedy.

At the turn of the decade, however, the La Follettes' house was a lively place. As unconventional as they were, large and rambling, it had obviously been built before 16th Street or Mt. Pleasant Street had been laid out on the hill overlooking the old city, and was left tucked away between the two streets, in the triangle made by them, facing on neither, partly hidden by new growth. But there was nothing quiet or retiring about the life within it. Talk, animated and varied, never seemed to pause.

In less sophisticated days, the adjective used to describe almost any social gathering in Washington was "brilliant." This called up images of society dramas in which diplomats in dazzling uniforms exchanged with bejeweled ladies repartee as glittering as their gems, while a statesman's whispered phrase changed the fate of a nation or a bill in Congress. If such gatherings occurred, we did not attend them. Over the years Washington social talk, like that of all single interest societies, is repetitious and dull. Politics tends to become gossip; and uninterrupted gossip is dull. Possibly politics laced with philosophy by Plato and with history by Thucydides might be enthralling. Unhappily, neither is available to imaginative Washington hostesses; and where the "salon" has been attempted, it too easily slides into a current events lecture, or a fencing match between political prima donnas. In recent years the founding of distinguished galleries and modest beginnings in other forms of art have brought a dilution — but only a dilution — in the steady absorption of "politics on the rocks."

At the La Follettes' one enjoyed two forms of self-entertainment or enlightenment, or both, which were soon to pass with the fading era. The first of these was to discuss matters in the merits of which the discussants were deeply concerned — in short, talk by those committed to action about what they were doing; not talk by observers about the gamemanship of more or less professional performers. One of the first columnists, delightful Frank Kent, who wrote "The Great Game of Politics" for The Baltimore *Sun*, observed that the weakness of the La Follettes was in deceiving themselves by their own bunk. He meant hardly more than that the La Follettes' intensity and zeal in advocacy heightened their belief in their cause — a fair enough observation; though he conveyed also the growing sense of detachment from the issues of politics and increasing absorption in the techniques of the art. As this attitude has become predominant in political discussion in Washington, talk has become more arid. One hears more discussion of the views of the commentators and less discussion from the artists themselves. This was not the case at the La Follettes'. There one never heard about the mysteries of "timing" — which appears today as the heart of the po-

litical process. But one did hear passion and indignation and conviction.

More fun — and a good deal more instructive — were the evenings when the Senator played the lead in Shakespeare readings.
He had histrionic ability, with a delightful touch of ham about
him, had once wanted to be an actor, so he said, and, perhaps,
had achieved his ambition. The word "great" could become almost a paragraph when the Senator put his heart into it. He took
the best parts, often several in the same play, and both starred
and directed. Phil, as I remember, was rather better than Bob.
Fola had been, perhaps still was, on the stage and, when available, was conceded the female lead. The evening would build up
to what might be called the Senator's great arias. One could imagine that he spoke of himself in Wolsey's speech in *Henry VIII*.

> ". . . I have ventured,
> Like little wanton boys that swim on bladders,
> This many summers in a sea of glory,
> But far beyond my depth . . ."

and in reporting the Cardinal at the monastery door:

> ". . . 'O, Father Abbot,
> An old man, broken with the storms of state,
> Is come to lay his weary bones among ye;
> Give him a little earth for charity!' "

He, too, was soon to need it.

We were coming to the end of an era in many ways other than
politics. Before the decade of the twenties was half gone, a majority of the Court I first knew had gone too. Soon even its habitat was destined for change, and with this something of its aura,
too. The old courtroom in the Capitol, which had been the Senate chamber of Benton, Henry Clay, and Webster, combined
dignity with truly republican simplicity. I felt about it the way,

years later, a security officer of mine felt when I pointed out to him the spot not far from the Place Royale in Paris on which Henry of Navarre was murdered. "Gee, Mr. Secretary," he said, "there's a hell of a lot of history around here!"

The main axis corridor of the Capitol cut off the courtroom on the east side from the Clerk's office and the combined robing and conference room on the west. On days when the Court sat the Justices, having robed, notified waiting Capitol policemen, who stopped and held back traffic in the corridor until, led by the Chief Justice, the Court solemnly walked across. It was all very simple and intimate.

Mr. Taft, on becoming Chief Justice in 1921, made it a first order of business to get under way the new Supreme Court Building, facing the Capitol across the park. Justice Brandeis was strongly opposed and never moved into the offices set aside for him. He found more than symbolic importance in having the Supreme Court midway between the Senate and the House, almost directly under the dome of the Capitol, accessible to the main flow of life through the old building. He thought it a great mistake to give the Court, the other branches of government, and the country the sense of its aloofness which came from setting it apart in a palace of its own.

Since the Capitol had no space for chambers for the Justices, they worked at home. Each Justice was entitled to a set of federal court reports, a messenger, whom he inherited from the Justice whose place he took, and one other employee as desired. Most of them chose a stenographer-typist. Justices Holmes and Brandeis chose differently. They dispensed with the stenographer, answering their mail — when they did so — by hand, but consigning a satisfactory part to the wastebasket. For Justice Brandeis correspondence was not difficult. Short answers to proper questions, none to silly ones, and no explanations for refusals were his rules. He often mentioned the impression made on him by a man who wrote: "I regret that I cannot comply

with your request. So that you may know that my refusal is
final, I give no reasons." Justice Holmes corresponded volumi-
nously in the best eighteenth-century tradition. His letters, in his
fine hand, fill volumes. Many of them were written on the bench
while he was waiting for counsel to catch up with his understanding of their case. This gave him, he used to say, an unde-
served reputation for attention and industry. Opinion writing,
also, these Justices did in longhand, often so interlined and altered as to be almost undecipherable. The making of a fair copy
of these drafts fell to the Court printer, who must have employed
a gifted cryptanalyst.

Instead of a stenographer-secretary, first Holmes and then
Brandeis supplemented their messengers by a June graduate of
the Harvard Law School, chosen (in my time) by Professor Felix Frankfurter. They believed that these young men, fresh
from the intellectual stimulation of the law school, brought
them constant refreshment and challenge, perhaps more useful in
their work than the usual office aides. Very soon the idea caught
on and Congress made a choice no longer necessary. Today the
practice of using as "law clerks" current graduates of all the leading law schools has spread pretty generally throughout the federal
judiciary and to many state courts. The insight into the working
of the judicial process which young lawyers gain by their experience is of incomparable value.

But in 1919, my colleague with Justice Homes and I felt the
zest of pioneering at the end of an era a wholly new and unique
institution.

4

"OUR COURT"

MR. JUSTICE STORY in later life referred to the Marshall Court, to which he was appointed as its youngest member, as "the Old Court." To me the Supreme Court of the United States, as constituted at the beginning of the nineteen-twenties, will always be — in Justice Brandeis's phrase, solemnly pronounced with a forward gesture of the right hand — "Our Court." Was it only the illusion of perspective which made eminence and individuality more easily discerned in our youth than later? My mind tells me that many men, including judges whom I have known by their first names, have a greater claim to distinction than many members of that Court. But I do not feel it in my bones, as I do that on the day of judgment "Our Court" will be sitting in their robes before the Throne, handing down decisions in the more difficult cases.

In the preceding chapter I spoke of the old courtroom in the Capitol, drenched in history. In fitting accord two men taken out of the heart and turmoil of American history sat in the center of its bench — a Confederate soldier in the middle chair and a Union soldier on his left. On some anniversary, I forget what, perhaps of one of Holmes's wounds, the Chief Justice would bring him a red rose to be pinned on his robe. Chief Justice White was not a great Chief Justice, but a beloved figure. Justice McKenna put it very well:

. . . our associate in duties, our companion in council, our friend and intimate[.] He was all of these to us, and by them animated and directed our work; his precedence veiled under a considerate courtesy, our intercourse with him made a real enjoyment. . . .

. . . .

In private life he was a gentleman in the best sense of that much-abused word. He was considerately kind and courteous, and not in passing show, for he was incapable of artifice or dissimulation.

He was a large man with a small face, centered about a little shrewd nose and eyes, surrounded by high forehead, fleshy cheeks and jowls which shook under emotion.

The Chief Justice would often be brought and left at Stoneleigh Court by his chauffeur to talk with Justice Brandeis. It fell to me to walk him home the two blocks to Rhode Island Avenue, for his eyesight was too bad to permit crossing streets alone. His talk, easy to start, made these walks a delight. One day we were walking home along Connecticut Avenue, soon after Mr. Elihu Root's argument in the *National Prohibition Cases*. This group of cases, involving a number of issues raised by the then new constitutional prohibition of intoxicants, produced one of the oddest situations in the Court's history. The Court was able to agree on how the issues should be decided, but not why. As Justice Brandeis once said to me, "Some questions can be decided which can't be answered." That was the case here. So the judgments were supported by eleven "conclusions of the Court" regarding the Eighteenth Amendment and the Volstead Act; but no attempt was made to relate these conclusions to the disposition of the several cases. This precedent, as Justice McKenna observed, "will undoubtedly decrease the literature of the Court if it does not increase lucidity."

Whatever their differences, however, no member of the Court was persuaded by Mr. Root. I hoped to draw out the Chief Justice on one aspect of his argument. Mr. Root drew a long bow, nothing less than that the Eighteenth Amendment to the Constitution was itself unconstitutional. His argument employed the "entering wedge" or "slippery slope" technique: " 'the Constitution,' " quoting Chief Justice Chase, " 'in all its provisions, looks to an indestructible Union, composed of indestructible States.' . . . The so-called (sic) Eighteenth Amendment *directly* invades the police powers of the States . . . and absolutely withdraws from them their right to local self-government. . . . In other words . . . the States are not in truth indestructible . . . the Eighteenth Amendment . . . would authorize the complete subversion of our dual and federal system of government. . . ." "The Civil War amendments," were not a precedent because they were germane to an original federal duty. I reminded the Chief Justice that, when he had pressed Mr. Root on the similarity of prohibiting slavery and prohibiting liquor, Mr. Root thought that the pressure of war had, perhaps, distorted the symmetry and logic of our governmental system. The Chief Justice had inquired whether the pressure of war was not as valid a factor as symmetry or logic? After recalling this exchange, I mused that the Chief Justice's position had been a most "interesting" one.

The old gentleman came to a full and palpitating stop. "Young man," he bellowed, his jowls quivering, "I know what you're thinking." So did I, and feared that I had imposed too far on his good nature by hinting that the old Confederate soldier had come a long way. But his quivering ended in a chuckle. "Remember this," he added. "You'll be lucky when you're my age if you've only been a damned fool once." I am not so far as I should like from that age now, and already not that lucky.

The Chief Justice had a weakness himself for the style of argument just illustrated, with his individual touch to cap it. He would start with a reasonably fair statement of a litigant's position, followed by restatements progressively more disadvantageous to the side about to lose — each preceded by "or to put it another way," or "in other words" — until the position was palpably absurd. Then the guillotine would fall. "To state this proposition," he would conclude, "is to decide it," as, indeed, it was. It has been said of him that he had a tendency to believe that all facts were created free and equal. The Chief Justice's greatest dialectical coup, so Justice Holmes thought, was his invention of the "rule of reason" in the *Standard Oil* case for construction of the Sherman Antitrust Act. As he stated it, "the criteria to be resorted to in any given case for the purpose of ascertaining whether violations of the section have been committed, is the rule of reason guided by the established law and by the plain duty to enforce the prohibitions of the act. . . ."

"The moment I saw that in the circulated draft," Justice Holmes said to me, "I knew he had us. How could you be against that without being for a rule of unreason?" "Of course," he added with a twinkle, "the thought did occur to me that the rule might not prove to be self-elucidating."

The Union soldier was arresting, too; moreover, possessed of a grandeur and beauty rarely met among men. Like General Marshall, his presence entered a room with him as a pervading force; and left with him, too, like a strong light put out. Handsome, and aware of it, with thick white hair, intense eyes under heavy brows, and sweeping white mustache, he had style and dash. Mrs. Holmes was wrong in saying that he thought that a cock to his hat and a swagger made him well dressed. He was, in an impeccably Edwardian way — morning coat, striped trousers, and stiff wing-collar. Occasionally he, too, would open the door upon impressions and emotions of the war sixty years before — of Ball's Bluff, where he was shot in the heel, an inglorious wound, he would point out, were it not for the precedent of Achilles. But it could have been worse, he would add; for at one point, stretched out behind a rock which gave him some comfort, he glanced around to see his rear vulnerably above the cover. Homer offered no precedent for that contingency.

Others have written so exhaustively and authoritatively about Justice Holmes, his own letters and writings, legal and otherwise, fill so many volumes, and anecdotes about him are so numerous and so often retold — due to his sound instinct in conserving and reissuing good conversational and epistolary currency — that one relating his own experiences with the Justice can easily become a bore. So I shall do no more than give excerpts of talks with him to convey how intoxicating for a young man these meetings were.

Justice Holmes lived little more than a block from Justice Brandeis. Neither man would use the telephone. So my duties took me back and forth, carrying notes, drafts of papers, suggestions for opinions and so on. One rarely got away from 1720 I Street without what was called there "a chin." In these he gave the young a sense of great community of interest by his joy, eagerness, and delight in the beauty of life.

On November 29, 1919, I went there for a purpose long forgotten and had what must have been an exceptionally good chin, for on getting home I jotted down seven items of the great man's talk. I reproduce them here without editing or elaboration.

Nov. 29 — Conversation at 1720 I Street.

1) At the outset of our philosophy we take the step of supreme faith — we admit that we are not God. When I admit you, I announce that I am not dreaming the universe but am existing in it as less than it.

2) I have often done my part to amuse a bored god by trying to imagine how many universes might be existing in the same space at the same time without conflicting. Where we are sitting now a tyrannosaurus may be locked in a death struggle with some unnamed creature of another sphere from ours.

3) Man is a vain little creature with his pompous ultimates. If you want to realize his absurdity, think of a generation as the space of time within which the story of life could be passed on say from a man of eighty to a child of ten. Then realize that into one room you could get all the people who knew the story back to nothing.

4) Man is the leader of the whole pageant of the universe! Yes, he is the leader just as small boys lead a circus parade when they walk ahead of it. But if they turn down a side street, the parade goes on.

5) This little artichoke of a life of ours. We pull off a leaf of twenty-four hours and after all the waste and dullness of eating and dressing and sleeping and working, there is at most a few hasty moments when we are there with both feet — at most no more than a taste.

6) I remember once taking an essay I had written on Plato to Emerson — I was then nineteen. The sage read it and then, "When you strike at a king, you must kill him!" Rather fine for an old fellow to a young man.

7) I say sometimes, to give pain to my cultured friends, that everything twenty-five years old is dead. Civilization is a wave which progresses without moving its contents, and only that part within the wave length is alive. Each age orients itself anew. It finds a new touchstone which gives life meaning. This is not built wholly on the past, though the past shapes it. Therefore to the person with a developed mind starting out to think, I say, "read the most modern thing that you can find." As my old Uncle Charles Jackson used to say, "When you forget the color of the heroine's eyes, drop that book!"

Then as one reads on, learns in any field, he will find that he is carried further and further back. Only then the past takes on its real meaning.

Young girls say to me, "Oh, Judge Holmes, I love Euripides." And I tell them, "My child, you love Swinburne via Gilbert Murray." The real meaning of the classics is so simple that only a sophisticated mind can appreciate it. To read the classics first, one has to put in a lot that isn't there in order to bear them.

Take Plato: —

The notes break off with this imperative. What the Justice did with Plato has gone from my mind. No more entries were ever made in the book. For years I was convinced, and often said, that I had burned it when my wife pointed out the dubious propriety of making notes of confidential conversations. In fact, constant repetition has made a dramatic picture: my wife in the role of "Stern daughter of the Voice of God"; I penitently touching a match to the offending document in the fireplace in our living room. Discovery of the notebook a few weeks ago among some old papers somewhat impairs my part in the drama; but the lady refused to have her role questioned.

A few of his opinions of people stand out in the notes or from memory. "What," I asked, "was Justice Peckham like, intellectually?"

"Intellectually?" he answered, puzzled. "I never thought of him in that connection. His major premise was, 'God damn it!' But he was a good judge." As to Justice John Marshall Harlan, the elder, "Harlan's mind was like a vise, the jaws of which did not meet. It only held the larger objects."

John Hay, at their first meeting, made an unfavorable impression which persisted. As an immaculately dressed staff officer, he waked Holmes, dirty and unshaven in a box car in the Alexandria freight yard, with orders for his company, sent with other units of the Army of the Potomac, to screen Washington from a Confederate raid. "I thought of him as a dandy without much weight. But he has been useful to me in checking notions I have had about Henry Adams." Adams was important; Hay, merely a point in getting a triangulation.

I have no defense to the charge often made that from the first moment I saw Justice Holmes I succumbed to hero worship. So, in summing him up, I turn to the views of Alexander M. Bickel, who never knew him: ". . . He was, of course, one of the towering figures of his time, a many-colored Renaissance Man not to be enclosed within the conventional boundaries of the legal profession or of any other discipline he might have chosen. It has been remarked that no other man of comparable intellect and spirit has been a judge in the United States, or for that matter among English-speaking peoples."

The senior Associate Justice was Joseph McKenna of California, who, intending to become a priest, became, instead, a Congressman, a friend of William McKinley, and, by his appointment, Attorney General and Associate Justice of the Supreme Court. It is not recorded that the Justice ever quoted Cardinal Wolsey — "Had I but serv'd my God with half the zeal I serv'd my King, he would not in mine age have left me naked to mine enemies." Far from naked, the Justice appeared in all seasons with white scarf, overcoat, and rubbers. ". . . A little, bearded, birdlike man, McKenna had occasional flashes of insight into the nature of the new social and economic problems that came, more and more during his tenure, to be at the core of constitutional issues; but he was just as capable of having no insights."

I think of him always in company with Mr. Justice William R. Day, his contemporary and colleague in the McKinley Cabinet, another small, frail man whom a breath of air would carry off. A balding head, too large for his body, over which the skin was stretched tight, and protuberant ears seemed to qualify him more for membership among the Seven Dwarfs than the nine judicial Olympians, where President Theodore Roosevelt put him. This impression, I am sure, does him far less than justice, for Brandeis has characterized him as "a hot little gent." But to me one of his attributes was outstanding and provided ground for continual speculation. He was the only man I had ever spoken with who had been Secretary of State. To be sure, after a few months he had gone off to negotiate peace with Spain and been succeeded by the famous Mr. John Hay. What sort of an office was it which could have been occupied by this diffident little man? Reading his opinions gave no clue, and the impenetrable mists of the future shrouded from me the mode by which the answer would become clear.

Justices Van Devanter and Pitney were both, quite appropriately, appointees of President Taft. They shared a qualification which he admired and sought in prospective appointees to the Supreme Court, prior judicial experience. This is a good asset. It is not captious to say that it is not the best, adding, at once, that one should not expect all members of the Court to possess the best. Almost of an age, they practiced law two thirds of a continent apart: Pitney in New Jersey, the congenial habitat for large corporations; Van Devanter in Cheyenne, Wyoming, a frontier community — not the "New" but the last of the old frontier. Both men were active in Republican politics in their own states; both came to Washington in the days of McKinley — Pitney to the House of Representatives; Van Devanter as an Assistant Attorney General for the Department of the Interior concerned with public lands and water rights. Both men had judicial experience on the highest courts of their states; and Van Devanter, on the United States Circuit Court of Appeals for the Eighth Circuit.

By the time they came to the Supreme Bench both men's minds were firmly set in conservative laissez-faire beliefs. These views impeded but, at least in Pitney's case, did not wholly block insight into the new social and economic problems which "came, more and more during [their] tenure, to be at the core of constitutional issues." Pitney, wrote Holmes, "as Brandeis always said and, I came to think, truly had intellectual honesty that sometimes brought him out against his prejudices and first judgment." This was true in the series of employers' liability cases culminating in the *Arizona* cases in 1919. The principle of liability without fault, not by contract between employer and employee, but by legislative fiat, was hard for the Chief Justice and Justices McKenna, Van Devanter, and McReynolds. It was not easy for Pitney and Day. These two, however, were essential for a majority. It was Pitney who by dint of prayerful study had developed the rationale which held the whole Court together in the prior, simpler cases and, in the last and toughest, still garnered the essential Day, when a sweeping generality of Holmes's, who was first given the opinion, lost the Chief Justice and threatened to lose Day. Justice Brandeis, who had no small part in helping

Pitney through his travail, believed that "But for Pitney, we would have had no workmen's compensation laws."

In April 1920, another Arizona labor statute came before the Court in *Truax* v. *Corrigan*. The statute forbad Arizona courts to enjoin strikes or peaceful picketing, and a state court, accordingly, refused to do so. The Supreme Court voted 6 (the Chief Justice and Justices McKenna, Day, Van Devanter, Pitney, and McReynolds) to 3 (Justices Holmes, Brandeis, and Clarke) to hold the statute unconstitutional. The opinion was assigned to Pitney. This was during my service with the Court. Justice Brandeis prepared and circulated a dissenting opinion before Justice Pitney had prepared anything. After considering this document and further reflection, Pitney concluded that he could not "write in accordance with the vote" and circulated a memorandum in the opposite sense. In this state of affairs, the Chief Justice died, leaving the Court equally divided. The case was restored to the docket and reargued in October 1921, after Chief Justice Taft took his seat. He joined the former majority and wrote the opinion of the Court. Justice Pitney remained firm in his dissent, despite Taft's powerful influence with him, and filed his own opinion.

Superior performance on the Supreme Court of the United States is not to be determined solely by decisions in those cases of the highest constitutional importance where the Court is performing functions which in any other society but ours would not be thought functions of a court of law, but rather of a *curia regis* or *genro*. In these uniquely American cases the justices are asked to be statesmen possessed of wisdom, restraint, and selflessness very rarely achieved, perhaps hardly achievable, by man. Because of the rare abilities required to deal with them, prior judicial experience gives no assurance of the highest eminence on the Supreme Court. Justice Frankfurter's paper on the subject leaves no doubt about that. Aside from brilliant exceptions — in our own times Justices Holmes and Cardozo — the great figures on the Court have come from careers more closely connected with the life of the country. But to say this does not dispose of our appraisal of Justices Pitney and Van Devanter.

As judges they had achieved and maintained a high standard of excellence in one of the most civilized and difficult roles in any society. Their minds, as judges, were not only open but disciplined and controlled, and their exercise of power was limited and restrained, by the law as it existed in the precedents. Here lay both the value and the limitation of their prior judicial experience in preparing them to exercise the functions of our highest court.

A present vogue in judicial practice and theory is to turn from the ideal of restraint in the exercise of judicial powers, from restraints imposed by respect for precedent and predictability in the law, as well as from deference to legislative and executive judgments and prerogatives in the constitutional field, to a more "activist" and "result-minded" role. The role would use vague and general phrases of the Constitution, in some instances, to veto legislation contrary to the contemporary ethos of democracy as the particular judge understands it; in other instances, to prod reluctant legislatures forward to achieve it.

I can hear objection raised that what is novel is not the veto but the prod; and there is truth in this so far as constitutional decisions are concerned. But truth goes deeper. What seems to me novel is the self-consciousness of the "activism" both in constitutional decisions and in less far-reaching but still important ones applying historic statutes and common law conceptions. By self-conscious activism I mean an acknowledged desire for change in the law in accordance with the decider's own conception of right. He may conscientiously be seeking to administer justice, but it is personal justice — the justice of Louis IX or Harun al-Rashid, not that described on the lintel of the Supreme Court Building, "Equal Justice Under Law." One of our younger judges has been quoted to the effect that, whenever a precedent of which he disapproves is cited to him, he wants to smash it. This reflects, perhaps, a passionate and crusading temperament, but hardly what has hitherto been regarded as a judicial one.

Pitney was a man of grace and charm; Van Devanter, of solid Dutch strength and good judgment, beneath which ran a subtle capacity to understand and deal with his brethren. This made him a valuable man in conference in resolving those differences less than vital, often founded in mere stubbornness but none the less troublesome, with which one experienced in meetings is only too familiar. Equally valuable were his "returns" — that is, his comments and suggestions on draft, pageproof opinions circulated by his colleagues. Justices Holmes and Brandeis almost always accepted his wise and penetrating editing. Increasingly with age, writing became a labor and his output of opinions fell far below his colleagues'.

One day, sent to his house on 16th Street and ushered into his study, I was stopped by his peremptory command to "watch out for my opinion." Little piles of United States Supreme Court Reports covered the floor of the study, each pile with a memorandum on top. "Take care," said the Justice, "that's my opinion. If you knock those piles about, a week won't straighten them out."

Mr. Justice James Clark McReynolds of Tennessee was a different kettle of fish. The ogre of the liberals, a deplorable judge, an outrageous old curmudgeon, or, to put it in another's supreme understatement, "a man of numerous and abrasive personal idiosyncrasies," he remained my friend until death. Perhaps refuting — or, at least, confusing — the Lincoln-Brandeis dictum of men being responsible at forty for their faces, McReynolds had a magnificent head. One evening at a public dinner Jo Davidson, the sculptor, pointed him out to me in great excitement, exclaiming, "Look at that head! It could be a Roman Senator or a Medici Pope!"

Before my arrival on the scene, McReynolds had ceased speaking to his brethren Brandeis and Clarke because of some imagined slight on their part. This bothered Justice Holmes, who was most sensitive to personal friction near him and rendered acutely unhappy by rudeness. He struggled to mend matters, but McReynolds would neither explain nor forget. Knowing this, though not from my chief, I undertook with some trepidation my first mission to McReynolds's chambers in the Rochambeau (now demolished) on Connecticut Avenue between H and I Streets. But apprehension was unwarranted by the event. The Justice received me courteously, explained with complete frankness that he was not on speaking terms with my employer, but that this had nothing to do with me. He would treat me with consideration and would expect the same treatment from me. Furthermore, he added, I was not to smoke in his apartment (which I had no intention of doing) or before coming to it, since he could only too readily detect the repulsive odor which hung about a smoker. At first, our easy and friendly relations produced a sense of disloyalty, which I confessed to Justice Brandeis's amusement. He assured me that any ease of strain had his blessing.

Justice McReynolds came from practice in Nashville to be a trust-busting Assistant Attorney General in Theodore Roosevelt's Administration. He busted the tobacco and other monopolies, and followed that by a stint at practice in New York City, interspersed with special antitrust assignments for the Attorney General. All this sounded like liberalism to Woodrow Wilson, who made him, sight unseen, his first Attorney General. This post he held for a stormy year, rowing with Senators who charged him with using secret agents to spy on federal judges and influence their decisions and whom he defied by refusing in the public interest to supply information demanded of him. In 1914 President Wilson appointed him to the Supreme Court with evident relief and a disregard for the interests of the Court and the country, in which among Presidents he was not unique.

Thirty-five years after the Justice's appointment and some years after his death, I met the messenger, Harry Parker, whom he inherited from Mr. Justice Lurton. Justice Frankfurter had induced him, by the bait of a talk with the Secretary of State to cook one of his superior soufflés for our lunch in the Justice's chambers. We got onto the subject of Justice McReynolds. Was he, I asked, as hard to handle in domestic affairs as he was in official relationship? Parker was emphatic that this was not so, except at the very beginning of their association of thirty years. The crisis came over an afternoon reception of Mrs. Pitney's.

The Justice wanted to wear his morning coat. Harry Parker was laying out his clothes while the Justice had a haircut in his bedroom. When the striped trousers were put out, McReynolds objected; wanted to wear gray flannel trousers. Harry was outraged. A morning coat was formal; so were striped trousers. Flannel trousers were "dishabille." "Formal and dishabille just don't go together," Harry told him. The Justice appealed to the barber. "That barber was nothin' but a yes man," Harry reported. "He said flannel pants were fine." So they were worn.

Harry hurried off to tend the front door at the Pitneys' party. When Justice McReynolds came in, Mrs. Pitney was talking with Miss Patten. "You remember her, Mr. Secretary, a nice lady but a mighty sharp tongue. 'Good afternoon, Mr. Justice,' she says. 'Do I take it that you are bereaved?' 'Bereaved, ma'am?' he says. 'I don't follow you.' 'Well,' she says, 'why else would you be wearin' your pants at half-mast?' " That was when Harry Parker left.

The Justice returned to the apartment full of sound and fury. He accused Harry of laying out the flannel trousers, a travesty upon the truth, of having urged their propriety, an even greater travesty; he denounced him for having represented himself as experienced in valeting gentlemen. Parker recounted how he demolished these false accusations by an overwhelming array of fact and then, coming with fearful dignity and scorn to the last sneering reproach, "And as for valetin' gentlemen," he concluded, "I was valetin' gentlemen when some folks as thinks they's gentlemen were drivin' mules in cornfields." After that, he reported, there was no more trouble.

A statement made earlier — that Justice McReynolds was "a deplorable judge" — needs a word of explanation to those whose memory of the years before the Second World War is either nonexistent or misty. Justice McReynolds's views were rigid and ultraconservative; his temperament was passionate. These ingredients could hardly do other than produce a Colonel Blimp of the Bench. As he himself put it, "an amorphous dummy, unspotted by human emotions" is not a "becoming receptacle for judicial power." His most spectacular display of temperament and views occurred on February 18, 1935, in the courtroom of the Supreme Court when, following the announcement by Chief Justice Hughes of the Court's opinion in the *Gold Clause* cases, supporting legislative and executive action regarding the value and redemption of the dollar in gold, it fell to him to announce dissenting views of "The Four Horsemen," who included himself and Justices Van Devanter, Sutherland, and Butler. The following account is taken from Solicitor General Perlman's report to the Supreme Court of the Minute of the Bar at the time of Justice McReynolds's death.

. . . He completely departed from his written opinion and went to the country with an extemporaneous denunciation of repudiation of contracts and devaluation of the currency which electrified his auditors, sympathetic and unsympathetic alike. No stenographic transcript of what he said was taken. His remarks were quoted only fragmentarily, in the press. It was feared that they would be lost to posterity. Justice McReynolds himself prepared a revision of his remarks, which was published by the Wall Street Journal as the most authentic version. Many who heard the utterance will remember passages that do not appear in that version and will remember differently many that do appear. He has often been quoted as saying, "The Constitution is gone." It is believed the expression he used was, "The Constitution, as we have known it, is gone."

Among the stronger expressions contained in Justice Mc-Reynolds's own revision are the following:

". . . The record reveals clear purpose to bring about confiscation of private rights and repudiation of national obligations. To us, these things are abhorrent. . . .

"First, the President is granted power to depreciate the dollar. He fixed sixty cents. Next, attempt is made to destroy private obligations by 'A Statute to Regulate the Currency of the United States.' Also to destroy Government obligations. The same language — the same section — covers both. Having put out five hundred million Gold Clause bonds in May, Congress declares in June that these promises so to pay in gold are illegal and contrary to existing public policy, although this had been consistently observed for many years and had been approved by the courts.

"After this effort to destroy the gold clause, the dollar is depreciated to sixty cents. Prices are to be estimated in deflated dollars. Mortgages, bank deposits, insurance funds, everything that thrifty men have accumulated is subject to this depreciation. And we are told there is no remedy. . . .

"It is said that the National Government had made by these transactions $2,800,000,000 and that all gold hypothecated to the Treasury now may be used to discharge public obligations! If the dollar be depreciated to five cents or possibly one, then, through fraud, all governmental obligations could be discharged quite simply.

"Shame and humiliation are upon us now. Moral and financial chaos may confidently be expected."

Attorney General Clark added, "Those who were present . . . report that Justice McReynolds was almost beside himself with feeling as he spoke extemporaneously in dissent."

His prejudices extended beyond legal doctrine to women lawyers. Whenever a woman rose to address the Court, he pushed back his chair and left the Bench. Curiously, when the responsibility of presiding at sittings of the Court in the Chief Justice's absence fell to him as Senior Associate Justice, he was the soul of courtesy, welcoming women lawyers graciously, and listening with apparent attention and benevolence to arguments from lawyers of both sexes, which doubtless raised his blood pressure to the bursting point.

The Justice enjoyed social relations in congenial company. Always courtly, he was also kindly and could be amusing. His Sunday morning breakfasts for young people were famous and good fun, unless some unfortunate and forgetful youth absentmindedly lit a cigarette. Of all the Court it was McReynolds who organized and paid for annual trips to the circus for the pages.

Sometimes his penchant for gallant remarks to the ladies ran into bad luck, which puzzled but rarely bothered him. This happened once when he was dining with us, and once when we were with him. Being the ranking guest at our house, he made the move. Turning to Miss Laura Harlan, an elderly lady, the aunt of future Justice John Harlan, he asked for the pleasure of escorting her home. The lady bridled coquettishly and asked the company whether it would be altogether proper for her to go off with so handsome a bachelor. The Justice, intending a compliment to the well-known blamelessness of her character, replied with a bow, "Miss Laura, a lady like you would be safe with anyone." It seemed all too likely.

On another occasion at his apartment my wife had admired the excellent aquatints on the dining room walls. As we rose from the table, the Justice observed that he had even better ones in his bedroom, which he invited her to see. Gay Mrs. Owen J. Roberts complained that no such invitation had ever been extended to her, upon which he bore both ladies off for a tour of the gallery.

Justice McReynolds was woefully miscast on the Supreme

Court. He acquired a reputation from his deficiencies and became a figure with which law professors frightened their students. Abilities and qualities were obscured which might have brought him a substantial distinction and real regard in a less exalted and demanding position.

My memory of Justice John H. Clarke of Ohio, the faintest of all memories of that Court, is of a quiet, courteous, gray-haired gentleman, but carries neither sense of quality or personality, nor recollection of any conversation with him or where he lived, except that a sister was said to keep house for him. It was no secret that he was unhappy on the Court. Justice McReynolds's vendetta made daily life on the Court distasteful and he lacked compensating interest in its work. His great interest was the League of Nations. Justice Clarke was quoted as saying that, as he ascended the judicial hierarchy, he found it less rewarding. Like many more distinguished judges, he was happy in the trial court, as a District Court judge in Ohio. There, in his own phrase, he was lord of all he surveyed, not having to adjust at every turn to the views of colleagues. Beyond this, he delighted in being the embodiment of the law where people met it in action, in the commotion of trials, with split-second decisions to make, for which his simpler qualities of strength and character stood him in good stead. On the Supreme Court every decision, even when the Court should sit, had to be discussed with eight colleagues. And the issues seemed to him to concern either trivialities (under the jurisdiction as it existed before 1925) or disembodied intellectual abstractions. In an address in 1922 he said that unless one "sits on the Bench of the Supreme Court and hears, day after day, the astonishing discussions and distinctions there presented, no man can fully realize the extent to which ingenuity and refinement of constitutional discussion are rapidly converting the members of our profession in this country into a group of casuists rivaling the Middle Age schoolmen in subtlety of distinction and futility of argument." Frankly, the apellate process bored him.

Because the work of the Court lacked interest for him, one may question whether it engaged all his energies. He was curiously unpredictable. Sometimes he would be with Justices Holmes and Brandeis upholding modern legislation to meet the needs of an industrial age; again, he would desert them to write the opinion of the Court in sustaining the more hysterical persecutions of opinion growing out of the Espionage Act. For six years he endured the life, and then resigned to do all he could, so he said, to promote American entrance into the League of Nations, a cause already hopelessly lost.

Such, with my employer, of whom more later on, was "Our Court," from 1919 to 1921, made up of the selections of five Presidents — Cleveland, McKinley, Theodore Roosevelt, Taft, and Wilson, made over nearly a quarter of a century from 1894 to 1916. As I look back on them, it is with great respect, and with not only that but with respectful affection. And this is not because those were days of easy relations on the Court. The two years after the First World War were years of passionate division, in which two Justices, sometimes three, dissented from the majority on questions which aroused the deepest feelings: labor relations and civil rights.

I was a strong partisan and I still am. I still believe that the dissenters were right and the majority of the Court were wrong. But it never entered my mind to believe that the majority were not disinterested; I never doubted that they were subjecting themselves as much as men could within the system of their limitations to the restraint and to the discipline of the law.

5

WORKING WITH BRANDEIS

JUSTICE BRANDEIS'S STANDARD for our work was perfection as a norm, to be bettered on special occasions. Hard work he took for granted; but mere hours spent at a desk did not impress him. He would recall an observation made by Mr. Herbert Croly, editor of the *New Republic*, about Secretary of State William Jennings Bryan. Mr. Bryan had been criticized for neglecting official duties to lecture on the Chautauqua circuit. He replied that on the basis of careful investigation he sat at his desk fully as long as his predecessors. Whereupon Mr. Croly observed that the American people did not employ him to use that end.

The Justice worked long and hard, but he insisted that it be with a fresh mind and at top efficiency. As soon as he felt the let-down of fatigue, he stopped and either took his morning drive, or stretched out on the couch in his study and napped for exactly twenty minutes. When he found himself reading sentences over again, he knew that, worse than wasting time, he was missing the point of what he read. "More men," he would say, "have gotten into trouble by the inability to say no, and the failure to take vacations than by more familiar vices." And again, "A year's work can be done in eleven months, but not in twelve months." In short, he worked with intensity, or recharged his reserve of energy until he could.

He was not given to praise in any form, nor to blame in any

usual way. But his displeasure was made unforgettably evident. My first, and last, experience of his displeasure came at the beginning of our relationship. Again, it was Mr. Elihu Root and a prohibition case, *Jacob Ruppert* v. *Caffey,* which got me into trouble. Mr. Root had brought suit on behalf of Colonel Ruppert, a brewer, but better known as the owner of the New York Yankees, to enjoin enforcement against him of the Volstead Act prohibiting the sale of beer containing "one-half of one per centum or more of alcohol by volume." The Colonel's beer contained 3.4 per centum of alcohol by volume, but counsel alleged and wanted to prove that it was not, in fact, intoxicating. The lower court had refused to listen. We were even more unkind; we buried the argument that the fact was relevant under fifteen pages of footnotes. The idea of footnotes was the Justice's, but the compilation of them was mine. They established a world's record in footnotes to that time and constituted 57 per centum of the opinion by volume. They were a noble work, worthy of a better cause.

The footnotes collected the legislation and court decisions of all the states and territories to show their conclusion that regulation of intoxicating liquor could not be effective if made to depend on the "issuable fact whether or not a particular liquor . . . is intoxicating," that nearly all states had adopted a fixed alcoholic content as the test, and that the content fixed by Congress was within the range chosen, and hence a reasonable exercise of power. Only one state, we callously pointed out, had adopted a test of alcoholic content as high as the Colonel's beer. Even the footnotes did not win the concurrence of Justices McReynolds, Day, and Van Devanter.

On the Monday when the opinion was due to come down, I courted displeasure by knocking off work to listen in Court. While other opinions were being announced, a page kept bringing Justice Brandeis volumes of reports. This seemed strange and vaguely ominous. At length, when the Chief Justice nodded to him (he was then the next to the most junior Justice), he shook his head. Something was very wrong. Back at the office, I waited. When he came, the Justice put two volumes of state reports on my desk. "Did you read all the cases cited in the footnotes?" he asked. I answered that I had. "Suppose you read these two again," he said and went into his study.

The cases had nothing whatever to do with the propositions for which they were cited. Plainly, having made from the digests a list of cases to look up, I had checked two wrong ones for what some other cases had held. The explanation was too stupid to bother making. When I expressed chagrin and regret, he dismissed the matter with a sentence — "Please remember that your function is to correct my errors, not to introduce errors of your own." I remembered.

Our work would begin on Monday mornings following a Saturday conference of the Court with the receipt from the Chief Justice of an assignment notice, a paper on which were written the docket numbers of the cases assigned to Justice Brandeis for an opinion in accordance with the vote. The inhuman practice of those days was to hold the conference on Saturdays beginning at noon. Today they are held on Fridays beginning at ten o'clock. The Justice's mild protest was to rise at five o'clock and say, "Chief Justice, your jurisdiction has now expired and Mrs. Brandeis's has begun." With that he would leave for home.

From the assignment slip, the Justice would indicate the cases on which he would start drafting and those on which I was to start. If there was a dissenting opinion to be written, he would give instructions about that. He drafted in longhand; I, on a typewriter. When he reached a point where he wanted his draft checked, he would give it to me and take mine from me in whatever state it was; sometimes using parts of it, sometimes not. My instructions regarding his work were to look with suspicion on every statement of fact until it was proved from the record of the case, and on every statement of law until I had exhausted the authorities. If additional points should be made, I was to develop them thoroughly. Sometimes my work took the form of a revision of his; sometimes of a memorandum of suggestions to him. He was remarkably tolerant of physical alteration and often dissection of his sheets.

When, at length, the time came for a fair copy, the court printer made it from the nearly undecipherable manuscript put together with the aid of scissors and paste. The printer's proof was, in turn, subjected to further revision. When we were both satisfied, the final proof was circulated among the Justices for their editing, suggestions, and concurrence or dissent. A touching part of our relationship was the Justice's insistence that nothing should go out unless we were *both* satisfied with the product. His patience and generosity were inexhaustible.

An extreme example occurred in *Sutton v. United States,* an appeal from the Court of Claims, which today could not be taken to the Supreme Court. I thought that the decision of the Court was unjust and wrong legally. Due to the error of a government officer, a dredging contractor was required to do more than his contract with the government required and claimed on an admittedly fair basis, more than Congress had appropriated for the work. The Justice had written that, since Congress had provided that no contract "shall bind the Government to pay a larger sum . . . than the amount . . . appropriated . . ." no implied contract by reason of the error could obligate the government for more. When I objected to the inequity of this harsh rule, the Justice told me to try my hand at an opinion the other way, reminding me that it was not a question of what we "felt" was "right," but of what the law permitted and required. His opinion was held up until, after an earnest but futile attempt, I agreed with him.

Very early in our association I awakened to the fact that the law library did not contain all the tools of our trade. The Justice demanded the most exacting, professional, and imaginative search of the legal authorities. But to him this was more often than not the beginning, not the end, of our research. Too many of the issues which came to the Court were framed by social and economic conditions unimagined even a generation before. The debate might be carried on in the language of the cases; but the judicial weighing of the interests involved should, he believed, be made in the light of facts, sociologically determined and more contemporary than those which underlay the judicial approach to labor questions at the time of which I write. This rested on the law of conspiracy as devised by the Court of Star Chamber under the Tudors and developed by the common law courts of the Enlightenment, and the doctrine of "liberty of contract" developed in the early nineteenth century. (Justice Holmes used to say, "When my brethren talk of liberty of contract, I compose my mind by thinking of all the beautiful women I have known.")

So I spent my days not only in the Supreme Court Law Library — then in the basement of the Capitol under the courtroom — but in the stacks of the Library of Congress and with civil servants whose only recompense for hours of patient help to me was to see an uncatalogued report of theirs cited in a footnote to a dissenting opinion.

After working with the Justice for a few weeks, it was clear to me that his working papers would be an invaluable aid in any future appraisal of his mind and methods of approach to his work. So, with his consent, I began to collect them, a practice which my successors continued. For over twenty years every scrap of paper connected with his opinions and memoranda was preserved. Each case had its own red manila envelope, marked with its title and docket number. Into it went everything — the assignment slip, his and his law clerks' drafts, notes exchanged between them, printer's proofs with the changes made on them, the "returns" of the other Justices with their comments, the final product. Some envelopes bulged; others were thin. On leaving,

I instructed my successor in his duty and told him to pass the orders on. On his retirement, Justice Brandeis turned all these papers over to Justice Frankfurter, who in 1954 placed them in the library of the Harvard Law School. Both Justices used them extensively in their work. The first product, and a worthy one, of this rich mine was Professor Alexander M. Bickel's excellent book, *The Unpublished Opinions of Mr. Justice Brandeis.* I have drawn heavily on it in this volume. For the lawyer who wants a full-length view of Justice Brandeis's judicial methodology it is indispensable.

Justice Brandeis was not a simple man. His approach to his opinions was not a simple one, was not aimed merely to produce a scholarly and sound rationalization of the Court's decision. Opinions were addressed to two audiences — first, to his colleagues on the Court, and, second, to counsel in the cases and the bar beyond them. In dissent he often had another audience also in mind, the politically sophisticated public.

His method and purpose in addressing his colleagues played a large part in the increasing influence which, over twenty-five years, he exerted on some of the views of some of them. The purpose was education and persuasion; the method, that of education — patience, repetition, understanding the interests of the learner and meeting them. His style rarely sparkled; he avoided the epigrams and generalizations in which Justice Holmes delighted, the doubtful logic in which Chief Justice White and Justice McKenna sought to entrap the reader, and viewing with alarm the horrendous consequences of other views, so appealing to Justice McReynolds and Mr. Elihu Root. He understood the philosophical principle of antinomy: that inferences drawn from principles equally true may be in direct contradiction with one another, and that, in consequence, as Justice Holmes put it, "general propositions do not decide concrete cases."

He sought continuously to make the case before him as concrete as possible, to develop fully all the facts involved in the dispute and, beyond them, the great body of factual knowledge which surrounded the particular episode. "The change in the law," he wrote during my time with him, "by which strikes once illegal and even criminal are now recognized as lawful was effected in America largely without the intervention of legislation. This reversal of a common-law rule was not due to the rejection by the courts of one principle and the adoption in its stead of another, but to a better realization of the facts of industrial life." Justice Brandeis was the means by which this realization — and others — came to, at least, some of his brethren. His object was to narrow the issue and, with it, the area of judicial choice, of judicial discretion. Where part of the area of choice had been occupied by a statute, his effort was to give the legislative choice full scope, both by sustaining the legislative power and through interpretation, by giving full scope to its purpose and intention.

From the beginning of Justice Brandeis's tenure the possibility of obtaining a majority of the Court in support of labor legislation depended on Justices Pitney and Day; and Day depended on Pitney. In the preceding chapter something was said about the relations between Justices Brandeis and Pitney. These had a solid basis in mutual respect. Brandeis's influence with Pitney was also strengthened by his method of judicial approach, just mentioned. Where the path to understanding was blocked for Justice Pitney by "judgment or intuition more subtle than any articulate major premise," Justice Brandeis's method was to bring them out into the open and flood them with the light of learning. His reliance, as already said, was on Pitney's innate honesty of mind. To illustrate, I enlarge on a matter already mentioned.

In *Duplex Printing Press Company* v. *Deering*, argued during January 1920, two United States courts had refused to enjoin a machinists' union in New York which refused to install a press made in Michigan by a company whose machinist employees had failed in a strike to unionize the plant. The legal issue was whether this case was a dispute between an employer and em-

ployees within the Clayton Act, which was relied upon in denying the injunction. It was argued that, although the New York
union and the Duplex Company were in dispute, this was "secondary" to the "primary" dispute in Michigan. But the "legal"
issue may not always lie at the heart of the matter. There may be
a deeper and more subtle judgment or intuition directing or, at
least, affecting analysis. What I am about to write does not
prove but mildly suggests it here.

Each Justice in those days had a docket book, bound in red
leather over steel back and covers, joined by a locked clasp. I
had a key to our docket book, in which it was my duty to enter
on a separate page the name and number of each case, with minimum essential data, as it was assigned for argument. At the bottom of each page, in tabular form for voting purposes at the
Court's weekly Saturday conference, were the names of the Justices and, after each, columns marked "Aff.[irm]," "Rev.[erse],"
"Dism.[iss]," and — a larger space — "Remarks." One of the
joys of being a law clerk was to open the book on Saturday
afternoon and learn weeks ahead of the country what our mas-
ters had done.

On that Saturday afternoon — no five-day week for the
Court in those days — I turned to *Duplex v. Deering*. It was no
surprise to see that the Court had affirmed the injunction, which
would mean a dissenting opinion for us. Hidden away in the
"Remarks" column was the gem. After Justice Pitney's name
Justice Brandeis had written "P. says no such thing as peaceful
picketing," and after Chief Justice White's, "C.J. saw peaceful
picketing at Raleigh Hotel yesterday." Justice Pitney wrote for
the Court holding that the Clayton Act properly construed did
not permit a "secondary" strike or boycott, and reversed the
lower courts which had held to the contrary.

Justice Brandeis ended his dissenting opinion with a paragraph
looking toward the future. His conclusion that existing law gave
industrial combatants the right to push their struggle to the limits

of the justification of self-interest in no way meant that he attached "any constitutional or moral sanction to that right." And he went on:

> All rights are derived from the purposes of the society in which they exist; above all rights rises duty to the community. The conditions developed in industry may be such that those engaged in it cannot continue their struggle without danger to the community. But it is not for judges to determine whether such conditions exist, nor is it their function to set the limits of permissible contest and to declare the duties which the new situation demands. This is the function of the legislature which, while limiting individual and group rights of aggression and defense, may substitute processes of justice for the more primitive method of trial by combat.

This seed was soon to bear fruit. *Truax* v. *Corrigan* was argued three months after *Duplex* v. *Deering*. Here the legislative command was clear beyond doubt. Arizona's courts were forbidden to issue injunctions against picketing in labor disputes. In the preceding chapter I described the conversion of Justice Pitney in this case, brought about by a memorandum of Brandeis's, which later became his dissenting opinion. As soon as it was completed it was sent to Pitney. Again, as in *Jacob Ruppert* v. *Caffey*, the task of historical and legal research was assigned to me. Hours in the library are embalmed in the equivalent of eight full pages of footnotes. Together we wrote, and documented, a major work on the evolution in England of the law of conspiracy in labor disputes from the first Elizabeth's time to the present, with its separate and diverse history in this country from the eighteenth century on.

What stood out — and was meant to stand out — was that the law was in different stages of development in different common law jurisdictions. The common law of Arizona had been stated by its highest court to forbid peaceful picketing, as — at that time — did the law of New Jersey (as declared by Chancellor

Pitney), Massachusetts, California, Illinois, Michigan, Texas, Washington, and other states. But the legislature of Arizona had changed that rule. Its statute law was in accord with the court-made law of New York, Ohio, Indiana, Minnesota, Montana, Oklahoma, and other states. Justice Brandeis's point was that the Fourteenth Amendment to the Constitution could not possibly prevent Arizona from achieving a result, unquestionably legal in a large and forward-looking part of the nation. He believed that Justice Pitney would find the point unanswerable — as, indeed, he did — and would bow to reason. That a majority of the Court in all probability would not did not invalidate his belief or deflect his purpose.

The Justice had for a large segment of humanity — which did not include his law clerks — a tolerant view of their capabilities and modest expectations of their achievements. When I asked him one day whether he thought a certain person, temporarily prominent, was intelligent, he paused as though giving the question careful thought. "Intelligent?" he responded. "Yes — certainly. Perhaps not great intelligence. Rather, the intelligence which counsels one not to stand in front of a locomotive." I never screwed my courage to the point of asking him — as I often wanted to do — why he was so much more lenient toward his colleagues than his law clerks. The question remained unasked partly because we all knew that discussion of "Our Court" was out-of-bounds. But the answer would have been clear — he was the ultimate authority (though he never exercised it) in the selection of his law clerks. As for his colleagues, what fate gave one accepted, and used or suffered, as might be.

Chief Justice White died in May 1921. From then until the Brandeises went off to Chatham on Cape Cod for the summer, I would attempt to draw the Justice out on possible successors to the Chief Justice. My guess was former President Taft; but this suggestion was brushed off as "impossible." No explanation was given or needed, for I remembered well that, at the time of Mr.

Brandeis's nomination to the Court in 1916, Mr. Taft with others signed a statement that Mr. Brandeis was "not a fit person" to sit on the Court. Why I do not remember, but suspect that it stemmed from the Ballinger investigation. Not long after the Court reconvened in the autumn I noticed on the Brandeis mantelpiece a photograph of the new Chief with a warm inscription. An attempt to get an explanation was coldly ignored. The mantle of membership on "Our Court" had encompassed Mr. Taft's ample frame. Any suggestion of frivolity or criticism was out-of-bounds. Within a year evidence appeared that even the new Chief Justice was not wholly beyond the reach of my then former employer's seduction.

United Mine Workers of America v. *Coronado Coal Company*, first argued — and ably argued for the union by Mr. Charles Evans Hughes, soon to be Secretary of State — at the beginning of the October Term, 1920, was not decided until the last day of next term, June 5, 1922, a year after I had left the Justice for practice. In the meantime, a death, a new appointment to the Court, and a great deal of work made a vast difference.

The case was an action against the union for treble damages under the Sherman Antitrust Act for the destruction during a strike of a plant at a coal mine in Frogtown, Arkansas. Judgment had been recovered for $625,000. The company's legal theory was that the union was attempting to restrain interstate commerce. The minute amount of coal involved made the claim fantastic enough, but beyond that the unreality of the idea appeared between and on thousands of lines of the interminable record. Had the Duke of Wellington been induced to page this record — an utterly impossible assumption — "Old Nosey," remembering Ciudad Rodrigo and Badajoz, would have known that an assault on Frogtown was building up, and that, once it was launched, no one could control the troops. In drafting our opinion, the task was a novelist's — to make reality shine through the legal haze.

The first vote of the Court was five to four — Chief Justice White in the majority — to affirm the judgment. Shortly after this the Justice started me to work on a draft of dissenting opinion, which he soon took over from me as he began his own. "The facts," I wrote, "present a picture of a primitive struggle clothed in the forms of industry. . . . There was no conference with the men, nor was there any process of law to determine the justice of this proposal to sacrifice standards of work and living in order that operation might continue at a profit. . . . There is a refreshing absence of hypocrisy about this matter; both sides understood clearly that the conflict between cheap labor and union standards was to be settled on the basis of power — physical, economic and legal — with no interference from principle. Both sides armed. . . . Conditions became like those in a country occupied by a small invading force. . . . Engagements took place between small parties of the invading force and the inhabitants."

Then came a brief account of the union assault on the strikebreakers and these comments on the legal situation: "There is no legal right to live, much less to a standard of living. There is a legal right to use or disuse one's property as one chooses, to employ whom one likes at whatever wages offer a more attractive alternative to starvation, and to protect one's property by repelling force with force."

The Justice adopted this shock method of forcing attention upon the realities behind the jargon of the legal record. But he made it more stark by avoiding conclusion for brutal, unadorned, uncolored statement of fact:

In the mountains of western Arkansas, near the village of Frogtown, were nine small coal mines which Bache and Denman managed as a business unit. . . . The Bache-Denman mines had been so operated since 1903, when the first of them was opened. In 1913 (or before) the business became unprofitable. Bache and Denman were led to believe that this was due to union exactions and restrictions. The superintendent proposed operation on the open shop basis; but he advised that the change would involve "a bitter fight" and that "the success of this plan means the utter annihilation of the union so far as our mines are concerned. . . ."

Recent occurrences in Colorado, known as the Ludlow Massacre, made clear how bitter the fight might become. But Bache and Denman decided upon the course proposed and made appropriate preparations. It was arranged to begin with one mine. . . . Then the mine was shut down and all employees were discharged. Soon guards arrived, men furnished by a private detective agency, experienced and well supplied with rifles and ammunition. All removable inflammable material around the mine was taken away. A wire rope was stretched around the enclosure. Notices were posted warning all but employees off the premises. Electric lights were placed at intervals with reflectors throwing the light outside of the enclosure. As soon as the entrenchment had been completed, non-union men, from neighboring States, were brought in at intervals, in small numbers. On Saturday, April 4, 1914, operations at the mine were resumed but as an "open shop."

On the Monday following came what the defendants call a demonstration and the plaintiffs a riot. Union miners and other citizens from all the surrounding villages gathered at a schoolhouse near No. 4. The band played. Speeches of protest were made. The excited crowd pressed forward, attacked the guards and the non-union employees and beat them up badly. Unconditional surrender followed; and on the tipple was hoisted a banner with the legend: "This is a union man's country." Two days later an injunction was secured. Additional guards furnished by the detective agency arrived — increasing the number to sixty or seventy — all armed with long-distance rifles and supplied with many thousand rounds of ammunition. Throughout the next three months conditions grew ever more menacing. There were evictions from company houses to provide shelter for the new employees, and the dispossessed families settled in tent colonies near by. Finally on July 17 came what is called "the battle." Armed men, undoubtedly unionists, surrounded Mine No. 4, and opened fire upon the guards and the employees. These soon beat a hasty retreat. Some of them were caught and brutally shot. Fire was set to the tipple and other buildings and was fed by all procurable furniture, furnishings and supplies belonging to the company. Then the process of wanton destruction, in part by dynamiting, was extended to other Bache-Denman mines. One of these mines had not been run at all for more than two years. And at others there had not yet even been an attempt to operate on the open-shop basis.

Throughout these trying months the operators acted strictly within their legal rights. The unionists, on the other hand, had been lawless aggressors, violating grievously the laws of Arkansas and also in many respects the injunction issued by the Federal Court. No fact urged by them in extenuation would, if established, afford legal justification for any of the injury inflicted. . . .

To destroy a business is illegal. It is not illegal to lower the standard of working men's living or to destroy the union which aims to raise or maintain such a standard. A business is property; the law protects it; and a statute which denies to its owner the right to protection by injunction against striking employees violates the Fourteenth Amendment, although there is no threat of violence or of injury to tangible property. *Truax v. Corrigan*, decided December 19, 1921 [257 U.S. 312]. A man's standard of living is not property; and the law does not protect by injunction or otherwise. Statutes designed to maintain or raise the workingman's standard of living, by affording labor unions protection against employers discriminating against union members, are unconstitutional. *Adair v. United States*, 208 U.S. 161 [1908]; *Coppage v. Kansas*, 236 U.S. 1 [1915]. Even the right to self-help by means of a strike against such discrimination has been denied to the unions in some jurisdictions. And, although the employment be at will, persons may not be solicited to join the union while so employed, if they have agreed as a condition of employment not to join the union. *Hitchman Coal & Coke Co. v. Mitchell, supra.* Nor may a union protect itself by a refusal of its members to work upon the product of an employer who is attacking the union, if the necessary effect of such refusal is to injure a third person. *Duplex Printing Co. v. Deering*, 254 U.S. 443 [1921]. Such being the law every citizen should obey it; and the court must enforce it. It may be morally wrong to use legal processes, great financial resources and a high intelligence to lower miners' standards of living; but so long as the law sanctions it, economic force may not be repelled by physical force. If union members deem the law unwise or unjust, they may, like other American citizens, exercise their political right to change it by new legislation, and, if need be, by constitutional amendment. But no government may tolerate willful disobedience to its laws.

The cause of action here sued on, however, is not for malicious trespass upon property or persons. The suit is brought under Section 7 of the Anti-trust Law for injury done to the plaintiffs' business and property by reason of a combination or conspiracy to restrain interstate commerce.

This dissenting opinion was destined to remain unpublished for nearly thirty years; for it was never delivered. Fate intervened in a way perhaps unique in the Court's history. On May 19, 1921, Chief Justice White died. No majority opinion had been circulated; and there was now no majority. On July 11, 1921, William Howard Taft became Chief Justice of the United States. The case was restored to the docket and reargued in March 1922. Justice Brandeis stated his views strongly in conference. The new Chief Justice at first agreed with the view of the former majority and assigned the opinion to himself. Brandeis continued to expound his dissent.

Toward the end of May 1922 Brandeis put a few finishing stylistic touches on his dissent. Evidently he expected to deliver it. But Taft, as he tried to write out the conclusions he had voiced, changed his mind. The end of the term was now approaching — the June days, which, Brandeis once said before passage of the Twentieth Amendment, "are like March 3rd in Congress." Taft's opinion, holding the union not liable, was handed down on June 5, 1922, the last day of the term. It spoke for a unanimous Court. "They will take it from Taft but wouldn't take it from me," Brandeis commented later. "If it is good enough for Taft, it is good enough for us, they say — and a natural sentiment."

In the preceding term of Court the Justice had taken the same infinite pains to assure an exposition of the economic and social history underlying a legal issue (in this case a construction of the La Follette Seaman's Act) by circulating a memorandum in *Strathearn Steamship Company* v. *Dillon*. My note inserted in the folder tells the story.

This opinion was prepared at a time when it appeared that the decision might have gone against the interpretation of the act which is here advocated. The Chief Justice was wavering, Pitney, Van Devanter, Day and McKenna were contra. I don't remember whether a copy was sent to the Chief or not. But eventually it was decided according to this view and Judge Day wrote a poor opinion.

This took the Justice two weeks of hard work while court was sitting.

As already suggested, Justice Brandeis's opinions were addressed not only to his brethren on the bench but to counsel as well. As a member of the bar himself, he neither expected nor desired to deprive losing counsel of their historic privilege of "cussing the court." But both counsel in the case and those following the decisions were entitled to know — and, indeed, in his view, confidence in the Court required that they should know and believe — that the questions raised were understood and disposed of with the highest professional competence and candor. It was not enough that a judge could carry conviction of believing passionately in the correctness, or justice, or wisdom of his decision. Importance lay in what paths led him to that conviction and whether they were legal paths which he followed to the point where choice had to be made. This choice might be which of two valid principles should prevail over the other — for instance, the state's duty to maintain order or its duty to respect freedom of expression — or which of two views of the facts the Court chose. Whatever it was, the Court should state with candor what moved it. In the first case, for example, was the state or public order really endangered, or was the state en-

titled to be free of foolish obstruction in time of emergency?
The purpose of making known the Court's view was not primar-
ily to persuade others that it was the correct view, or even to
serve as a precedent, so much as to be honest in explaining the use
of power.

In dissent, the Justice was always keenly aware that the case
was only an episode. There would be other cases. Justices in the
majority in this instance might be saved from the burning in another. "Our Court" and "my brethren" might have fallen into
error, but on all occasions they were treated with the greatest
deference and respect. He never gave way to bad temper because his views had not prevailed, nor dealt disrespectfully with
the arguments of the majority, as too often occurs. His attitude
in dissent was in one way different from and, in another, similar
to his attitude when writing for the Court or before final decision. His educative purpose continued; he was careful to leave
no wounds, to narrow and not widen the gap between majority
and minority. But, since in that particular case the final vote had
been taken and no precarious majority needed to be held together, he was free to look to the future and point out to a wider
audience than the Court or the bar the nature of the issue, where
its roots lay, future trends which would affect its later manifesta-
tions, the possible course of legislation, and so on.

It was this larger audience he had in mind during a talk which
my notes report on November 22, 1919. We were talking of the
purpose he had in mind in the series of dissenting opinions we
were preparing in the Espionage Act cases — that is, prosecu-
tions for publication of views said to impede prosecution of the
war. "The [his] whole purpose, and the only one," he said, "is
to educate the country. We may be able to fill the people with
shame, after the passion cools, by preserving some of it on the
record. The only hope is the people; you cannot educate the
Court." I am sure he meant "on this subject."

At the start of our work together what seemed variations of

purpose and method and of style puzzled me. For a long time apparent inconsistencies in his use of certain cases led to my being constantly overruled in attempts to produce uniformity. These were such cases as *Lochner* v. *New York, Coppage* v. *Kansas*, and *Adair* v. *United States*, in which, over Justice Holmes's dissent, the Court had declared unconstitutional statutes, today accepted everywhere, affecting labor relations. While the Justice declined to be bound by them, I argued that as a matter of principle he should never make use of them to make a point in dissenting opinions. He answered only that the Court had gotten into these errors and must not be permitted to escape the consequences.

At first this attitude seemed to me an Old Testament one like Lincoln's conception in the Second Inaugural that it might be God's will that the war continue "until all the wealth piled by the bond-man's two hundred and fifty years of unrequited toil shall be sunk, and until every drop of blood drawn with the lash, shall be paid by another drawn with the sword. . . ." But I came to see that this was not so. His purpose was not retaliation but education. He wanted some of the brethren to see both that they could escape from the bondage of the language in these cases and that their doctrine might be very costly if developed.

The Justice's severity in his analysis of fact, in reducing the issue involved to the minimum possible, in confining the effect of prior decisions to the controlling facts involved, misled many of his admirers about his basic nature. I remember one evening during the twenties listening to Professor Manley Hudson of Harvard (later Judge Hudson of the World Court) hold forth on Brandeis, the Scientist of the Law, who had brought the methods of the laboratory into the courtroom, who put facts through test-tube treatment, and so on. While this was going on, I found out that the Justice was free and would receive my friend and me. It was easy to guide the conversation to the growing political issue of prohibition and, in the course of it, to provoke Mr. Hudson into asserting that moral principles were no more than generalizations from the mores or accepted notions of a particular time and place.

The eruption was even more spectacular than I had anticipated. The Justice wrapped the mantle of Isaiah around himself, dropped his voice a full octave, jutted his eyebrows forward in a most menacing way, and began to prophesy. Morality was truth; and truth had been revealed to man in an unbroken, continuous, and consistent flow by the great prophets and poets of all time. He quoted Goethe in German and from Euripides via Gilbert Murray. On it went — an impressive, almost frightening, glimpse of an elemental force.

When, at length, we were on the sidewalk in front of Stoneleigh Court, I asked Hudson what he thought now about the Scientist of the Law. He stood there shaking with emotion, making little gestures as though trying to get his cuffs out of his coatsleeves. "Monstrous!" he kept saying. "It's monstrous!" Here, indeed, was proof of my thesis expounded to Felix Frankfurter, "that if some of his [Brandeis's] admirers knew him better they would like him less."

What was truly surprising was not that Brandeis had absolutist convictions on the nature of truth, but that he kept his beliefs and emotions so sternly, even rigidly, disciplined and controlled in the performance of his judicial duties.

In two respects my work with Justice Brandeis was different from the current work of many law clerks with their chiefs. This is sometimes closely concerned with the function of deciding. The Justice wanted no help or suggestions in making up his mind. So I had nothing to do with petitions for *certiorari*, petitions to the Court's grace or discretion to review a judgment of a lower court which the Supreme Court was not required by law to review. At the time of which I write — before 1925 — the area of required review was both large and burdensome, so that petitions were far fewer than today. But the Justice was inflexible in holding that the duty of decision must be performed by him unaided, and adhered to this after 1925, when the greater part of the docket consisted of these petitions.

He was equally emphatic in refusing to permit what many of the Justices today require, a bench memorandum or précis of the case from their law clerks to give them the gist of the matter before the argument. To Justice Brandeis, one of the great advocates of the American bar, this was a profanation of advocacy. He owed it to counsel — who he always hoped, usually vainly, would be advocates also — to present them with a judicial mind unscratched by the scribblings of clerks. He went further, and even refused to read the briefs before hearing the argument. Briefs, he would say, should be memoranda of the oral argument, elaborations of it, in many cases, with excerpts from the authorities for convenience. But they were not to perform the same function. Counsel who used his hour to read from his brief, or a condensation of it, wasted it, so far as Justice Brandeis was concerned.

An oral argument was to him a work of art, and the statement of the case lay at the very heart of it. The metaphor he used to describe a proper statement was that of a pebble dropped into a still pond from which widening concentric circles flowed outward. The point where it entered the water was the first statement made to the Court; each of the circles, a statement of fact complete in itself, raising no question in the hearer's mind, satisfying it, occupying it wholly. From such a statement followed another, also complete in its relevancy, leaving no loose ends to puzzle, and so to delay, the listener in marching with the developing story.

If one is opening the argument, the first sentence should tell the Court what kind of a case is before it — for instance: "This case involves the constitutionality under the Fourteenth Amendment of the Oregon Minimum Wage Law for Women." The second should begin its procedural history: "The case comes here on direct appeal from the highest court of Oregon." The Court now knows that the question of the validity of a state statute has gone through the hierarchy of the state courts and comes to it for final decision. It is ready to learn what the Supreme Court of Oregon did and why, what sort of an action was filed in the trial court of Oregon, and what happened there. So far nothing unexplained has been said which should cause any question.

Counsel is now ready to state what the statute provided and what the facts were in the case at bar, relating them to the statutory command. All too often counsel are likely to state their case in this way: "If the Court please, my client, Mrs. Mary Jones, a poor widow of Portland, Oregon, for a decade since the death of her husband in a railroad wreck has been the sole support of her three children, the eldest of whom is not yet of an age to be gainfully employed under the laws of that state. She supports them by her labor in a laundry on the outskirts of the city." To which the mind answers, "And so what? Why tell us all this?"

But the statement, as the Justice would have developed it, brings the Court to the issue: Does the case fall within the statute; and, if so, is the statute a valid one? In the latter event, more facts will be adduced. These will steer the case away from — or toward, depending on counsel's necessity — prior positions taken by the Court. If the desire is to distinguish, hope may lie in the specific facts of the particular case or, perhaps with better prospect, in changed economic or social situations surrounding the relationship involved.

This method of statement should avoid questions from the bench until argument is reached upon the issue which brought the case to the Supreme Court. No skill can, or should try to, avoid questions here. Whether at this point or earlier, however, a question means a puzzled mind which will not be listening until its problem is settled. So it should be answered at once, not postponed. "Never say," the Justice would admonish, "Your Honor, I am coming to that in a moment." One will have lost the attention of the questioner until his problem has been met. Furthermore, pert and overconfident answers seemed to him to suggest lack of candor on the part of counsel or lack of intelligence on the part of the questioner. In every case worthy of the Court's attention, lurk difficult questions for both sides. These should be dealt with seriously for what they are, either questions arising out of the technical complexities of the subject matter, and, hence, subject to explanation, or the question demanding decision — or close to it — and, hence, requiring persuasion. In neither case does cockiness help.

Years ago a gifted Solicitor General, now a judge, demonstrated his mastery of this branch of advocacy. Interrupted by a deeply disturbing question, he paused to give his full mind to the problem, then said, "Ah, your Honor, how often I have asked myself that question; and more and more seek its answer along this way." From then on counsel and Justice joined in a common search for truth and light.

Nothing is more disturbing to an experienced advocate than to have a judge who has read extensively in advance of the argument put ultimate questions before his colleagues have had a chance to listen to a full statement of the case. Here lay the one instance which comes to me when the Justice believed ignorance to be a benefit.

So far this account of working with Justice Brandeis has been all of work. To leave only this impression would be quite wrong. Each day we talked. I pumped him on the headlined news and usually drew him out. For a time, as I said, I kept notes. During October and November 1919, the news centered about strikes in steel and coal industries. To give his views now after forty-five years involves no impropriety.

October 1919, at the beginning of the first Industrial Conference:

D.A.: What hope is there of a conference with Judge Gary [head of U.S. Steel] in it giving labor new rights?

L.D.B.: The struggle for rights is over. They are now recognized as much as anything ever is in a world where you cannot expect unanimity. The thing to be preached now is the correlative duty to one's mates and to the job.

D.A.: But what about Judge Gary?

L.D.B.: Oh, he's an anachronism. An English civil servant in the labor service said to me the other day that our employers amazed him. They were living in the world of a hundred years ago.

Some days later, after Judge Gary's refusal to recognize collective bargaining and the consequent breakup of the Conference:

D.A.: Are you so sure that the struggle for rights is over?

L.D.B.: Well, perhaps a little remains to be done.

Later, after reports of police raids on socialist and labor offices and meetings and arrests:

D.A.: Don't you sometimes feel so discouraged that you want to go to an island in the South Seas?

L.D.B.: Not discouraged; simply deeply humiliated and filled with a sense of sin that we with the greatest possibilities of any people should waste ourselves on these age-old methods of oppression.

[Returning to the subject:] You asked me if I were discouraged. I am not because I have profound faith in our people. They are the best stock in the world. Only the British equal them. They are the most civilized people in the world.

D.A.: Yes, but isn't much of our idealism simply the exhilaration of people on a fast toboggan amid glorious scenery?

L.D.B.: Perhaps, but the people have great stuff in them. The stuff that our private soldiers showed is in the whole people.

D.A.: Do you think that Garyism is an attempt to smash unionism all along the line as the Knights of Labor were smashed [in 1887]?

L.D.B.: No, we cannot go backward; but it will drive labor into radical leadership. We shall pay dearly for this injunction.

A month later, after newspaper reports that Governor Harding of Iowa was trying to get the coal-producing states to take over the mines and operate them on the basis of the union demands pending settlement by agreement:

D.A.: Don't you think that industrially the evil has occurred which the Founding Fathers feared politically, the paralysis of the states and the absorption of power by the Federal Government, controlled by the dominant economic interests? I am a States rights man!

L.D.B.: Of course, so am I. What I have had impressed on me in my public life and private practice is that man's activities have outrun his abilities. He must go back to the smaller unit. I remember saying to Filene of Boston when he had extended his activities from his own business to the Boston Chamber of Commerce, then to that of the State, then to that of the United States, then to the International Chamber of Commerce, that he was only waiting for communication with Mars for new worlds to conquer.

By the way, have you heard the news about the Attorney General [that he was on the verge of a nervous breakdown]? It reminds me of a story of my brother's: A man convicted of fraudulent bankruptcy proceedings was asked by the judge whether he had anything to say before sentence was pronounced. "O Judge," he replied, "I have such a bad headache!"

November 27:

L.D.B.: The coal situation seems worse.

D.A.: I should think that any miner would be justified in thinking of revolution. Isn't there some man who will head a movement of protest?

L.D.B.: There will be a reaction of protest all right. The

situation is forcing it. We are being governed by a set of insane men — inanity is not the word for this sort of thing.
They have lost all power to see and weigh consequences.

November 28:

L.D.B.: How do you like the coal mess today?

D.A.: Isn't there any way out?

L.D.B.: Yes, and the men will find it, if only their money
holds out and the west freezes for a couple of weeks.

D.A.: What about the injunctions?

L.D.B.: They can't arrest everyone. I wish they would get
out four thousand injunctions and see that they are all perfectly useless. We shall never get anything better until our people are convinced of that. The conduct of the miners has been
most wonderful — every possible provocation, all the forces of
the Government, capital and the press against them, and yet
they have kept their heads and maintained perfect order. It's
wonderful!

D.A.: Isn't there some big man to lead the liberal thought of
the country? I wish you could take a few months off.

L.D.B. (with a laugh): Well, the miners did ask me to be their
counsel once, but I couldn't do it. Things will go right if only
their money holds out.

D.A.: You are an incurable optimist.

L.D.B.: Oh, yes. Oh, yes.

In these fragments passion, indignation, faith in the very basis
of the democratic dogma came to light like potsherds in a digging. The vases of which they formed parts belonged in his inner life, rarely glimpsed in his judicial writings, which were
sternly channeled by reason and learning. Together they
formed a man of impressive influence on all who came near him.
Twenty years later I attempted to describe this influence when,
two months to the day before Pearl Harbor, I spoke at his funeral.

The other strand in these memories is all the more vivid because of the times in which we have lived. We are the generation which has lived during and between two wars. We have lived in the desert years of the human spirit. We have lived in the barren years of disillusionment — years when the cry was, "What is truth?" — years when men with a little new-found knowledge believed that they had pried into the mainsprings of the human mind and spirit, and could make mankind work for any end by playing upon its fears and appetites.

These were years during which we were with the Justice and saw in action his burning faith that the verities to which men had clung through the ages with verities; that evil never could be good; that falsehood was not truth, not even if all the ingenuity of science reiterated it in waves that encircled the earth.

We have heard him say almost in the words of Saint Paul, "Whatsoever things are true, whatsoever things are honest, whatsoever things are just, whatsoever things are pure, whatsoever things are of good report — think on these things."

But to him truth was less than truth unless it were expounded so that people could understand and believe. During these years of retreat from reason, his faith in the human mind and in the will and capacity of people to understand and grasp the truth never wavered or tired. In a time of moral and intellectual anarchy and frustration he handed on the great tradition of faith in the mind and spirit of man which is the faith of the prophets and poets, of Socrates, of Lincoln.

And so today, whatever dark days may lie ahead, the memory of the Justice will be a voice always saying to us, "Lift up your hearts."

6

LITMUS FOR LIBERALS IN THE TWENTIES

DURING THE LATE Wilson and the Harding years we knew our liberals. We had tests, which those who congregated at the Brandeises' met. It was not enough just to meet some of these tests. The litmus paper must turn blue in each of the whole series. Mr. Charles Evans Hughes produced a heavenly blue by opposing the expulsion of the Socialists from the New York legislature, but was very muddy-colored on the League of Nations. The tests of the twenties were specific and unequivocal, tests of firm belief in certain goals for immediate achievement. When these goals were achieved — and surprisingly quickly — liberals were often left confused and rudderless in meeting emerging problems of the thirties. Some were then charged with having turned conservative; others with being fellow-travelers. In fact, their points of view had usually not changed at all.

It is typical of American liberalism to be specific rather than ideological. This was true of the Progressive Era, the ancestor of the Wilsonian. In both periods liberals wanted to use the powers of the state to restrain the strong from dominating and using weaker groups. But the beneficiaries were not the same in both cases. As in other countries, the weakest groups had to wait longest for help. From the outset of the Progressive Era to the present, liberals have advocated the regulation of business and conduct which affects the rest of the community or an especially vocal section of it. Regulation has run from railroads and grain elevators to communication through space satellites. The first groups to win the ear of the state were unorganized but numerous, vociferous, and politically significant groups of businessmen and farmers who complained of what they regarded as monopolistic and oppressive practices of large banking, transportation, and industrial combinations.

However, when liberals tried to get government to regulate, they found that the "interests" they wished to curb controlled legislatures and executives. So liberals went to work on methods to evade established institutions and procedures. For more than a decade they experimented in techniques which proved to be a blind alley. Out of it came the primary election of party candidates, the initiative, the referendum and recall, including that wild doctrine, the recall of judicial decisions. If legislators and officials refused to act, the people themselves would legislate, remove officials, and overrule decisions of the courts.

An example of this faith in direct popular government lies before me, a yellowing and brittle editorial page of the *New York American* for Thursday, April 22, 1920. In a box stretching across the top of the page appears this pronouncement:

MEASURES THAT WOULD CURE MOST OF THE TROUBLES AND
TENDENCIES WHICH DISTRESS AND ALARM US TO-DAY

(1) To nominate for the Presidency by direct nomination and to elect by popular vote.
(2) To elect the Cabinet officers and make them responsible to Congress.
(3) To deprive the President of the power of patronage; to put all public offices as nearly as possible under Civil Service, and have appointments made by a committee of Congress.
(4) To elect Federal Judges, including the Supreme Court Justices, by popular vote.
(5) To apply the Initiative, the Referendum and the Recall to national matters.

Happily, this "degradation of the democratic dogma," in Brooks Adams's phrase, was about over, though we still have the primary and, on the Maryland ballot, some legislation referred for the final judgment of the sovereign people. A letter from Justice Brandeis in the summer of 1920 gives his view of what he called "democratic façades":

May 3/20
Old Lane Farm
Cherry Garden Lane
Meadowhew Thicket
Berks.

My dear Acheson:

Doesn't that give you the flavor of the Old Country? We plan to sail for New York on the Zeeland Aug. 19. But this early return need not change your plan of returning to Washington Sept. 15, as we purpose going to Kentucky for a visit to my brother before returning to Washington.

England is joyously interesting. The struggle onward is proceeding intelligently and in good temper. Public opinion is an omnipresent potent factor; and one feels himself in a land where there is a real democracy, manfully applied. None of your "democratic façades" here — nor constitutional cure-alls of initiative, referendum and recall or primary elections — and like machinery, as a substitute for thought and attention to matters of public interest. I would swap the whole job-lot of them for a few letters to the Times, backed by the determined spirit of men who protest when their supposed rights are being infringed upon.

There is little real redness here. But most of the British world are dyed with a very faint pink which color blind Americans might take for scarlet. Our greetings to the family.

L.D.B.

However, belief in two innovations in the democratic process remained necessary to color the liberal litmus paper. In 1913, the election of United States senators by direct vote of the people, instead of by the legislatures of the states, was required by the Seventeenth Amendment, a great liberal triumph. Seven years later the beneficial effect of this reform was still in the realm of faith. In August 1920, women became entitled to vote in all elections, federal and state. The effect upon the national tone and judgment was not immediately or noticeably elevating.

A half-century ago supporters of woman suffrage and popular election of senators believed that both would so improve the electoral process as markedly to improve its products. A persistent American illusion drives us, in domestic and foreign affairs, to strive unceasingly for improvement of what we call political "machinery." As Chief Justice Taft said of President Hoover's urge to improve "legal machinery," "You know, he really thinks it is machinery." Today it would be hard to demonstrate that either of these reforms for which the faithful went on crusade made much of any change. This, of course, is quite consistent with the belief that for quite different reasons the reforms were desirable.

In the early nineteen-twenties a liberal still believed strongly in government regulation. This was based on the believed necessities of the public interest. These necessities continually expanded and, with them, the need for regulation. Regulation led to administrative bodies — like the Interstate Commerce Commission and the Federal Trade Commission — to do the regulating. If every decision of these bodies had to be retried in the courts, the system broke down. So those in favor of regulation properly sought considerable scope for finality of administrative judgment. The interests regulated wished to narrow it. To support their position liberals developed a dogma, the mystique of the administrative process, the conception that such expertise was involved in these regulatory decisions as to escape "the artificial reason and judgment of the law," as King James I judges explained their training, and as to require very limited review.

The liberals' purpose — prompt decisions and terminable litigation — was good. The dogma advanced had little merit. It obscured the desirable purpose, and also a real danger in it — a tendency toward bureaucratic arbitrariness growing from the arrogance of unreviewable power. For a long time conservative effort in this country was to attempt to insure justice in each case by meticulous judicial review, an unworkable method. The British chose a rougher system which we might call administrative tyranny tempered by assassination by Parliament and Royal Commission, as in the notorious Crichel Down furore, before which even Mr. Churchill had to bow.

The details of the long and passionately fought battle over judicial review have ceased to be important. I have mentioned it here because as a youth I believed strongly in the dogma; and, in middle age, as Chairman (in 1939–1941) of the Attorney General's Committee on Administrative Procedure, was able to help point the debate away from a confrontation of absolutes to find solution in a reform of administrative procedure itself.

Connected with the battles over regulatory procedure was another belief which became a doctrinal test of liberal faith. One method of regulating great combinations of public utilities was by competition. To provide it liberals advocated conservation of natural resources and public development of water power, beginning with the Muscle Shoals Dam on the Tennessee River. Senator George W. Norris's faithful advocacy of it made him a high priest of liberalism. Beatification was snatched from him in 1928 by Calvin Coolidge's veto. But he pressed on to become under FDR the patron saint of the world-renowned Tennessee Valley Authority.

The time was not far off — about a decade and a half — when a wholly new concept would become almost the supreme article of liberal faith, that of managing the whole economy to eliminate the recurrent cycle of "boom and bust." But that is ahead of our story. The nineteen-twenties began with a depression. The depression led to unemployment and to widespread strikes and lockouts. These conditions and the fresh memories of world war brought about a change in the beneficiaries for whom the liberal sought the help of the state.

At home these beneficiaries were laboring people, poor and propertyless people — men, women, and children, pathetically weak and defenseless in bargaining for their only asset, their labor. Abroad the beneficiaries were even more vaguely sensed — humanity, the age-old victim of the scourge of war. At the pinnacle of liberal belief in domestic affairs stood the trade union movement; in foreign affairs, the League of Nations. The liberal believed in the trade union movement as the instrument, often misguided as it was, devised by working people themselves, to redress gross inequities. But they found redress impossible of achievement without reform of the whole gamut of constitutional decisions, common law doctrines, and statutory enactments which hampered the labor movement, practically eliminated the strike and boycott as instruments for improvement of pay and work conditions, and denied to government itself, state and federal, any power to interfere by law. We repeated to one another, as a creed, words from Justice Holmes's dissenting opinion in *Lochner* v. *New York:* "The Fourteenth Amendment does not enact Mr. Herbert Spencer's Social Statics."

Today it seems impossible that ideas, now so long accepted as commonplaces, should for two decades have divided the country, the Congress, and the Court. But American liberalism from 1910 to 1930 was curiously like Tory liberalism in England a hundred years before, the liberalism of Lord Shaftesbury and the Factory Acts. This should not be surprising; for the time between was the century of American isolation, the century in which the conquest of a continent cushioned America against the brutalities of the industrial revolution, their social consequences, and the inevitable new role of the state in society. Liberals believed that they alone were awake and aware — aware of revolt around them, of troubles ahead, of need for immediate change of course. They read, or helped prepare, documents on which rested the Brandeis briefs in the wages and hours of work for women cases; they followed changing ideas and practice in Europe; they supported the Women's Trade Union Leagues and Florence Kelley's Consumers' League. They quoted the *New Republic*.

At the Brandeises' we met Andrew Furuseth, the craggy Viking head of the Seamen's Union, and heard at first hand of the last group of serfs or indentured men. Long after the Dred Scott Decision had been overruled at Appomattox Court House, a form of fugitive slave law for sailors existed throughout the maritime world. By international practice a deserting seaman, no matter what his wrongs, could be arrested in any port and returned in irons to his ship, where no appeal lay from the captain's will. Furuseth had labored endlessly, and with the earliest success of almost any labor group, for governmental intervention and amelioration. Perhaps he was too successful. At any rate, American shipping has had to rely more and more on government subsidies to survive foreign competition.

The grand old cigarmaker, Sam Gompers, President of the struggling American Federation of Labor, a caller we heard about by report, was received in private audience. Professor Felix Frankfurter of the Harvard Law School, a frequent caller, would tell us about the Bisbee deportation of Wobblies (Industrial Workers of the World) from the copper mines of Arizona, which he had investigated as counsel for President Wilson's Mediation Commission, and of the condition of the itinerant agricultural workers in the Southwest, which Steinbeck immortalized in *The Grapes of Wrath*. Belief in his current absorption — the bill in Congress which later became the Norris–La Guardia Act, limiting the power of federal courts to issue injunctions in labor disputes — was almost a test of liberalism in itself.

Not all involvements in the labor struggle were so impersonal. Among our friends were the William Hards, Bill and Anne. They lived in Georgetown, a block only from a house which was soon to be ours, for now over forty years. Bill was a newspaper man, a liberal with a high but not perfect score. He had latent tendencies: one, high-church Anglicanism, was to lead him to Rome; another was to bring him by easy stages to an editorial position in the *Reader's Digest*. But, in the days I write of, Bill played with fire. One evening I was asked to come to his house on 28th Street within a few doors of historic Evermay, whose surrounding trees, it is said, were laid out by General Washington himself. It was the time of the great coal strike of 1919 and of Attorney General A. Mitchell Palmer's anti-Red drive.

Bill had with him two or three union officials from the mine field of West Virginia. When I arrived, they were launched upon the state of affairs in the struck mine fields. The company stores had stopped credit. Scanty union strike benefits provided little more than a starvation diet. Evictions from company houses enforced by the Cossacks, the state police, were increasing. The Cossacks, too, broke up union meetings and demonstrations; a barrage of injunctions, state and federal, pinned the men down and led to the arrest of the leaders for contempt of court, should they attempt any act of leadership. Despair mounted around every minehead.

The government, they said, was rigged against them — the sheriff, his deputies who constituted the mine police, the governor, the legislature were all beholden to the coal interests; the United States court was distant and hostile. This whole combination went so far beyond the reach of their action and their votes that they could do nothing about it. They could handle the county all by itself. It had a salable product and needed no outside help — or so they thought; they could handle the mine police if not reinforced. Wasn't President Wilson's right to self-determination almost as hallowed as the Ten Commandments? Why shouldn't their county secede from the state and go on its

own with laws which self-respecting people could live under?
They were willing to stay within the Federal Union if the
courts would leave them alone. Mr. Hard had written articles on
the strike sympathetic to the miners' plight; they wanted his help
on how to get ahead with their plan.

As they talked, one saw that here were no frustrated liberals
imagining themselves manning the barricades with John Reed
and finding heroes' graves in the Kremlin wall. These were desperate men ready for action, both very foolish and very dangerous. The Espionage Act was still in effect, with its conspiracy
section and penalties of twenty years' imprisonment, a penalty
only recently handed out to an old man and his girl co-
conspirator for throwing out of a Brooklyn tenement window
leaflets, which Justice Holmes had called "poor and puny anonymities." Attorney General Palmer and the Bureau of Investigation hovered, ready to pounce on such subversive gatherings as
ours. Clearly it was no place for a law clerk of a Justice of the
Supreme Court.

So I pointed out to our friends that what they were planning
was no less than insurrection against a sovereign state; that if plan
ripened into action, the Governor would proclaim it insurrection, call out the National Guard to suppress it, and, possibly, ask
the President for the aid of federal troops. The outcome could
never be in doubt. If, unhappily, anywhere along the line of action someone was killed, our friends and others might well swing
as did John Brown of Ossawatomie for action no more mad or
less well — perhaps even nobly — inspired.

While they digested this somber prediction, I said that I must
be off, and left feeling far from a hero, but less like a conspirator.
Nevertheless, the essential role of labor unions in the scheme of
our times was to me no longer a purely intellectual conclusion. I
had passed the first test of a liberal; it was a conviction.

Today it seems very odd indeed that until this century was
more than four decades old the Supreme Court was of the opin-

ion that the Founding Fathers had put it beyond the power of any government in the land to protect those historic wards of the law, women and children, from exploitation by the owners of machines. As the textile industry and the needle trades grew, the plight of the child and woman worker resembled, as I suggested earlier, that of their counterparts in England a century earlier. But when the legislatures, federal and state, attempted to intervene, the Court barred the way. To Congress it said that the manufacture of goods was not interstate commerce and could be dealt with only by the states. So an Act to prohibit the movement in interstate commerce of the products of child labor was held unconstitutional. The goods themselves, the Court said with the wisdom of Solomon, were not harmful like guns, prostitutes, or liquor. When Congress attempted to take the profit out of child labor by imposing a tax upon the product, it declared this a subterfuge to accomplish an unconstitutional purpose, although the subterfuge had proved permissible when employed to protect dairy farmers against competition of other farmers through cheaper oleomargarine. Not until 1941, in *United States* v. *Darby*, did the Court penetrate suppositions which would have justified Mr. Bumble's conclusion that "the law is a ass," and found legal basis for safeguarding the national interest in the physical growth and education of its young citizens.

Working women were not only denied the protection of the federal government but of state governments as well. The states were bowled out by the fast-breaking ball which so depressed Justice Holmes, "liberty of contract." The development from ancient to modern law, Sir Henry Maine had pointed out, was from a system based on status to one based on contract. Whether or not this was true, to a majority of the Court the curious phrase, "liberty of contract," seemed to mean that women had escaped from a status approaching slavery, requiring them to work for bare subsistence, to a new liberty, to meet the pressures of poverty and starvation by working under contract for the same bare subsistence. The Constitution guaranteed women the enjoyment of this right free from interference by a state to alter or dictate the contract she was free to make or not to make. All this was accomplished by the Fourteenth Amendment, a product of the Civil War, which declared that no state should deprive any person of life, liberty, or property without due process of law, nor deny to anyone the equal protection of the laws.

If all this fills the reader with the baffling frustration of an argument from Humpty Dumpty (" 'When *I* use a word,' Humpty Dumpty said in rather a scornful tone, 'it means just what I choose it to mean — neither more nor less. . . . The question is . . . which is to be master — that's all.' "), it filled liberals with the same frustration half a century ago. The Brandeis brief in the Supreme Court — filed for liberal organizations appearing as *amici curiae*, friends of the court — sprang from a patient faith in the educative process and the power of reason. These briefs proved with a wealth of authoritative detail what today is obvious — and, indeed, had been for some centuries to those whose minds, in Burke's phrase, the law had not sharpened by narrowing them. They proved that women were different from men and hence could be classified differently for protective measures; that their biological functions warranted protective measures; that necessitous women were not free women, and so on. The undeniable was added to the obvious, and the self-evident piled on top of that — "What Any Fool Should Know," as I described the Brandeis briefs to Frankfurter, quoting the Justice himself.

Every few years a new case was brought and a new assault made upon the entrenched Old Guard on the Court. But, though beleaguered and hard pressed, the flag of Liberty of Contract still flew. When Mr. Brandeis became Mr. Justice Brandeis in 1916, Felix Frankfurter took up the role of counsel in the *Adkins* case. After that and two other cases had fallen before the Old Guard, Frankfurter thought a new face might bring a change of luck. Hence it fell to my lot to suffer martyrdom as counsel for *amici curiae* (six states) in the last of these cases to be lost. *Morehead* v. *New York* ex rel *Tipaldo*. In the very next term of Court, Justice Roberts switched his vote, leaving the Four Horsemen in dissent.

Only the National Woman's Party grieved at the defeat of the Old Guard. To these embattled successors of the suffragettes, their three leaders embalmed in granite in the basement under the Capitol dome, bitter against the legal and political disabilities of women, sex had become a complete irrelevancy. The liberal of the twenties saluted them by requiring belief in woman suffrage as the test of liberalism; but, at the same time did his best to frustrate their proposed amendment to the Constiution which would have prohibited any differentiation in legislation by reason of sex. This would have undone a half-century battle for the protection of working women.

Close on the heels of belief in the labor movement as a test of liberalism, came the civil rights issue, a quite different one from that of today. The hysteria which swept the country in 1919 and 1920 was quite as great as that of thirty years later, which added the word "McCarthyism" to the language. The word for the earlier period was "Palmerism," in acknowledgment of the zeal of Attorney General A. Mitchell Palmer in fomenting it. The earlier hysteria, like the later one, followed the emotionalism and the fears of a great war. Just as one now hears it said that McCarthyism is dead, so it was thought a generation ago that Palmerism was dead. The truth, in all likelihood, is that these fears always lurk just below the surface, waiting for the circumstances and the man to exploit them.

Attorney General Palmer was such a man. "There is a condition of revolutionary intent in the country," he told the House Judiciary Committee, "of sufficiently widespread a character . . . to destroy or overthrow the government of the United States by physical force or violence."

Judge Elbert Gary saw the same movement leading the steel

strike: "If the [steel] strike succeeds, it might and probably would be the beginning of an upheaval which might bring on us grave and serious consequences. You know that the questions involved in the strike, which is led by Foster, the acknowledged revolutionist, are higher than the Steel Corporation." "Judge Gary," contributed the *Wall Street Journal*, "is fighting the battle of the American Constitution." And Judge Kenesaw Mountain Landis, whom Justice McReynolds would never have considered "an amorphous dummy unspotted by human emotions," told a meeting of the American Protective Legion in Minneapolis on January 31, 1920: "What we need is a new definition of treason. Then we could use the side of a barn for those who would destroy our government. . . .

"Now I am not the kind of a man to be in office in North Dakota [he was a federal district judge in Chicago] but, my God, I'd like to hold court there for about a week."

Fortunately brave men, true patriots, stood out against this madness. Federal District Judge George W. Anderson told the Harvard Liberal Club on January 12, 1920:

> . . . It is a depressing, — almost appalling fact, — that, as an aftermath of our "war to make the world safe for democracy," real democracy now seems unsafe in America. It is increasingly clear that America's loss of valuable lives and of money in this war was as nothing compared to her loss of moral, social, and political values.
>
> . . . Many, — perhaps most, — of the agitators for the suppression of the so-called "Red menace," are, I observe, the same individuals, or class of forces, that in the years '17 and '18 were frightening the community to death about pro-German plots. . . .
>
> Let us stop being scared at our own shadows. It is a time for calmness, for critical and dispassionate search for truth, for facts. We are over-fed with alarming rumors and wild imaginings. One aspirant for high office issues a pamphlet wildly in-

quiring whether "America is worth saving." It is, and it is fairly
safe; even if he is not elected to the office to which he aspires.
There will be no sun-strokes in Massachusetts this month.
There will be no Red revolution this year. . . .

The heresy-hunter has throughout history been one of the
meanest of men. It is time that we had freedom of speech
for the just contempt that every wholesome-minded citizen has
and should have for the pretentious, noisy, heresy-hunter of
these hysterical times.

Mr. Frank I. Cobb began an address before the Women's City
Club of New York on December 11, 1919, with this sentence,
"For five years there has been no free play of public opinion in
the world." Here are other paragraphs from the same speech,
provoked by the temper of the times:

. . . The Bill of Rights is a born rebel. It reeks of sedition.
In every clause it shakes its fist in the face of constituted authority and thunders, "Thou shalt not," and because its ulti-
matum is "Thou shalt not," it is the one guarantee of human
freedom to the American people unless they themselves destroy
their safeguard.

We are in danger of forgetting this under the terrorism of
mass thought, but we can forget it only at our imminent peril.
There is revolution in reaction as well as in radicalism, and
Toryism speaking a jargon of law and order may often be a
graver menace to liberty than radicalism bellowing the empty
phrases of the soap-box demagogue.

Writing from Paris to Abigail Adams, Thomas Jefferson said
that: "The spirit of resistance to government is so valuable on
certain occasions that I wish it always to be kept alive. It will
often be exercised when wrong, but better so than not to be
exercised at all." . . .

. . . The protection of the people against crime and violence
and the destruction of property is an elementary function of
government. But government protecting the American people

against revolutionary propaganda is a new manifestation of paternal authority. I wonder what old Sam Adams would say to that? Or Patrick Henry? Or Benjamin Franklin, with his grim joke about hanging together or hanging separately? Or Thomas Jefferson? Or George Washington? Or all the rest of that noble congregation of rebels who to their defiance of George III pledged their lives and their fortunes and their sacred honor? . . .

God forbid that our supreme achievement in this war should be the Prussianizing of ourselves!

Perhaps the best measure of the retreat from reason and principle of those days is found in "An Appeal to the People of the Churches of America" by a group (named in the Notes at the back of this book) of eminent and conservative clergymen.

We the undersigned ministers of the Church of Christ, believing that the political institutions of our country commend themselves to the reason and conscience of mankind sufficiently to stand the test of such freedom of speech as has hitherto, in times of peace, been accorded by our Government to the aliens who have come to us for asylum as well as to our citizens, are moved to make an appeal to the people of the Churches of America on account of certain measures, inconsiderately undertaken, which threaten the basic principles of our Government. We have in mind, in particular, the deportation of men without judicial trial; the proposed repressive legislation now before Congress, threatening the primary rights of free speech, free press and peaceable assembly; the suspension of Socialists by the New York State Assembly; and other evidences of an excited mood on the part of many of our people. We have long been saying that constitutional changes can be effected without violence in America, because of our right to free expression of opinion by voice and ballot. We cannot now deny this American substitute for violence without directly encouraging resort to revolution. In the conviction, therefore, that our American institutions will survive because they have the willing allegiance of the majority of our citizens, we urge the people of the Churches of America to use their influence for the return to that old faith in the fundamental principles of our civil liberty.

As a result of the anti-Red raids, persecution for opinion, exclusion of minority views from the second-class mails, and so on, dissenting opinions by Justices Holmes and Brandeis sputtered along the line of fire. But the greatest of them all came at the beginning of my service. The *Abrams* case, which I have already described, was argued on October 21, 1919, and decided on November 10. Justice Clarke circulated an opinion for the Court, sustaining the savage sentences. Justices Holmes and Brandeis indicated that they would dissent. Justice Holmes was then waited on by three of his colleagues, who brought Mrs. Holmes with them. At the time my classmate at Yale and the Harvard Law School, Stanley Morrison, who later combined teaching of law at Stanford University with practice of it, was Justice Holmes's law clerk. The Justice asked him to stay in his room with the door into the Justice's study open.

One of the callers has faded from my memory of Morrison's account. The other two were Justices Van Devanter and Pitney, for whom Holmes had warm regard. They laid before him their request that in this case, which they thought affected the safety of the country, he should, like the old soldier he had once been, close ranks and forego individual predilections. Mrs. Holmes agreed. The tone of the discussion was at all times friendly, even affectionate. The Justice regretted that he could not do as they wished. They did not press. Thus, fortunately, survived a most moving statement of liberal faith in freedom of thought and speech.

In this case sentences of twenty years imprisonment have been imposed for the publishing of two leaflets that I believe the defendants had as much right to publish as the Government has to publish the Constitution of the United States now vainly invoked by them. Even if I am technically wrong and enough can be squeezed from these poor and puny anonymities to turn the color of legal litmus paper; I will add, even if what I think the necessary intent were shown; the most nominal punishment seems to me all that possibly could be inflicted, unless the defendants are to be made to suffer not for what the indictment alleges but for the creed that they avow — a creed that I believe to be the creed of ignorance and immaturity when honestly held, as I see no reason to doubt that it was held here, but which, although made the subject of examination at the trial, no one has a right even to consider in dealing with the charges before the Court.

Persecution for the expression of opinions seems to me perfectly logical. If you have no doubt of your premises or your power and want a certain result with all your heart you naturally express your wishes in law and sweep away all opposition. To allow opposition by speech seems to indicate that you think the speech impotent, as when a man says that he has squared the circle, or that you do not care whole-heartedly for the result, or that you doubt either your power or your premises. But when men have realized that time has upset many fighting faiths, they may come to believe even more than they believe the very foundations of their own conduct that the ultimate good desired is better reached by free trade in ideas — that the best test of truth is the power of the thought to get itself accepted in the competition of the market, and that truth is the only ground upon which their wishes safely can be carried out. That at any rate is the theory of our Constitution. It is an experiment, as all life is an experiment. Every year if not every day we have to wager our salvation upon some prophecy based upon imperfect knowledge. While that experiment is part of our system I think that we should be eternally vigilant against attempts to check the expression of opinions that we loathe and believe to be fraught with death, unless they so imminently threaten immediate interference with the lawful and pressing purposes of the law that an immediate check is required to save the country. . . .

Such gallant men as these kept alive faith in the Republic's great traditions of rationalism and restraint. Soon the hysteria passed. But those who had been infected by it were not cured. Distressingly soon they and their spiritual descendants were in its grip again.

The test which most liberals passed with flying colors was belief in the League of Nations, a belief held with passion, first as a fighting faith for battle, and after battle as love of a lost cause. No faith could have been more ideally suited to the American spiritual inheritance and ethos. The conception of the inherent rationality of man, which came from the Enlightenment, and of his perfectibility through Progress, the contribution of the nineteenth century, fused by Locksley Hall — "the common sense of most" leading to the furled battle flags, "the Parliament of man, the Federation of the world," "lapt in universal law" — took institutional form with the help of the American nostrum, political and legal "machinery." When the vision faded under the harsh light of normalcy and its repudiation by Senator Nye and the neutrality legislation, whole armies of liberals dissolved and straggled home like Crusaders, beaten, tired, and spiritually impoverished.

The fight, though lost, was not without effect. It left in the country a lingering sense of guilt, so that, when the Second World War burst upon us, there was much breast-beating and crying of "peccavi" — that, if only the country had joined the League of Nations, the Second World War would never have come. Here, again, our exaggeration of the role of "machinery" obscures the truth. The League might or might not have been a more effective instrument to carry out its declared purpose had the United States been a member. I am inclined to think not, that the difficulties lay elsewhere. It is hard to believe that our membership would have altered the trends which were developing in America, Europe, and Asia, that those in authority would have understood any better what was occurring in the world around them and acted differently than they did. The failure of the League's successor to achieve its purpose lay in the failure of the assumption upon which it rested, the assumption of postwar cooperation by the Soviet Union with the West. The same sources of failure, and others beside, undermined the League, and would have done so, I suggest, regardless of our membership.

To have written this a quarter of a century ago would have disqualified me as a liberal — and, perhaps, does so now.

7

STARTING AT THE TOP

As I look back over my life, I am amazed how unplanned it was, what slight pushes turned it this way and that, what a vast part luck played in it. Whatever we may think, surely it is this way with all of us. Not long ago a friend wrote to me, "We tend to think that no one has more than his fair share of luck. In truth I think that for spectacular achievement a man must have more than his fair share." It was the good fortune of my relationship with Felix Frankfurter which led to his choice of me from among others as well qualified to go to Justice Brandeis. As June 1920 approached, the Justice asked me about my plans. I had none; but thought vaguely of teaching law and had had an offer. He suggested staying with him another year, and I agreed at once. Later, when asked about this departure from the one-year procedure, he would speak of a concern for my prospective clients.

The second year was even better than the first, and, in addition, brought an opportunity which had not existed a year before. This time, I bestirred myself, writing to a lawyer in Springfield, Illinois, who was at the time counsel for District No. 12 of the United Mine Workers to ask whether he had an opening in his office. His polite reply is before me, saying that he would be glad to see me, but that he could not then say "whether an opening exists for a connection with this department." Now, listening to dull speeches, I sometimes amuse myself by wondering how Mr. John L. Lewis and I might have hit it off — we have long been friendly acquaintances — and what might have developed out of that exploration had it succeeded.

While I considered possible practice in San Francisco and another teaching offer, luck pushed aside my puny efforts and assumed control. It took the form of our good and kind friend, Norman Hapgood, who told me that a friend of his was looking for a young man to work on an international case to be argued at The Hague a year later and that Norman had recommended me. An interview with Mr. Edward B. Burling, a newcomer to the Washington bar, was arranged, and, thus began an association and friendship which has been one of the privileges and treasured joys of my life for now over forty years. What was offered me seemed too good to be true; but was both true and as good as it seemed.

Mr. Burling had been retained by the Norwegian Government as counsel before a special panel of the Permanent Court of Arbitration at The Hague to pass upon a claim of the Norwegian Government to payment for the taking of Norwegian-owned property by the United States during the First World War. My job would be to work on the pleadings and briefs and then go with Mr. Burling to Norway and The Hague as general handyman. The pay seemed princely, a fifty per cent increase over a law clerk's, when the dollar was worth $3.00. What more could one ask? Especially when, after our first talk, I was sure of what I have never since doubted, that in Mr. Burling were centered rare originality and power of mind, a teasing sardonic wit, and a gift for unpredictable and willful friendships and dislikes. What took longer to learn was how true a friend he could be. In some of these respects, moreover, he was a proper member of a remarkable trio. I shall come back to him again when I have introduced the other two.

The firm was a young one in the summer of 1921, not yet three years old, and small. "Covington & Burling" — soon to become "Covington, Burling & Rublee" — was its style. A dozen years ago, after a period during which various names were added and dropped, the firm went back to its original and simple title. Judge J. Harry Covington, an Eastern Shore Marylander, had resigned as Chief Justice of the Supreme Court of the District of Columbia to open a Washington law office, where Mr. Burling joined him on January 1, 1919. President Wilson had put him on the bench some years earlier in recognition of stalwart services as Congressman from the first congressional district of Maryland, the Eastern Shore. In 1912 Judge Covington had led the fight in Maryland for Wilson delegates to the Baltimore Convention. At a critical moment in the convention he split the Maryland delegation, instructed for Clark, leading off a swing to Wilson. One of President Wilson's first acts when the "New Freedom" came into power was to call for the amendment of the Panama Canal Tolls Act which exempted American-flag vessels from Canal tolls, contrary — so the President contended — to specific treaty obligations. To call for repeal of the offending sentence was one thing; to accomplish it, quite another. For the Act had been passed only a year or two before, after the Democrats had gained control of Congress in 1910, as part of the harassment of the much harassed President Taft.

All the Democratic leaders had taken part in the frolic, and most found it embarrassing to do an about-face at President Wilson's call. But not Congressman Covington. In later years, when I knew him well, I came greatly to admire an expression which gave perfectly his attitude toward an unpleasant political obligation which honor forbad him to duck. "I have it to do," he would say. Never, "I have to do it," which carried the implication of external compulsion, instead of something which lay before him to be done. So he told the President that he would take on the task. He asked for help of two kinds: one, a letter from the President to him saying that if the Act was not repealed, the President would face hazards in our international relations (which should remain unspecified) with which the President would not know how to deal. The other help was considerable latitude in withholding and granting patronage in important doubtful congressional districts. With these aids repeal was accomplished.

That same year Congressman Covington gave major help in piloting the Federal Trade Commission Act through the Congress, and, in this, worked alongside the third member of the partnership, George Rublee of New Hampshire, who was to join the firm in the autumn of 1921. The Judge, before going on the bench, formed with Senator Isidor Rayner and Senator John Walter Smith the triumverate which ruled the Democratic Party in Maryland before the Ritchie empire. They would sit for business, so he told me, in the lobby of the Emerson Hotel in Baltimore, in sight, but out of earshot, of the general public, receiving advice or petition, a perfect example of a useful political technique, secret covenants openly arrived at.

Judge Covington was a great talker, and had every qualification to be one. He was an encyclopaedia of American politics, of Maryland history, a rare raconteur, an authority on eighteenth- and early nineteenth-century furniture, aquatints, and prints, a gourmet of talent, a great bird-shot, and the best-natured man one could wish to know. I went through a very difficult time with him years ago, when, under considerable strain and worry, he was before a Master for days on end, giving testimony, and with counsel for nights on end, preparing it. Never once did his equanimity fail, nor his patience fray.

For me George Rublee began as a tradition — his name carved in lonely eminence on an oaken panel as the first graduating class of my school, appearing again in the gymnasium as the captain of every team, and in the folklore of the place as the winner of prizes, the setter of standards. For the last thirty-five years of his life we were colleagues, partners, and friends.

In the fifty-odd years before I knew him as more than a tradi-

tion and imposing figure, a character of the most intriguing sort
had developed. The Rublees, a Huguenot family, long settled in
Vermont, in 1839 went west to Wisconsin to farm and lumber.
There George was born in Madison about as General Grant was
being elected President of the United States. The new President
appointed Horace Rublee, a founder of and a power in the Wisconsin Republican Party, Minister to Switzerland, where
George's childhood was spent. In Europe began the formation
of his tastes and interests. After this diplomatic interlude the
family lived for two years in Boston, where Mr. Rublee was
the "temporary editor" of the *Daily Advertiser;* then returned to
Milwaukee in 1881, where he became a part owner and the editor of the *Milwaukee Sentinel.*

Milwaukee in those days had an atmosphere of cosmopolitan
culture which few American cities have today. Its leading citizens included numbers of Germans, Swiss, and French to whom
the languages, literatures, and music of Europe were natural and
loved inheritances. Here George lived until he came east to
school and Harvard, returned for two years to Europe, then
back to study at the Harvard Law School. There he made three
friendships which were among the closest and most enduring of
his life — Edward Burling and Augustus Hand in the class before him, and Learned Hand in the class following him.

Back again in Wisconsin, George did not share his father's zest
in the life of the Middle West at the end of the century. A year
of practice without clients in Milwaukee, followed by two years
with Burling in Chicago, was enough. He left for the wider and
more glamorous life of New York to practice with the leading
authority on corporations, Victor Morawetz.

Now began, as in a symphony, the movement, first indistinct
and faltering, then repeated with growing clarity and insistence,
which was to dominate George Rublee's life, a movement with
alternating themes, one of contented languor touched with melancholy, the other a passionate, almost demoniacal seizure which

carried him to heights of brilliant and tireless effort, ending in the tragedy of frustration and failure, followed again by the melancholy languor.

The work in New York was hardly begun when George by fortunate investment made, for those days, a comfortable fortune. Off he and his wife went to Europe, where, universally admired, they moved in social, artistic, and sporting circles. George became a favorite tennis partner of the late King of Sweden. Several years passed and some of the fortune. The champagne of life began to go flat. The Rublees returned to New York, he to practice law again, this time with the late Joseph P. Cotton and Senator John C. Spooner of Wisconsin.

Then came the first of the seizures. In 1910 the Progressives and Young Turks were in full revolt against President Taft and, most especially and particularly, against his Secretary of the Interior, Richard A. Ballinger. The Robin Hood of this adventure was Gifford Pinchot; the St. George was Louis D. Brandeis, retained by *Collier's Weekly* to conduct the case against Secretary Ballinger before the Senate committee investigating charges against him. Rublee became St. George's squire.

The dilettante of the previous year was inexhaustible, infinitely resourceful, passionately committed. The dragon was slain. The Taft Administration was mortally hurt. The Bull Moose sounded his call and George marched to Armageddon with TR through the Chicago convention, the resurrection of the Square Deal, persuading his leader on the way first to transfer his advocacy of the recall of judges to the recall of judicial decisions, and then to soft-pedal the whole matter — all to the martial strains of "Onward Christian Soldiers." The crescendo mounted, then crashed to disaster, complete, total, absolute. There was a breathless moment of silence. Then began the theme of quiet melancholy.

This time it was short. Brandeis sent for him again to work out for the new professor President the first of his prophylactic antitrust measures, the Federal Trade Commission Act. The act was passed. President Wilson nominated Rublee to be a member of the first Federal Trade Commission. Opposition immediately developed. It was charged that he was not a regular Republican. Senator Sherman's opinion was that "the President may think he is doing the wise thing in selecting two members of the bull moose party, but, as the boy out in Illinois said about ghosts, 'there ain't no such thing.' " Much more potent was the opposition of Senator Gallinger of New Hampshire, where Mr. Rublee had his residence. He stated that Rublee was personally obnoxious to him. The battle lasted a year and a half; the Administration defied the Congress with a recess appointment for Mr. Rublee and threw in its reserves in his support. In the bitter end it was defeated by senatorial courtesy. Again crescendo, again the silence.

A year went by and the First World War burst upon an astonished America. Rublee's sympathies were quick and strong. He was soon deeply committed. His friend Raymond B. Stevens of New Hampshire, who had been a member of Congress and an ally in the Federal Trade Commission battle, had become Vice Chairman of the United States Shipping Board. At Stevens's invitation, Rublee joined in that great innovation in international organization, the Allied Maritime Transport Council, where, through a skilled staff of civil servants, which included that amazing person Jean Monnet, allied shipping tonnage was pooled and allocated for war use. He was instrumental in getting Ned Burling to come on from Chicago to be Chief Counsel for the Board. Purely as war work the task was absorbing. Gradually a vision as mystical and inspired as that of the Holy Grail began to come to this brilliant and devoted group. It seemed to them that here in this body of disciplined men, a technical staff, might lie the secret of subordinating national interests in the creation of a new world order. Reason and knowledge could be, they thought, so powerful as to overwhelm prejudice and narrow interest.

As the war ended, conviction grew; and Rublee, with the

others, threw himself into the fight for the League of Nations with a passion transcending anything he had experienced before. Again the end was the same. Again all was turned to dust, ashes, and frustration.

More than a decade passed before the spirit possessed him again. During this time he enters our story. But I shall jump to his last passion to complete the mystery of this man. In 1938 President Roosevelt persuaded Rublee to become director of the Intergovernmental Committee on Refugees, which was attempting by negotiation with Nazi Germany to save by emigration the German Jews. Once again the magnitude of the cause fired George Rublee to overcome towering obstacles. One difficulty after another was met, as conference followed conference up the Nazi hierarchical scale. At last the impossible seemed accomplished. At Hitler's direction Goering was made the Fuehrer's deputy with power to act. George threw himself into the final effort. He believed that he had won Goering over. The Red Sea seemed to have parted to open the way to a new deliverance. Then came the war, and the deaths of six million people in the concentration camps and gas chambers of Germany and the ghettos of Poland.

This was the last passion; the fire, even in the inner recesses of his nature, had gone out. Why was he fully extended so intermittently? Why did his potentiality so often seem to elude him? Who can say? Perhaps the favor of fortune was a handicap. Perhaps the discipline of a harder environment would have made dominant those qualities which, on occasion, could burst into blazing possession of him. Would he have been as beloved if he had attained his full potentiality? Probably not. For, although he always seemed to slip from one's grasp, few men have ever so absorbed the interest and devotion of their friends.

Were ever three men more dissimilar, more diverse specimens, more children of a willful and wayward nature than these? Mr. Burling, born in Eldora, Iowa, went to work in a local grocery store at eleven years of age. His mother, a lady of great character and probably the dominant influence in his life, had a good deal to counteract. One of Ned Burling's set pieces deals with the advantages of having a ne'er-do-well father — no psychoses, no omnibrooding presence to oppress. His father had a natural aversion to work and spent his time reading, largely Latin and Greek. He contributed a small remittance to the support of his family, principally sustained by his wife's salary as a schoolteacher and what the boys could earn. Years later the son sat in the father's bedroom as the old man reclined, propped up by pillows, his beard spread over his chest, seemingly unconscious, awaiting death. Suddenly he sat up, his eyes open and flashing; in a voice which could be heard a block away — never used before — he cried out, "I am a Roman Senator, and I shall address the people!" With that, his last illusion, he died.

Ned made a great mistake, he has always maintained, when, high school finished, he left the grocery store and went off on scholarships to Grinnell College, thence to Harvard College and the Harvard Law School. A brilliant student, this introduction to the life of the intellect fatally weakened his natural drive toward the acquisition of power. In a delightful Walter Mitty dream, he sees himself moving from clerk to owner of the grocery store, then to a mighty chain, and on to be Super-Grocer of the United States. From that eminence he would unite the Burling power with the other separated powers under the Constitution into a really formidable counterbalance to the Soviets.

Alas, we cannot live our dreams! Mr. Burling became a successful lawyer in Chicago, was brought from there to the Shipping Board in Washington at the beginning of the war, and was shortly its Chief Counsel.

Typical of his gay irony is a tale of a summer afternoon at the beautiful Maryland Eastern Shore place of his son and daughter-in-law. They were entertaining in an expansive way. One of the guests who had wandered off met Mr. Burling coming home from a walk dressed in unfashionable country clothes and trying to slip into the house unobserved by a back way. The guest engaged this obvious "character" in talk, learned that he did not live thereabouts but had a log cabin in Virginia (a truthful reference to a retreat in the woods along the Potomac), and that his name was Burling.

"Any relation to our host?" asked the guest.

"Father," said Mr. Burling.

The guest's curiosity was now rampant. Further questioning revealed this shy father had no "regular" job, only worked when something came along. Discretion thrown to the winds, the guest ventured further.

"Mr. Burling, would I presume too far by inquiring why, with this beautiful estate in the family, you live in a log cabin?"

"You see," replied Mr. Burling, the picture of simple innocence, "I didn't have the advantage of a rich father!"

In 1921 the partners with six young lawyers to help them were happily overworked, chronically disorganized, and pleasantly prosperous. Their principal practice came from the flood of claims, by and against the United States, which form the aftermath of war. The claim which engaged me was the largest single one of these. Everyone was so busy that no problem of delegating responsibility existed. It was lying about everywhere to be picked up. I found myself even more completely on my own than I had been with Justice Brandeis.

The glamour which surrounds international law cases gives rise to a good deal of myth. They are supposed to be very "different" from domestic litigation, much more "interesting" and infinitely more "important." This is true if they are compared to the numerical bulk of the civil cases in our state and federal courts, which are accident cases. But aside from these, the nature of the issues and the work is remarkably similar. There is a difference in lawyers' methods between the civil-law lawyers of the Continent, who go in heavily for abstract "principles" of law, and the common-law lawyers, whose training leads them to dwell at length and in detail on the facts of the specific case. So far as interest is concerned, a case which may take one to foreign countries is always more interesting than one involving a trip to the local courthouse, or another American city, or even to the Supreme Court in Washington. Comparison between intellectual challenge and importance of the issues involved defies generalization. But one can say that the balance tips in favor of domestic practice if one compares only the more important cases in the more important courts.

However, it could fairly have been said of my entrance into the practice of law that I started at the top and could confidently expect to spend the rest of my professional life working down. Certainly it took forty years to bring me back again as counsel to the Peace Palace at The Hague.

My new assignment proved at once to be as interesting as what had gone before. It presented an intellectually challenging problem upon which hung a considerable amount of money. Norway claimed that the United States had taken from her citizens contracts with American shipyards for oceangoing vessels for which her citizens had paid large sums and which had great value. The amount of its claim was approximately $16 million, including interest for five years. The United States admitted that something was due, but denied that it had taken the Norwegians' contracts. On the contrary, it claimed, what was taken was "work in progress" in the shipyards, evidenced by such physical material as had been assembled for the several ships. The fair value of this work in progress could be assumed, unless more was proved, to be equal to the progress payments already made by the contractors to the shipyards. The amount offered was $2.5 million. No interest was to be paid.

As I sat in my empty new office and looked at the treaty of arbitration and some files of unhelpful correspondence, the problem was where and how to start. It was plain that the man one had to convince was the Swiss President of the Tribunal, Mr. James Vallotton, an eminent authority on international law. The American and Norwegian members were expected to and would press the views of their governments, since this was a court of arbitration. To approach the Swiss President with metaphysical and legal arguments only was quite wrong. The correct path lay through facts not theory, as I had been trained for two years to believe.

The first task was to unearth everything that could be learned about what the Shipping Board, the Emergency Fleet Corporation — the United States agencies in charge — and their agents had done and reported about the whole shipbuilding program in general and this group of requisitions in particular. If one knows one's way about the Library of Congress, particularly the area of congressional hearings and reports, the record rooms of the various government agency libraries, and similar collections of dust-gathering, ephemeral official literature, presided over by custodians, usually female, who are eager to help the rare visitor, then the amount of information available is overwhelming. There is no need for secret or private files. Our government is a continuous and compulsive reporter of every aspect of every action. All one needs is the key or keys and out it pours.

My plan became to let official United States Government documents, freely available to the public, prove our case for us. It took time and digging. But the result left no doubt that over and over the government had said at the time and reported later that it had taken over — not merely in our cases but in all cases — the contracts with the yards, stepped into the shoes of the former contractors, sought to enforce the contract terms, and that it had in all prior settlements with claimants repaid them the premiums they had paid in purchasing the contracts as the measure of their fair value.

The result of these researches, "The Case of Norway," filed February 6, 1922, was an impressive document. It led our opponents to redesign their defense and build a strong secondary line, disclosed in their "Counter-Case," filed May 22 and hammered home in their "Argument" of a month later. There this line, referred to as "the taint of Hannevig," was developed in an eighty-page section asserting that $13 million out of $16.4 million was "claimed on the purely speculative features of transactions" conducted by a colorful Norwegian, Christoffer Hannevig, who had had important interests both in the shipyards and in the ship companies involved in the case. The lawyers representing the United States did not minimize the sinister conclusions drawn from their evidence. Here they are:

(a) That the "taint" of Hannevig and his methods is upon every one of the fifteen claims.

(b) That the well proved identification of Hannevig and Hannevig's methods with every claim is more than enough to throw suspicion on the claims, even without the many other suspicions and significant circumstances that are apparent in the record.

(c) That the claims are not legitimate claims for compensation for property requisitioned by the United States, but are demands that the United States underwrite the speculative transactions of men who "bought a chance."

(d) That there is grave reason to believe that many of these transactions were not bona fide, even as speculations, but were devices for the threefold purpose of

(1) Magnifying claims against the United States.

(2) Unloading on a deluded public, stock of companies formed and founded on contracts which the Supreme Court of Norway has shown to be worthless except as "a purchase of a chance."

(3) Procuring loans from banks, either deceived by these speculators or associated with them, on the prospect of big indemnities from the United States.

(e) That on August 3, 1917, not a single claimant had any interest whatsoever in the property requisitioned by the United States, and that the only interest they may now have was acquired with their eyes wide open to the facts of requisition and to the gamble involved in their transactions.

(f) That the prices allegedly paid for the contracts did not represent real value, but fictitious values conceived, created and magnified with a view to obtaining large sums of money from the United States.

(g) That in some cases it is doubtful if the prices claimed were actually paid, the indications being that the prices allegedly paid were only pretended prices.

(h) That requisitioning, at least in claims 7 to 15, inclusive, and probably in all the cases instead of damaging the owners of August 3, 1917, actually saved them from great if not total loss.

(i) That the amount conceded by the United States in these cases is far more than the former owners of the nine Hannevig hulls could ever have received if there had been no requisition.

(j) That the amount conceded by the United States is complete and just compensation for the property requisitioned.

In this document our opponents were not only constructing a new defense but mounting a spirited counterattack against the very *bona fides* of the claims. Nor were our opponents men to be discounted. The argument was signed by Mr. William C. Dennis, Agent for the United States, a lawyer experienced in international matters, later President of Earlham College, and by Counsel for the United States, former Senator George Sutherland of Utah, later Mr. Justice Sutherland of the Supreme Court of the United States. So we in turn made new dispositions. Mr. Burling associated with him, as a counterweight to Senator Sutherland, a Chicago friend, Mr. Walter L. Fisher, who had succeeded Mr. Ballinger as President Taft's Secretary of the Interior, and we started off for The Hague a month early via Christiania (now Oslo) to gather evidence to refute our opponent's new attack.

The S.S. *Stavangerfjord*, even then an old ship, took us by the long route north of the British Isles to Bergen and along the beautiful coast of Norway to Oslo. There the task of interviewing our indirect clients, the shipowners, and digging into their relations with Hannevig fell largely to me. It wasn't an easy one, due to their gift for narrative and lack of a sense of relevance. At length, however, at considerable length, the resulting documents in part diminished "the taint of Hannevig," and in part diminished the effect of the association with him upon the fair value of the contracts. Nonetheless an odor of Hannevig remained; and inevitably I became the expert on this complicated and uninviting part of the case.

Our stay in Oslo was enlivened by an audience with King Haakon, a handsome and agreeable monarch. In preparation for this my brother, a student who had come along with me and been pressed into service, was sent to the palace to distribute our calling cards, as protocol required, among the boxes of the royal household. As he did so, he learned from the old servitor who had him in charge that he had worked for twenty years in the silver factory in our home town of Middletown, Connecticut. They adjourned for a beer and reminiscence in the servants' quarters.

The anteroom to the King's study, where he received us, was a Victorian period piece, filled with photographs of family scenes involving most of the crowned heads of Europe before the First World War — picnics, yachting parties (the King was an enthusiastic sailor), birthdays, weddings. We were told that our meeting would be informal — as informal as one can be in a morning coat — and that the King would indicate its end. I was to become the occasion for his doing so. After some amiable conversation, His Majesty discussed the case on which we were engaged. His briefing seemed to have been deficient, for he expressed the view that his government would have done better if, instead of litigating the matter, it had relied upon the generous impulses of the American Government and people to do the right thing. This produced a somewhat embarrassed pause until Mr. Fisher, a forthright man, explained that the American Government's idea of the right thing, as expressed by its offer of payment, was one seventh of the Norwegian Government's idea of the right thing, and that, so far, no audible protest had come from the American people, if, indeed, they had heard about it. Another of my seniors changed the subject.

In due course, it led around to what seemed a harmless enough subject, the international monetary problems which the First World War had produced (and which the Second was to duplicate), owing to the flow of gold to the United States. As this group of unexperts became more entangled in this difficult problem, I — being farthest from the King — whispered an aside to George Rublee to the effect that perhaps our efforts were directed toward an important monetary end of which we had not been aware, the redistribution of gold. George chuckled nervously, attracting the King's attention, which flustered him.

"You said something, Mr. Rublee?" asked the King.

Like a schoolboy who is caught red-handed and panics, George answered lamely, "Mr. Acheson did."

The inquiring look turned on me. My prayer for a thought went unanswered. At length, as lamely as George, I confessed to the observation, which sounded even sillier to me the second time. The King was not amused. No one had a diversionary idea. The King rose; the audience was at an end.

Our argument opened at The Hague on July 22 and went on for six weeks. We met each morning at the Peace Palace in the smaller courtroom for three or four hours. The President, flanked by his colleagues, Messrs. Chandler Anderson and Paul B. Vogt, an American and a Norwegian diplomat respectively, sat at a raised bench. Counsel addressed them from an elevated pulpit. The proceedings were dignified but relaxedly disorganized. Issues were taken up one by one; first counsel for Norway spoke for a day or so, then opposing counsel replied, after that often a rejoinder, and so on. Each afternoon and evening I worked with one of my seniors on material for the next day.

We lived out of The Hague on the sea at the Grand Hotel in Scheveningen, a vast company of us — our American party, a group from the Norwegian Foreign Office, and all our ship-owner clients with their camp followers. But it was great fun, with the boardwalk and the beach for exercise, the Kurhaus for opera, when we could get to it, and good Dutch restaurants. The younger ones commuted on bicycles with swarms of Dutch.

As the days went by we got the feel which comes to counsel in a long case that our main points were going well, but that the "taint of Hannevig" persisted and was having a corroding effect. Our opponents worked at it and held the attention of the President. Mr. Burling decided that we had to face it at length and in detail. A council of war agreed, but produced no volunteers — each senior pointing out the qualifications of another. After the meeting Mr. Burling asked me to take on the job, pointing out in his amused, sardonic way that, after making my first court argument in the Peace Palace, I might find what was left of my legal career something of an anticlimax. That was the least of my worries; I jumped at the chance.

Almost a month after the argument of the case had started, I found myself, nervous but prepared, aloft in the counsel's pulpit, guiding the tribunal through the intricacies of Hannevig's dealings. These centered particularly on the last nine claims, those of companies in which he was interested, organized solely to contract with a yard which his company owned but which in August 1917 was only partially built — "phantom ships upon phantom ways," our opponent's brief called them.

The argument had its problems. After a day of exposition and explanation, it seemed to me that some way must be found to make our opponents themselves limit the bearing of the "taint of Hannevig" to the value of our property, excluding the claim that

it went to the character of the property, the validity of the claimants' ownership, or the *bona fides* of the claims. To attempt this
required taking a chance. I decided to take it. To the surprise of
a tranquil courtroom, I said:

> In the Argument of the United States some very severe things
> were said about these claims, things which look to us as though
> they related more to the validity of the claims and to the good
> faith of the purchasers, and, perhaps, in some cases they tended
> to reflect somewhat upon the Kingdom of Norway in present-
> ing these claims. We have waited patiently after putting in our
> New Evidence to hear some statement by the Agent of the
> United States in this regard. We felt that some statement was
> due us. We felt that some statement was due the Kingdom
> of Norway. No statement has been made. These claims are
> not yet closed, and we trust that before they are some state-
> ment of a more positive nature than these remarks, that they
> dealt solely with value, will be forthcoming from the Agent of
> the United States.

About halfway through this passage Mr. Burling scribbled on
a pad and reaching above his head put it on the lectern before
me. A large scrawl read, "Shut up." The time for that had
passed. I pressed on for want of an alternative. The President
broke in:

> I think it is well understood that the validity of the assign-
> ments is no longer disputed. Is that not so, Mr. Dennis? As I
> understand, the validity of the assignments is not disputed but
> it is a question of the amounts?
> MR. DENNIS. We freely concede that the amount which we
> state in the Counter Case of the United States is due . . . we
> are willing to pay the amount to the Kingdom of Norway.
> MR. FISHER. I think it would clarify the situation if we
> could have a little clearer statement as to the admission of the
> claims so far as validity is concerned. I hope that there is not a

reservation in the mind of counsel on the other side that what they are doing is merely admitting the validity of the claim to the extent which they offer. It would be a curious thing, for instance, if the Tribunal would conclude that a thousand dollars more was due than is offered, that under that kind of an admission they would have to stop and see if they admitted the validity.

THE PRESIDENT. It is only the amount, as I understand it, that is disputed.

MR. FISHER. It is only the amount that is disputed, as I understand it. Is not that so?

(Mr. Dennis apparently nodded in assent.)

MR. FISHER. Say it so the stenographer will get it.

THE PRESIDENT. I think that is quite clear. Proceed.

This was not bad for a beginner's try. Afterward, I got a good going over for risking an all-out attack on our whole position; but results are what count and the risk had been justified by the outcome. The "taint of Hannevig" was contained but not removed. When the award was handed down, Mr. Anderson abstaining, our principal positions had been accepted by the majority; but the valuation of the last nine claims suffered materially. We had claimed, before interest, $11.5 million. The award was for $12 million including interest; but the last nine claims received $1 million less than was claimed.

The award was paid on February 26, 1923, accompanied by a letter from Secretary Hughes criticizing it on two grounds — because it appeared to impose stricter standards upon a belligerent state when requisitioning property of neutrals than of nationals, and because the exact calculation of each award was not spelled out. To the recipients the payment outweighed the criticisms.

For Senator Sutherland, also, consolation was at hand. In October 1922 he took his seat on the Supreme Court of the United States, where as a member of the "Four Horsemen" he helped put the Supreme Court athwart the trend of the times, which brought it into head-on collision with the Roosevelt Administration, and produced the constitutional crisis of 1937. A minor satisfaction came not long after Justice Sutherland's appointment, when he acted as the voice of the Court in *Omnia Commercial Company* v. *Russell,* in applying the legal principle which he had failed in urging upon the tribunal at The Hague.

As August 1922 wore on, our Norwegian friends wearied of the daily grind at the Peace Palace. A summer without gaiety was to them a summer lost. One who takes his view of Norwegians solely from Ibsen would be sadly misled. At length a ship of one of our party came into Rotterdam. As if by spontaneous combustion, the idea of a gala on board — dinner, dancing, supper, more dancing, daylight breakfast, champagne, music from Amsterdam, each added a new and glittering suggestion. Not the least brilliant of which was my brother's contribution in inviting a group of American college girls whom he had encountered just as their enthusiasm for sightseeing in The Hague had reached a low point.

The party was worthy of an Icelandic saga. The feasting gargantuan, mead flowed ceaselessly, Vikings danced with maidens on deck in the moonlight. Long after dawn, sustained by a parting refreshment, we made our way back to Scheveningen, pausing there for a final roll call. One maiden was missing and one Viking, a burly former sea captain in his sixties. His friends took a pessimistic view, but not my wife, who had assumed responsibility for the girls. Spotting a parked taxicab on the town's deserted grand circle, she organized a posse to investigate. In the car we found our maiden and, facing her on a jump seat, the captain. "No, no, Captain," she was saying, "it goes this way — Pease-porridge hot! Pease-porridge cold!"

"Nothing to worry about," my wife explained to the Norwegians. "It's an honors requirement in every girls' college at home."

8

AND WORKING DOWN

BACK IN WASHINGTON, after a vacation in England, the warning of a year before that my employment might be limited to The Hague case only proved unnecessary. The firm's business was growing so rapidly that it needed more, not less, help. So I settled into the routine of a busy office. One of the first assignments had its amusing side. We were employed to continue litigation with the government over Hannevig's wartime shipbuilding, in the course of which each party changed sides with the other in its legal theory. The government now tried to enforce contracts, which at The Hague it argued had never been taken over; while we insisted that the government's own actions inspired by the war had rendered the contracts impossible of enforcement. The innumerable changes which the Macy Board had ordered in wage rates and job classifications, alterations in ship design and specifications, higher material costs resulting from still further government orders — all these made it virtually impossible to calculate what amounts should be added to the original contract prices, regardless of the legal theory adopted. So for two years, as counsel for the receivers of the shipbuilding companies, we battled out an accounting with the government for more than $60 million advanced to finance the building of the ships. Each side accused the other of unconscionable inconsistency; and it all ended, as it had to do in the very nature of the facts, in a dead heat.

The decade of the twenties took its frenzied course to economic disaster. Washington, somnolent under *le roi fainéant*, Calvin Coolidge, relaxed after the excitement of the Teapot Dome scandals and the Fall, Sinclair, and Doheny trials. The functions of a capital city were turned back to New York. There our friends were rumored to be amassing wealth, while we, in our quiet backwater, went on learning our trade.

The required three years membership in our local bar having expired, I became a member of the bar of "Our Court"; and soon after made my first appearance there. It was not an unalloyed success. On a Monday morning before the Supreme Court was to meet at noon an out-of-town lawyer telephoned Mr. Burling and, finding him out, ran down our short list of names until he came to mine. He had a simple request, to move in a case pending before the Court to substitute as a party a successor executor for one deceased. To me, however, it was a great responsibility for which I must be fully prepared. Forgetting that I was not decorously and somberly attired for court appearance, but rather sportingly in tweed and colored shirt, I hurried up to the Capitol, got the briefs and record from the Clerk's office and absorbed them while admissions to the bar and opinions occupied the Court. If, after I recited my simple and formal request, a Justice should ask me a question about the case — an inconceivable supposition — I would know the answer.

At length I heard Chief Justice Taft ask whether there were any motions, went to the lectern, and made my motion. It was followed by complete silence, a sort of perplexed, almost astonished silence, at length broken by an irrelevant question from the Chief Justice — what was my name? I gave it in an agony of apprehension. "Mr. Acheson," he went on, "you have been in the courtroom this morning?" I had. "How strange," he added. "We handed down our opinion and disposed of your case not more than two minutes ago." Retreating amid titters toward the door, I had covered half the distance when the Chief Justice called me back to the lectern.

"I am afraid that I exaggerated," he said. "It could not have been more than a minute and a half ago." The courtroom relaxed into a good laugh. Justice Brandeis was not smiling.

For a decade my education as a lawyer through practice continued. It is a baffling experience to describe. Out of disparate activities, often of minor importance, largely unconnected in substance comes training rarely achieved by other means. Perhaps the phrase "largely unconnected in substance" should be modified in my case in one respect. Through most of my work ran the thread of some action of the federal government, actual or potential, favorable or unfavorable to a client's interests or desires. An account of "cases" undertaken turns into an unmitigated bore, as the recent epidemic of "histories" of well-known law firms so amply proves. And yet by some alchemy this base material can be turned into insight, judgment, and inventiveness. Alexis de Tocqueville, himself a lawyer, remarked a hundred and thirty years ago that the study and practice of law produced certain habits of orderly thought — as he put it, "a kind of instinctive regard for the regular connection of ideas" — and spoke of the lawyers of the young country as men of "information and sagacity." More than a century later, another perceptive Frenchman carried the analysis further.

Some years ago M. Jean Monnet, on a visit to this country to attend a dinner in honor of an American lawyer friend, discussed this matter. One of the brilliant men of his generation, he has stayed in the background while contributing greatly to such imaginative innovations as the Schuman plan for the European Coal and Steel Community, Euratom (the joint European development of nuclear energy for peaceful purposes), the Common Market of France, Germany, Benelux, and Italy, and the European Defense Community, which France herself tragically defeated. He talked about the rare and valuable combination of qualities found in few men — the capacity for origination joined with the practical knowledge and ability to translate dreams into operating institutions. In America, throughout his own long ex-

perience in business, in two wars, and in the aftermath of the
second, he had found this combination in the world of affairs
chiefly among lawyers. He spoke, among many others, of the
late Dwight W. Morrow, lawyer, member of the banking firm
of J. P. Morgan & Company, Ambassador to Mexico, and United
States Senator from New Jersey; of Mr. Donald Swatland,
whose services in procurement for the Air Corps during the Second World War were phenomenal; and of M. Monnet's friend,
Mr. John J. McCloy, lawyer, Assistant Secretary of War in the
Second World War, President of the World Bank, High Commissioner to the German Federal Republic, Chairman of the
Chase Manhattan Bank, Presidential Adviser on Disarmament.

These men, he noted, were from firms in downtown New
York and had dealt with large business and financial matters.
Another lawyer of the same rare ability and the same background was the late Mr. Joseph P. Cotton, Under Secretary of
State in the Hoover Administration. None of them was a court
lawyer. What had impressed M. Monnet was that lawyers of
this genre, by no means confined to New York, seemed pecu-
liarly able to understand at once the uniqueness of unprece-
dented situations and immediately to set about devising new and
practical ways of dealing with them. To be able to do each of
these is more unusual than appears at first glance. The unprece-
dented does not appear with a label around its neck announcing
it to be such.

Where does this practical statesmanship come from? How is
it learned? In large part from the role played for nearly a half
century by lawyers of the sort M. Monnet was speaking of.
While familiar with the clients' affairs as few lawyers are elsewhere, they have learned to remain detached from the emotional
involvement of their clients in their purposes or troubles. They
must see all around situations on which they are to advise,
whether they involve ambitious plans or unsought problems.
More than this, I have heard both Mr. Dwight Morrow and Jus-

tice Brandeis, in speaking of their years at the bar, say that, before starting on a complicated and difficult negotiation, they would spend as much time and thought on learning about and understanding the other party's business and problems as those of their own client. Their aim was to know more about the other fellow's business than he did, since both were persuaded that half of the controversies arose because of the faulty understanding by businessmen of their true interests.

It would be untrue to attribute the capacity for legal statesmanship to the bar generally. Mr. George Kennan complains, I think justly, of the disservice which lawyer Secretaries of State did to American foreign policy during the years when they directed most of our effort to the negotiation of nearly a hundred treaties of arbitration, only two of which were ever invoked. He is, of course, quite right that all this misguided effort sprang from a complete failure to see the enormous threat to world stability which the Germans were so soon to carry into action. Even after the First World War, the realities of power were still obscured to us by our peculiar American belief that salvation lies in institutional mechanisms.

Candor, I believe, requires us to go further and to concede that sometimes training and experience in the dialectics of legal or political controversy — a most useful aid in persuading others to accept a conclusion already chosen or imposed — can be handicaps in making a choice in the first instance. Lawyers, who are habituated to having their main choices made for them by the necessities of their clients, are often at a loss when, as in government, for instance, they have wide latitude in a choice of policy.

Secretary of State Cordell Hull, for years a lawyer and judge, then Congressman and Senator before heading the State Department, was, at first, a puzzle and then a source of delight in this matter of making a choice. For many years he would summon his principal assistants to a Sunday-morning conference in his office, a practice which should have been forbidden by the constitutional prohibition against "cruel and unusual punishment." During the winter the office was kept so warm that one had a half-fainting sensation of being detached from one's own body. He was sure at some point to ring for his assistant, an excellent Foreign Service officer, Cecil Gray, known as "Joe."

When he appeared, Mr. Hull would say, "Joe, look at that thermometer."

Joe would do so, and report, "Eighty, Mr. Secretary."

"I thought so," Mr. Hull would say. "Let's have some heat."

The main business of the morning was to review events and attempt to reach some decisions on future courses. For the first few weeks I thought that the heat was affecting my mind or Mr. Hull's, since he seemed to be taking contradictory positions on the same question. I soon discovered that this was his process of decision. He was trying out various views of the matter under discussion to find out how they went both with us and to himself. He would more likely than not settle on one which sounded the most convincing. This method of aural thinking and analysis is a long way from the working of the more sophisticated legal minds I have been discussing. It is not uncommon, however, as witness the apocryphal old lady who said, "How can I know what I think till I hear what I say?"

Toward the end of this decade of novitiate my work came back to international or — what is very like it — interstate disputes. The first involved a claim of Sweden against the United States for the "detention" of Swedish vessels in the United States by denying them the fuel with which to depart, in order to gain their use for Allied shipping needs. The second was in support of Arizona's struggle against the five other states of the Colorado River Basin and the United States over the division of the waters of the Colorado to be stored and then released for power, irrigation, and urban consumption through the Boulder Canyon Project in Arizona.

These tasks absorbed a little over two years of my life; both were unsuccessful; and both contributed much to my education in the broader sense. The decision to refer the Swedish claim to arbitration by a special treaty brought me the opportunity to work with a remarkable man whom I have just mentioned, Mr. Joseph P. Cotton of New York, then Under Secretary of State. Tall, handsome, able, cynical, and wise, almost unknown outside Wall Street's financial and legal circles, he could have been of immense usefulness in the years of crisis already upon us then. But in a few months he was to lose his life through medical mischance. It is told of him that, asked how to instruct an ambassador to deal with an embarrassing but trivial matter, he replied impatiently, "Tell him to laugh it off." Presently the officer returned. "Sir," he reported, "the code has no word for laugh."

Our tribunal in this case consisted of one man, a bearded, elderly, and learned Swiss gentleman, Mr. Borel. When I said to Ned Burling that he reminded me of my grandfather, Ned's comment was that he reminded everyone of his grandfather. This genial quality did not prevent him from deciding against the Swedish claim upon the not unreasonable ground that, whatever might have been Sweden's rights under the Treaty of Amity and Commerce with the United States — one of the first ever signed by the new Republic — neither the government nor its nationals had ever pushed to the limit its claim to have its ships leave without cargo and obtained a flat refusal. It was not enough that the negotiations had made it fairly predictable that such would have been the result of an unqualified demand.

The argument took place in Washington, a disappointment, but to prepare the case my wife and I spent the months of July and August 1930 in Sweden, largely in Stockholm, gathering material from the Johnson Line, whose ships were involved. Those months have left golden memories that have never dimmed. The Scandinavian summer pours out riches with wanton prodigality in its short span. Except for a few hours of semidarkness, there is "no night there." Only for records and routine does a new day begin. Life just goes on, especially for the young, who do not tire easily.

So much can be done when one banishes sleep. Work claimed only a third, sometimes less, of our time. The rest was left us to enjoy the beauties of a lavish nature. Never was so much water, salt and fresh, so used and so appreciated by so many. The entire population, working and idle, took to it — in or on it or both. Opportunities for land sports, too, were everywhere. And — the never-ending wonder — there was plenty of time. No scramble through paralyzing traffic to get in a set of tennis in the fading light before dinner. There was all the time until breakfast and no hurry. We sailed and swam, played tennis or golf, danced and dined, had long talks on the steamers going to Saltsjöbaden or on terraces in the endless evenings.

The city itself never ceased to work its spell. Stockholm has been called the Venice of the North; and properly so, if one stresses the word *North*. Here is always briskness and movement. Cumulous clouds hurry across its sky. Water swirls under its bridges and through innumerable rivers and canals which form their own aqueous street system. One begins to feel like an old resident as one learns to use the water ferries — vaporettos, they would be in Venice — which like those in Venice scurry everywhere, never tieing up at their landings, but just keeping their bows against the dock long enough for a spry passenger to land. One who daydreams may have an unintended tour of the waterways.

A continuing distraction while dressing in the morning was the pageant of the commuters' steamers which took place at the quay just under our window. We looked across a broad expanse of water to the Palace on the City Between the Bridges. From eight o'clock onward steamers from around the archipelago brought in their cargoes of office workers and herring. When each had disgorged its hurrying humans, trays of herring were stacked on the quay alongside. An old man near each stack placed an umbrella across his knees, opened his newspaper, and awaited the enemy. Clouds of gulls circled the stacks of herring trays, making sudden swoops first at one and then another. The guardians laid about them with their umbrellas, shouting, but the odds were against them and many fat herring never reached a smörgasbord. Finally trucks rolled up and the show was over for the day.

I had a small office in the Swedish Foreign Office — since we were counsel for the government — and another at the Johnson building, the headquarters of a remarkable man, Mr. Axel Axelson Johnson, a real entrepreneur of the classical period, a cultivated gentleman and the embodiment of Swedish determination. Gustavus Adolphus could and would have used him to advantage. Indeed, the Johnson steel plant at Avesta had been built to use the water power of the river to make munitions for the great warrior-king. In both offices we found plenty of companionship for lunches in the outdoor restaurants along the water and on the squares, as well as in the very fine ones on the terrace of the Grand Hotel and in the Opera House. Many of the younger Swedish Foreign Service officers were summer bachelors and knowledgeable about offerings for diversion. Some of those friendships have survived the years. One evening a company went with us to Nynäshamn, where my wife and I were taking the boat overnight to the island of Visby, one of the Hanseatic cities. When the steamer sailed at midnight, our friends came along, slept happily on deck and on the hotel porch, and used my razor. When, during the war, we negotiated purchase and supply agreements with Sweden to reduce materials available to Germany, one of these friends represented Sweden. Later he came back to us again as Swedish Ambassador.

We dutifully journeyed to the University at Uppsala to consult the sage of international law, Professor Unden, who later served for years as Sweden's Minister of Foreign Affairs. His utterances though impressive had the same ambivalent quality which characterized the oracle at Delphi, merely deflecting one's thought from the problem posed to the meaning of the answer. Over another weekend Axel Johnson drove us north to Avesta in Dalecarlia to spend his birthday. Here another, simpler Sweden brought to mind Justice Brandeis's views on the qualitative effect of size upon human performance.

The steel mill and those who worked in it were Avesta. The Johnsons' house, large and comfortable, was right in the middle of things, not aloof from them. At the bottom of the garden a path led over a canal, once used for water power, to the factory on the riverside. The rattle and clang of machinery started the day; its silence ended it. Across the street from the Johnsons' gate began the red-painted houses of the steelworkers, good socialists all. Our first evening we walked through the village, Johnson calling the men by name, introducing me, and stopping to chat with groups about the prospect of orders from Europe — an oil-cracking plant for Belgium or Rumania, and so on — upon which depended, if not their bread and butter, their meat and vegetables. The enterprise was intimate enough for them to understand functions other than their own. Manufacture was theirs, but selling was his, and selling in markets far from their country, which wasn't able to absorb all their speciality products.

On the morning of Axel Johnson's birthday we were awakened by the sound of music. A small stringed orchestra from the village was playing under his window, a tribute which told many things about the givers and the receiver. Later that day, a Sunday, we drove to Leksand on Lake Siljan to church on the lakeside at the end of an avenue flanked by double rows of giant beeches. Here, for churchgoing the congregation wore their gaily colored local dress, giving the day a fiesta atmosphere. This was my introduction to the Swedish national church, molded by the grandfather of Gustavus Adolphus, King Gustavus Vasa.

That wise monarch reformed the Church in Sweden with as

little outward and visible change as possible. Like Henry VIII in England, and at about the same time, he took over Church lands. Unlike him, he drastically changed the doctrines of the Church to those of Geneva Protestantism. But decoration, vestments, and ritual he left unchanged. The altar and crucifix, altar hangings, triptychs, reredos, embroidered and colorful vestments for clergy and their attendants, incense, all the trappings of religion familiar and comforting to the people, remained as they had been, and still remain. Gustavus Vasa approached the reformation of the Church as President Taft described his own approach to taxation, to get the most feathers with the least squawk.

The Colorado River Basin is about as different from Sweden as it is far away. The former is arid, while one ninth of the surface of Sweden is covered with lakes. The Basin states agreed on the necessity of storing the vast flood waters of the Colorado which annually took their destructive course to the Gulf of California in Mexico; they disagreed on the division of the water among them. Arizona in particular saw its whole future hinging upon a generous share of it. In advocating irrigation from Colorado River water, Senator Cameron of Arizona is said to have ended his peroration by declaiming that all Arizona needed to become a paradise was water and the right sort of immigration. To which Senator John Sharp Williams of Mississippi added, "That's all hell needs!"

Southern California, on the other hand, was receiving floods of immigrants — whether of the right sort or not may be arguable — but was running short of water and electric power for them. The federal government saw the opportunity of financing a large part of a multipurpose dam by selling water and power to Southern California, the only large cash market available. To Arizona water carried over the mountains was not only lost to Arizona but assured no return flow, as agricultural use in the Basin did, to satisfy the needs and demands of Mexico. Its interest lay in less grandiose and less costly dams for irrigation.

The unequal struggle went on first in the Congress and then in the Supreme Court. I worked for Arizona in both phases; preparing briefs for congressional committees, and as a Special Assistant Attorney General of Arizona, taking the lead in the litigation.

The litigation turned on the factual basis of the federal government's right to build a dam at all — the navigability of the Colorado River. The legislation purported to be improving the navigation of a navigable river; the rest was, in theory, trimming. The cases appeared to hold that God must have made a river navigable before Congress could legally improve upon His work; and, whether He had done so, rested upon facts to be proved. The courts would not become geographers in their own right or rely upon their own research. So after months of careful study we drew our bill of complaint reciting a host of evidential facts with their resultant facts establishing the condition of the river at important dates in history and concluding that the river was not and had not been navigable. Our pleading, we thought, was proof against a motion to dismiss for failure to state a cause of action. Moreover, we also thought, it was sure to produce a long hearing before a master to take testimony, during which the Court or a careful Congress might delay construction. Not only might we well win on the issue of navigability, but once hearings were ordered our position to bargain for a better deal would be greatly improved.

The argument, on March 9, 1931, went well. Arizona, one of the least populous of states pitted against the might of the federal government and five states gained sympathy like a David girt about by a host of Goliaths. We thought then that the imponderables were on our side. But we imagined a vain thing. Mr. Justice Brandeis delivered the blow, holding that the Court would take judicial notice that the Colorado was navigable and that the Congress might improve it, even at the cost of diverting a substantial part of its flow to the dry throat of Los Angeles. When I picked myself up and brushed off the dust, what was left for consolation was a note from Justice Holmes conveying his "felicitations on an excellent argument," and a notation at the end of Justice Brandeis's opinion — "Mr. Justice McReynolds is of the opinion that the motions to dismiss should be overruled and the defendants required to answer." A Daniel indeed, but unhappily not come to judgment.

At the end of the decade of the twenties some new assignments brought new and broader interests. At the time of the Democratic Convention of 1924 Governor Alfred E. Smith of New York was to us a romantic but vaguely known figure. For a time he brought whatever interest could be brought to the dreary gathering which we followed with pretty primitive radio receiving sets. But four years later the national and our own political situation had changed. We had found our hearts' delight, an eighteenth-century farmhouse with some land around it just north of Washington in Maryland, had registered as Democratic voters and become keenly interested in the approaching election. "The Happy Warrior," Wordsworth's phrase which Franklin Roosevelt had applied to Governor Smith when nominating him in 1928, gives the sense of joyous, affectionate exaltation his vibrant leadership inspired in us. For almost eight years the country, in a trance, seemed to have been following a hearse. Now at the touch of this prince in a brown derby, with his East Side accent, gay humanity, and common sense, came an awakening — at least, for a moment and for those not scaling the steep ascents of the stock market. The autumn of 1928 gave me the opportunity to find an outlet for this enthusiasm and to begin an education in public speaking by getting into the campaign in Montgomery County.

Justice Brandeis used to get off a Puritan maxim that I never much believed in. He would say, "The best vacation is a change of work." In the spring of 1930 George Rublee gave me a chance to try it. George had been in Mexico with his friend Dwight Morrow, who had been persuaded to go there as Ambas-

sador by his friend and classmate at Amherst College, President
Coolidge. Mr. Morrow's mission was to put right mutual griev-
ances of over a decade, growing out of expropriation of property
by one nation and armed invasion by the other. George had
gone along to help resolve another source of trouble, the controversy between Church and State over expropriation of Church
properties during the revolution. Their efforts had been spectac-
ularly successful. Then Mr. Morrow, after attending the London Naval Disarmament Conference, turned to a field still more
novel for him than diplomacy — politics.

The approaching congressional election of 1930 gave the Re-
publicans cold shivers. Mr. Hoover's majority of 1928 along
with the "new economic era" had drooped under the deepening
depression. The prospect might have depressed any Republican
candidate for office, but especially a former partner of J. P. Morgan & Company. Yet Mr. Morrow announced his candidacy in
New Jersey for the United States Senate. In November the Re-
publicans lost control of the Congress, but Mr. Morrow was
elected. His election was largely laid to his opening speech and
the repetition of its ideas during the campaign.

Many of Mr. Morrow's friends contributed to the work
which went into that speech. George Rublee was one. George,
also, contributed me. He overcame my qualms against this political apostacy by saying that the experience of working with Mr.
Morrow would be worth it. He was quite right.

We worked in the Morrow house in Englewood, coming up
from Washington for several days at a time and staying nearby.
An early meeting stands out. A cold had driven Mr. Morrow to
bed. He sat propped up and surrounded by books, pads, and
crumpled paper which spread from the bed to a table and over-
flowed onto the floor. From the bed to a fireplace the floor was
covered with pieces of linoleum. As he talked, Mr. Morrow
would nervously light a succession of cigarettes and, after gestic-
ulating with them briefly, throw them in the general direction of

the fireplace. Mrs. Morrow's protests could not overcome his absentmindedness, hence the resort to second-best methods to preserve the rug and prevent fire.

Dwight Morrow's mind was not like a rapier or a bludgeon, but like a pack of beagles, scurrying every which way through the underbrush, thoroughly disorganized, until one of them, getting a scent, gave tongue. Then the pack became a unified whole again, in hot pursuit. We spent some time exploring the thicket of possible issues for the best ones to pursue, before deciding to open his campaign for the nomination with a speech against prohibition. At first he was dubious about doing this, and many of his friends advised against it, but the more we explored the problem, the more enthusiastic he became as he began to develop a fresh, though not novel, approach. The whole discussion about prohibition had been preempted by moralisms. To President Hoover it was "an experiment noble in purpose"; to its other and supposedly overpowering supporters it was a moral crusade against man's depravity and the evils of alcohol, the saloon, wholesale violation of law and the corruption of government, youth, and a discriminating taste in wines.

As the beagles of Mr. Morrow's mind coursed around and through this issue, discussion of prohibition became a clinic on federalism. The troubles and evils we were suffering came from giving continental scope and enforcement to a regulation which did not have continental significance or acceptance. True, this had, to a very considerable extent, been forced upon the advocates of prohibition by the aggressive action of brewers and distillers, aided by unfortunate decisions of the Supreme Court, in forcing liquor into states and communities from which the majority wished to exclude it. Both the provocation and the remedy came of erroneous departures from the federal principle essential to a nation of continental size and varying local traditions and habits.

References to our early history and political thought developed this theme. It was not an original one; but it had important assets. It was true; it was fresh in its escape from the stalemated moral confrontation; it was timely in that the country, even though the politicians were still blind and deaf to the signs, was fed up with prohibition; and — as important as any — it made repeal of the prohibition amendment to the Constitution not merely respectable but in the true American tradition. It turned the moral tables on the Anti-Saloon League and the Women's Christian Temperance Union.

Reading the speech today, it is hard to believe that in 1930 it created a nationwide sensation. The day following it, the *New York Times* editorial was positively lyrical:

> Mr. Dwight Morrow's speech on prohibition last night is in the highest tradition of political leadership. When millions of citizens are restless and confused about an issue; when they see it breaking up parties and dividing families and setting cities against the country districts and arousing bitterness between whole sections of the country; when they look up to their nominal rulers and elected authorities and are fed only with platitudes and evasions; when they are conscious of wide surges of discontent and longing for some man to show the nation a way out of a terrible muddle — then is the opportunity for a public man of clear vision and calm courage to step forward with an accurate diagnosis and a definite remedy. This has now been done by Mr. Morrow. His New Jersey address makes him not merely the outstanding figure in that State, but a sort of path-breaker to whom the eyes of the whole nation will be turned. People everywhere will feel that at last a real leader has come to the front.

And even the less impressionable Baltimore *Sun* "could scarce forbear to cheer":

> . . . Dwight Morrow is the first major figure of the dominant political party to stand up in public and deal with the realities

of this business. Alfred E. Smith has done it with the minority party. Albert C. Ritchie has done it. Now, at last comes this first-class man of the Republican party to say what the Hoovers and the Hugheses and the Coolidges have dared not say. That is significant. We make headway.

Two years later, in the election of 1932, my efforts, more vigorous and public, inured to the benefit of my own party. My next-door neighbor and friend, Frank Page, an officer of the Postal Telegraph Company, suggested that I go to the Democratic Convention in Chicago with him, be equipped with credentials from his company permitting me to go anywhere, and stay with him and that delightfully eccentric character, Heywood Broun. To me this experience opened a new and fascinating world peopled with characters from wholly novel spheres. Rare good judgment led me to make up to the Sergeant-at-Arms and be admitted to the inner sanctum, where scotch and soda flowed. The right to bring guests to this exclusive club made one welcome even to the immediate circle of the leading candidate. Since my own hero, Governor Smith, seemed out of the front-running, I could observe proceedings with detachment and hear and pass on the fantastic rumors which are the life blood of our political conventions. Having observed one of these mad and not a little degrading spectacles, nothing would induce me to do it again.

That autumn I took an energetic hand in a rough local campaign — organized meetings, made speeches, met with the Democratic Advisory Committee, and as a member of the Roosevelt-Garner-(Senator) Tydings-(Congressman) Lewis Club took over the writing of political tracts. This interested me more than the rest. Nearly thirty years later, from 1958–1960, I organized this work on a national scale for the National Democratic Advisory Committee, writing a good number of the pamphlets myself and editing most. They laid out a series of real policy issues as had not been done for many years, and as the usual campaign speeches rarely do.

With very little respite after the great victory at the polls in 1932, preparatory work for the incoming Administration began. Our candidate had promised, if elected, to reduce government expenditures by one quarter. The President's spokesman in the Senate, James Francis Byrnes, Senator from South Carolina — who fifteen years later was to be my chief in the State Department — took charge of preparing some of the necessary legislation. On Judge Covington's recommendation, he accepted my volunteered assistance. Soon after March 4, 1933, invitations came to attend meetings at the White House, where the legislative program was being put together. Thus does one get drawn closer and closer to the flypaper of taking part in government.

9

BRIEF ENCOUNTER — WITH FDR

To MAINTAIN well into middle age an ambition for adventure is apt to produce unexpected results. It did for me. The young are admonished to choose their hearts' desires with care, for they may attain them in middle age. This was not the surprise in store for me; for I never had the adventure for which I longed; rather, one for which I had no desire at all, and which promised to be my last.

The adventure for which I yearned was to be Solicitor General of the United States, then the second officer of the Department of Justice, charged with supervision of the appellate litigation of the government and with argument of the most important government cases presented to the high court. From a professional point of view, no greater opportunity offered to exercise all one's powers toward excellence in an environment affording them scope. To all this was added glamour.

President Roosevelt had early decided on Professor Felix Frankfurter of Harvard as his Solicitor General. But the Professor was recalcitrant. He had been offered and had accepted the Eastman Visiting Professorship at Oxford University for the academic year 1933–1934, attached to Balliol College. The struggle was sharp but never in doubt. Frankfurter's plans remained unchanged. At his suggestion, the President proposed my name to the Attorney General, Mr. Homer Cummings of Connecticut. The reaction being immediate, violent, and adverse, the proposal was withdrawn. My youthful ambition faded "as a dream dies at the opening day." I never knew why until, my brief hour upon the stage over, I came home to see my father in his last illness. From him I learned the explanation of my misadventure. As Episcopal Bishop of Connecticut, he took a sternly adverse view of Homer Cummings's multiple marriages and forbad complicity by the Episcopal Church. Neither side gave, and the Attorney General sought ecclesiastic blessing elsewhere. Hence, as a possible Solicitor General, I was *persona non grata*.

This check to my fortunes was a crushing blow at the time, and I did not have the consolation — if it would have been such — of knowing that over the years I would twice be asked to leave the work I was doing to become Solicitor General. Hardly a twinge of regret was caused by the necessity of declining these appreciated invitations.

April is a good month in which to bear blasted hopes, for May lies ahead. As it was, in May, 1933, two old friends, Arthur Ballantine, the Republican holdover Under Secretary of the Treasury, and James Douglas, Assistant Secretary, also awaiting relief, asked me to lunch with them. The new Secretary, Will Woodin, was, they said, a man after our own hearts who would need congenial friends. Would I come to meet him at lunch? The lunch was gay, uninhibited; and the Secretary, the same. I was hardly back in my office before the operator announced Secretary Woodin calling. Would I become Under Secretary of the Treasury?

The Baltimore *Sun* put its editorial finger on the weakness of this appointment. Even at the time its witty, though caustic, comment seemed to be true.

FRESH POINT OF VIEW

In the light of the widespread complaint about academic theorizing by professors in government which is matched in volume by complaint about "practical" business men and bankers in government, the appointment of Dean G. Acheson, somewhat of Maryland, as Under Secretary of the Treasury, to succeed Arthur A. Ballantine, should cause widespread rejoicing. For Mr. Acheson, a lawyer heretofore engaged in general practice, has offended neither by making profound academic studies of Treasury finance nor by following its ramifications extensively in a "practical" way.

By virtue of that record of aloofness from contaminating contact with the subject-matter of his new post, Mr. Acheson should bring to it that which is so eagerly sought in these days when the ancient financial truths falter and the new ones seem cockeyed to those tutored on the old, a "fresh point of view." He also will bring to it a fine mind and a personality so gracious that, with Secretary Woodin to write the music for his lyrics, increases in Federal taxation and the public debt may soon come to seem merely incidents in an entrancing Treasury symphony.

The handicap of lack of previous "contaminating contact with the subject-matter" of my new post should have been foreseen, at least, by me. The second handicap was not foreseeable. Not long after I reported for duty Secretary Woodin's health broke down. Frail and — though we did not know it — dying, he went home to New York for unsuccessful treatment, returning only briefly as the end of our joint tenure drew near. His departure left me in first place in the Treasury, inexperienced in high office and untrained in monetary and fiscal affairs, at a time of change in monetary policy more revolutionary, as we shall see, than had occurred since the Civil War.

Relations with the President began well. Ten years older than I, he had left our school before I got there, but he regarded my having gone to it as a recommendation, and friendship with Felix Frankfurter as even more of one. Then, too, I was led to believe that he regarded Homer Cummings's conduct in the affair of the

Solicitor Generalship as petty and unfair. Up to this time my meetings with him had been minimal, once or twice at bill-drafting sessions and at a reception or two. After Mr. Woodin's illness they were frequent. Every week at the Cabinet meeting I sat on his left, across the table from Secretary of State Cordell Hull, slightly known to me as a friend of Judge Covington's and a courteous gentleman of the old school. Usually the President was wheeled into the Cabinet Room and helped into his chair while the members stood at their places. An abiding memory of those meetings is of the dreadful odor and anaesthetic effect of Secretary of the Navy Swanson's smoldering cigarette butts, which he never thoroughly stubbed out in the ashtray between us.

Then, too, came summonses to appear and report at the President's bedside while he breakfasted. Early bedside appointments started business for the President before the considerable period needed for him to be up and dressed. But they were not always as well adapted to the purpose as planned. After the tray was taken away, his daughter Anna's children — known as Sistie and Buzzie — often made a distracting entrance. Buzzie galloped about the room, while Sistie delighted in climbing onto the bed and sitting beside him. Then began a game not designed to improve communication between President and caller. The child, leaning innocently against her grandfather, would suddenly clap her hand over his mouth in the middle of a sentence, smothering the rest of it. The President's counterattack, a vigorous tickling of her ribs, brought her hand down in defense and produced joint hilarity. Conversation became intermittent, disjointed, and obscure.

Gay and informal as these meetings were, they nevertheless carried something of the relationship implied in a seventeenth-century levée at Versailles. We think of these as stiff and formal, yet Saint-Simon tells us how Madame de Bourgoyne won a bet that she could sit on a chamber pot in the presence of the Sun

King himself. This she did with the aid of her lady-in-waiting and her own voluminous skirts. Louis XIV could and did forgive her, his daughter-in-law. But, while the relations between royalty and all the rest of humanity, however exalted, could be informal, they crossed a gulf measured by light-years.

The impression given me by President Roosevelt carried much of this attitude of European — not British — royalty. The latter is comfortably respectable, dignified, and bourgeois. The President could relax over his poker parties and enjoy Tom Corcoran's accordion, he could and did call everyone from his valet to the Secretary of State by his first name and often made up Damon Runyon nicknames for them, too — "Tommy, the Cork," "Henry, the Morgue," and similar names; he could charm an individual or a nation. But he condescended. Many reveled in apparent admission to an inner circle. I did not; and General Marshall did not, the General for more worthy reasons than I. He objected, as he said, because it gave a false impression of his intimacy with the President. To me it was patronizing and humiliating. To accord the President the greatest deference and respect should be a gratification to any citizen. It is not gratifying to receive the easy greeting which milord might give a promising stable boy and pull one's forelock in return.

This, of course, was a small part of the man and the impression he made. The essence of that was force. He exuded a relish of power and command. His responses seemed too quick; his reasons too facile for considered judgment; one could not tell what lay beneath them. He remained a formidable man, a leader who won admiration and respect. In others he inspired far more, affection and devotion. For me, that was reserved for a man of whom at that time I had never heard, his successor.

Although my first experience with President Roosevelt was coincident with the Homeric battles and confusions within the Administration over monetary policy at its outset, I shall not attempt to write a history of the summer campaign of 1933 on the

Potomac. This has been done repeatedly and adequately. Rather, this chapter deals, as its title indicates, with a minor skirmish, my unsought, and unequal encounter with the President.

A word is necessary to explain what the row was all about. After the banking collapse of Inauguration week had been put in the way of solution, the Administration turned immense energy and resourcefulness to getting business of all sorts from factory and farm to store and service agency moving again. Central to many of these efforts was stimulation of a rise in prices, which had declined drastically during the depression. Rising prices, it was pretty generally believed, would increase production and payrolls in industry, and give farmers more money to spend in the market. The methods employed by the Administration were by no means radical, ranging from the historic ones of relief, public works, and the sort of price agreements which the anti-trust laws had frowned upon, to the equally historic devices of "reflation" — "inflation" had become a frightening word since the German experience in the nineteen-twenties.

Inevitably the place of gold in the monetary system came in for review, and with it the effect upon prices of increasing the price of gold and of major currencies expressed in dollars — in other words, of depreciating the dollar.

This all began during the bank crisis without controversy and, indeed, with general approbation. The President's proclamation of March 6, 1933, and use of broader power given him by the Emergency Banking Act of March 9, forbad the export, hoarding, or domestic use of gold or gold certificates (with minor industrial exceptions). Holders were ordered to turn their gold into the Federal Reserve Banks and were paid at $20.67 an ounce. While the United States was theoretically "off the gold standard," in that the dollar was not redeemable in gold, this was generally accepted as a temporary incident of the bank crisis, necessary to protect the government's gold reserve.

Controversy began with the Executive Order of April 20,

1933, and the action taken under it. By these steps the President made clear that the embargo on gold shipments was not a merely temporary measure. Later on he recalled April 20 as the decisive moment, and, even at the time, some of the more hysterical monetary conservatives described it as "the end of Western civilization" or as comparable to the "Oath of the Tennis Court" in the French Revolution. But the President's advisers were by no means certain how far he intended to go. As time went on, they became aware that he would not permit anyone, including Huey Long, to occupy a position to the left of him — not that he proposed to operate from the position but to preclude anyone else from doing so. For the same reason he now accepted the amendment of Senator Thomas of Oklahoma to the Agricultural Adjustment Act, which gave him discretionary powers, which he never used, to issue greenbacks, coin silver without limit at 16 to 1, and to reduce the gold value of the dollar. At the very time the President told the press about this frightening armament he was amassing, he also assured them that he hoped "to get the world as a whole back on some form of gold standard."

All these events occurred before I took office. Soon afterward came a step which caused more controversy than any which preceded it. This was the Joint Resolution of Congress signed by the President on June 5, 1933, declaring invalid the gold clauses in all public and private promises to pay money. True, it called for repudiation of contracts, public and private, deliberately made; but this act of high national policy seemed to me a necessary consequence of what had gone before, necessary to prevent hardships to debtors and windfalls to creditors, an invalidation of promises without damage. May and June 1933 were in a sense a lull in the campaign, a period of organization of opposing forces within the Administration and the furbishing of opposing ideologies. The Bull Run of this Civil War would take place not near the Potomac but on the banks of the Thames, at the London Monetary and Economic Conference.

President Roosevelt had inherited the London Conference

from President Hoover, as President Kennedy inherited intervention in Cuba from his predecessor. It was not the President's
own idea of policy, and at the critical moment he repudiated it.
But at the outset it appealed to echoes within him of Wilsonian
internationalism. In the Second Fireside Chat of May 7, 1933, he
described the conferences he was holding with the leaders of
other nations preparatory to London as having "four great objectives: first, a general reduction of armaments . . . second, a
cutting down of trade barriers . . . third, the setting up of a
stabilization of currencies . . . fourth, the reestablishment of
friendly relations and greater confidence between all Nations."
At this stage stabilization of currencies was a "great objective"
specifically underlined in the communiqués put out by the President successively with the premiers of Great Britain, France, and
Italy. And on this note the delegation, headed by Secretary
Hull, set out for London. A few days later another group followed, authorized by the President to discuss stabilization. It included George Harrison, Governor of the Federal Reserve Bank
of New York, Professor O. M. W. Sprague, adviser to the Treasury, and James P. Warburg, monetary adviser to the delegation.

In a very short time we were all in trouble. A temporary stabilization agreement for the duration of the Conference to steady
the relative values of the franc, pound, and dollar was cabled
from London. Rumors about it had strengthened the dollar, and
on June 15 stock market prices broke sharply. Secretary
Woodin at once denied that "suggestion of such a proposal has
been received here" and insisted that "any agreement on this subject will be reached in Washington, not elsewhere." On June 17
the President vigorously rejected the proposal, objecting that the
proposed rates overvalued the dollar, that "we must retain full
freedom of action under Thomas Amendment in order to hold
up price level at home," and that "far too much importance is
being placed on existing and temporary fluctuations."

On the same day, it became my duty as Acting Secretary to

brief the press on what had occurred. In retrospect one sees that the President, pressed by his deep concern about prices, was jettisoning one of the "four great objectives" of the Second Fireside Chat, reaffirmed as lately as May 16 in his message to the chiefs of state of the nations attending the London Conference. Perhaps he himself was not sure that his mind was made up. At any rate, my briefing contained the unwarranted suggestion that the third "great objective" was not dead, but slept. The *New York Times* for June 18 reported:

> Proposals for currency stabilization which have been submitted to President Roosevelt from the World Economic Conference in London are not agreeable to the American Government, Acting Secretary of the Treasury Acheson, said today.
>
> . . . .
>
> Mr. Acheson emphasized, however, that the United States should not be placed in the position of closing the door to stabilization proposals, adding that all realize the importance of currency stabilization.
>
> It was made equally clear that the United States did not propose to enter into any temporary or permanent agreement which again would give to foreign countries the economic advantage of deflated currencies at a time when the general recovery program in this country was beginning to bring about the much needed increases in prices.
>
> . . . "The delegation knows [I am quoted as saying] the President's views and what he is willing to do. It might be said that the communication forms the basis for further discussion . . ."

When on June 22 the delegation in London put out its own statement, it reflected the same ambivalence as had mine:

> The American Government at Washington finds that measures for temporary stabilization now would be untimely . . . because the American Government feels that its efforts to raise prices are the most important contribution it can make and

that anything that would interfere with those efforts and possibly cause a violent price recession would harm the conference more than the lack of an immediate agreement for temporary stabilization.

As to the ultimate objective, the American delegation has already introduced a resolution designed for ultimate worldwide stabilization of unstable currencies, and is devoting itself to the support of measures for the establishment of a coordinated monetary and fiscal policy to be pursued by the various nations in cooperation with the others for the purpose of stimulating economic activity and improving prices.

At the Conference the knowledge that Washington had turned down a stabilization proposal, as the *New York Times* put it, "naturally puzzle[d] the other nations. They think they detect a lack of unity in the United States delegation and an overshadowing uncertainty as to its course, which augurs ill for the success of [the] conference."

A truly delightful understatement!

On the same day that I was holding my press conference explaining the President's stabilization policy, he was leaving the port of Marion, Massachusetts, at the helm of the *Amberjack II,* en route to Campobello, New Brunswick. Thus both the President and the Conference were at sea and headed on collision courses.

In Washington what to do next was discussed at a meeting in Raymond Moley's office at the State Department. Mr. Bernard Baruch's spring of ideas was as dry as mine or any of the others. One Assistant Secretary of State, a veritable Mr. Pickwick, with patches of cottony hair on either side of a bald pate, a round, ruddy face, and steel-rimmed spectacles, inhibited thought by nervously pacing the room, flapping his coattails behind him and muttering, "Our wonderful recovery! They're endangering our wonderful recovery!" All I could think of was Alice's White Rabbit doing the same and in his anxiety murmuring,

"The Duchess! The Duchess! Oh my dear paws! Oh my fur and whiskers! She'll get me executed, as sure as ferrets are ferrets!" Finally, Moley himself cut the knot by deciding that he would go off into the blue, intercept the President, get the word, and carry it to the Conference.

The story of that fantastic and fatuous failure has often been told. It is enough to say here that it served as the crescendo leading to the grand crash of the finale, the Second Declaration of Independence of July 4, 1933. Moley's much heralded arrival in London occurred on June 28. The next day the President put in at Campobello as (so the *New York Times* reported) "the wild gyrations of the dollar today . . . created a situation that can be described only as a crisis for the World Economic Conference. Throughout the day the issue arising from the necessity for some measures to stabilize not only the dollar, but European currencies, too, transcended all others." But in New York stock market prices had recovered their losses of two weeks earlier.

On June 29–30 the text of a proposed Declaration on stabilization by the leading nations at the Conference was received in Washington and passed on to the President. Drafted in London, and approved by Moley, it was thought to fall within permissible limits as deduced from the President's recent cables, and to be "innocuous," though essential to permit the Conference to continue. It is reproduced in the Notes for this chapter.

George Harrison had come home from London to aid in getting the President's approval. We decided to enlist Secretary Woodin, if he was well enough, and Mr. Bernard M. Baruch in a final effort with the President. The next day, June 30, in New York, Mrs. Woodin's better judgment yielded to our importunity. Entering his bedroom, we were brought to a shocked stop. The portieres were drawn; the room, dim; a screen across the foot of the bed put it in deeper shadow. Will Woodin lay propped against pillows, motionless, without a trace of color, his eyes closed. He could have been a corpse. As the nurse spoke, he looked up, greeted us with a show of animation and had chairs brought. George quickly reported on the crisis in London; I, on the crisis at sea. A telelphone call was put in from his bedside to Moley to get the latest word. When it came through, the connection was bad. Mr. Baruch, sitting on the invalid's bed, bellowed ineffectively, then gave over to George. His hearing was better, his voice as loud; but the responses apparently lacked clarity. The tumult and the shouting went on.

A movement from the bed turned my attention back to Will Woodin. To my horror he was sliding slowly off the pillows, even whiter than they. Mr. Baruch had seen him, too. While I went to the door for the nurse, he tried to stop George Harrison, who was doggedly shouting away. As I turned back, he was shaking George and saying, "Stop it! Will's dead!" Will was not dead but had fainted, as the nurse and frightened Mrs. Woodin soon discovered. Understandably any resumption of our discussion was ruled out. We retreated to George Harrison's apartment on the East River to survey the stricken field.

Only one course was left. We would make a direct report and appeal by telephone to the President at Campobello. Strengthening ourselves for the effort with food and drink, we put in the call. Steve Early, the President's appointment secretary, who answered, told me that the President could not get to the telephone but that he (Steve) would relay the message and answer. We had better be quick about it, he added, as a thunderstorm was about to break. Our chances were low at best, but advocacy by proxy would surely extinguish them. I did my best, and waited, listening to the ominous crackle of electricity, while Early went to the President. In time he reported that the President was working on a message to the Conference through Mr. Hull, which would be his answer delivered directly. The connection went dead. The gambit was played out. By phone I prepared Under Secretary of State William Phillips for the worst, and went back to Washington.

On July 1 the President notified the "gold bloc" nations that he had rejected "in its present form" the Declaration submitted to him and that Secretary Hull would shortly make a statement. This Mr. Hull did, as he said, "in my capacity as Secretary of State and not as chairman of the American delegation, since the delegation has at no time had jurisdiction in this subject, which is purely a Treasury matter."

Two extracts from the message give its devastating tenor. It is reproduced in full in the Notes.

The President's Statement

I would regard it as a catastrophe amounting to a world tragedy if the great Conference of Nations, called to bring about a more real and permanent financial stability and a greater prosperity to the masses of all Nations, should, in advance of any serious effort to consider these broader problems, allow itself to be diverted by the proposal of a purely artificial and temporary experiment affecting the monetary exchange of a few Nations only. Such action, such diversion, shows a singular lack of proportion and a failure to remember the larger purposes for which the Economic Conference originally was called together.

. . . .

It is for this reason that reduced cost of Government, adequate Government income, and ability to service Government debts are all so important to ultimate stability. So too, old fetishes of so-called international bankers are being replaced by efforts to plan national currencies with the objective of giving to those currencies a continuing purchasing power which does not greatly vary in terms of the commodities and need of modern civilization.

The *New York Times* reported from London:

Tonight the delegations are still stunned and wondering what they would better do and they are in a terrible dilemma. Most of them would like to go home and do the best they can with domestic remedies, leaving aside all thought of international cooperation except such as they might severally arrange on their own account. And they dare not; the situation has become too serious for petulance.

So the probability is the Conference will drag along . . . hoping meanwhile that something will happen that may bring a change in the attitude of the United States.

This is what it did — drag along for three weeks until hope ended.

At this point fate intervened to give me a rest from monetary problems, albeit an undesirable one. On July 10 my very competent and perceptive secretary came into the office with a clinical thermometer and demanded my temperature. It alarmed us both. Since my family was away, my colleague Tom Hewes took me to his house, where for ten unpleasant days I was well cared for and not too aware of the world. July 22, which turned out to be a most significant day for me, saw me back again and in charge at the Treasury. For on that day the long upward climb of prices, which had begun in late April and had been checked only briefly in mid-June by the stabilization effort, stopped and a decline began.

All through the summer and early autumn the decline continued, producing near panic in agricultural areas quickly communicated to the White House through the press and Congress. The President spoke to me of the imminence of agrarian revolution and reported farmers' stopping milk trucks and pouring their contents in the gutters. Against this background, the debate between two groups of Presidential monetary advisers grew in intensity. One group under the political guidance of Henry Morgenthau, Jr., head of the Farm Credit Administration, an intimate of the President's mind and faithful executor of his will, had as their principal theoretician Professor George F. Warren of Cornell. This group were impressed by the fact that the rise in prices from April to mid-July was quite coincident with the fall of the foreign gold value of the dollar, which reached a depreciation of 31.50 per cent on July 18. From this they concluded that further depreciation of the gold value of the dollar was the medicine which would cure falling prices and produce the ruddy glow of rising ones.

The other group centering in the staff of the Treasury and the Federal Reserve Bank of New York had the sympathy of the Secretary and Under Secretary of the Treasury. It was led by Professor Sprague, Lewis W. Douglas, Director of the Budget, and James P. Warburg of New York, who in June had returned to private life. They pointed out that, although prices had risen while the dollar had declined prior to mid-July, after this time, except for a brief pause, prices had joined the dollar in its decline. The reply, of course, was that the dollar had not declined enough.

Accompanying a memorandum of recommendations, Professor Warren attached this summary:

I believe that the following are essential:

1. Raise commodity prices.

2. The only way to accomplish such a rise and hold it is by controlling the gold value of the dollar and forcing it downward.

3. The time for prompt and effective action seems to have arrived.

4. Provide some form of a more stable measure of value for the future. If an all commodity rather than a one commodity money is established, it will be an outstanding achievement in history.

A paragraph in the section of his memorandum dealing with methods of government buying of gold prior to fixing a lowered gold content of the dollar throws interesting light on what was to occur: "I would make the price of gold an odd number, depending on conditions at the time; for example, not 30 but

29.75 or 30.50, not $32, but $31.83, and would go far enough so that the pound would be at a premium."

In an answering memorandum Professor Sprague attacked specifically "the assumption that the price level is directly responsive to changes in the price of gold," and then took an even more far-reaching position:

> A general revival of business activity accompanied by a gradual disappearance of unemployment will be accompanied by an increase in bank credit and currency, and by a generally higher level of prices. It does not, however, follow that it is possible to reverse the order of events. To assume that an increase in the price of gold will bring about an increase in credit and currency and a higher price level that will hold and be accompanied or followed by a general business revival and higher standard of living, seems very definitely to be placing the cart before the horse.

In another memorandum to me at about the same time, Dr. Sprague reverted to the same theme. After advocating "a do-nothing policy" in the monetary field, attempting neither inflation nor stabilization, he concluded:

> I should hope that during the next few months good progress be made in distributing funds to the depositors of closed banks, and that it be made evident that virtually all open banks shall remain open. Acceptance of this quiescent course in the monetary field presupposes recognition on the part of the Administration that we have reached a stage in which further trade recovery is primarily dependent on action of a non-monetary character. No general rise in prices that will hold can be secured until we can bring about a general increase in the demand for materials and for labor. It is hopeless to attempt to induce this demand for materials and labor by an initial general increase in prices. That is putting the cart before the horse. Prices will rise when we have secured a general increase in the demand

My father,
the Queen's Own Rifles,
1885

The family in 1895

The author and Lucette

Prepared for
the Battle of Antietam

The pony had
no martial spirit

Residency 25, south of James Bay, northern Ontario, 1911

A track gang at Residency 10

Indians on
the Missinaibi

The author and friend

U.S. Supreme Court of 1916–1921
Standing, left to right: Louis Dembitz Brandeis, Mahlon Pitney,
James McReynolds, John Hessin Clarke. Seated, left to right: William
Rufus Day, Joseph McKenna, Chief Justice Edward Douglass White,
Oliver Wendell Holmes, Willis Van Devanter
(Harris & Ewing, Washington, D.C.)

Mr. Justice Holmes and Mr. Justice Brandeis leaving the Supreme Court room in the Capitol

SUCCESSOR—William H. Woodin (left) who retired on indefinite leave as Secretary of the Treasury, expresses his congratulations to Henry Morgenthau, jr., his successor. Dean Acheson, Undersecretary who resigned, appears at right.

Woodin congratulates Morgenthau.
From the Washington *Herald* for Saturday, November 18, 1933
(*Underwood & Underwood*)

GOLD-PURCHASE PLAN WAS HELD ILLEGAL BY TREASURY EXPERTS

R. F. C. COUNSEL ON OTHER HAND UPHELD POLICY

Hostile Opinion Credited For Recent Shake-Up And Acheson's Retirement

RULED CONTRARY TO INTENT OF CONGRESS

Author Unrevealed, But Views Believed Those Of Retired Official

By DEWEY L. FLEMING
[Washington Bureau of The Sun]

Washington, Nov. 26—Clashing opinions on the validity of the Government's gold-purchasing operations—opinions which were forerunners of the recent Treasury shake-up—came to light today in the wake of predictions that the President's managed currency policy would soon give way to a program of stabilization.

One of the opinions, revealed as the product of Treasury experts, denied the legality of the gold operations at every turn and said the use of Reconstruction Finance Corporation debentures for such purposes never was contemplated by Congress.

The other, prepared by Stanley Reed, counsel for the R. F. C., contends that the gold operations are entirely within the province of the Finance Corporation, are unquestionably legal, and do not run counter to the intention of Congress.

Acheson Guided Treasury Views

The Treasury memorandum is understood to reflect the views of Dean G. Acheson, the former Under Secretary of the Treasury, who went out to make a place for Henry Morgenthau, Jr., now Acting Secretary. Mr. Acheson, reputedly a "hard money" man and a foe of the gold-purchasing program, left his post without the usual exchange of correspondence with his

Gold Purchase Views Clash

STANLEY REED　　　　**DEAN G. ACHESON**

superiors and without discussion of the differences which led to his separation from the Treasury.

All who saw the newly-revealed Treasury document interpreted it as the substance of the arguments which Mr. Acheson made against the gold plan in his various talks with the President and with others in sympathy with the managed currency policy. As such, it was regarded as supplying the missing chapter in the story of the stormiest phase of the Roosevelt Administration to date.

Use Of R. F. C. Debentures Issue

In the very first paragraph the Treasury's adverse opinion on the gold-buying program asserts belief that the purchase of gold with R. F. C. debentures is "of doubtful legality."

Congress, the memorandum continues, contemplated that the issuance of R. F. C. obligations would be undertaken only as a revenue measure for the purpose of putting the R. F. C. in funds for use in connection with its authorized lending functions.

"It seems difficult under any stretch of the imagination," the opinion recites, "how one could possibly construe the present exchange of R. F. C. obligations for gold on the basis of a price in excess of the parity figure as an issue of R. F. C. obligations for a

revenue purpose, unless it be assumed that the R. F. C. intends either to obtain the gold at less than the world market price and then dispose of it in the world market at a profit, or to acquire the gold and hold it pending a rise in price at which the gold may be gainfully disposed of. And either of these two assumptions would result in the R. F. C. not issuing its obligations for revenue purposes but rather dealing in or speculating in gold for revenue purposes."

Question Of Sale Up

The unidentified author of the Treasury memorandum declared it was difficult also to construe an exchange of R. F. C. obligations for gold as a sale of such obligations.

"It would be remembered," the paper states, "that the emphasis in the exchange is on the sale of the debentures and not on the purchase of the gold, since the R. F. C. has no separate power to purchase gold.

"The question therefore is: Is the exchange of R. F. C. obligations for gold on the basis of a price in excess of parity a sale?"

Quotes R. F. C. Act

"The R. F. C. act states that the obligations may be offered for sale 'at such price or prices' as the corporation may determine. The use of the

Secretary Woodin bows out.
From the Baltimore *Sun* for November 27, 1933

Dean Acheson and Felix Frankfurter at Senate Committee's hearing on latter's nomination to be Associate Justice of the Supreme Court of the United States

Mr. Justice Felix Frankfurter and the author on a morning walk
to work in the early 1940's. (*New York Times*)

Practicing law by ear

for materials and labor, and our efforts should be directed toward bringing this about.

So the lines were drawn and the debate went on. To induce some order into it, toward the end of July I suggested to the President, through Secretary Woodin, that the preparation of recommendations on monetary policy should be centered in the Treasury, and that a carefully selected group of Treasury and other officials and outside economists of all schools of thought should prepare recommendations which the Treasury would pass along with its comments. Such a group was appointed, became known as the New York Group, since it met there under Mr. Woodin's chairmanship, and made two reports. These, which appear in the Notes for this chapter, were far less conservative than some of the historians of the New Deal describe them. But the President, under the pressure of falling prices and political discontent, was impatient. James Warburg has put the situation very well, referring to a meeting he had with the President on September 20:

> The President listened patiently to what I had to say, but when I was all through, he smiled and told me that all that was very pretty, but meantime how were we going to keep prices advancing? How were we going to relieve the debt burden? What were we going to do about the farmers?
> It was then that I realized with a sense of finality how impossible it was to combat successfully a group of advisers who had ready answers to all these questions, while the only answers those of us could give who felt that the cure could not be a purely monetary one involved a slow and more or less painful process of rebuilding.

I suffered from the President's impatience in August as a result of my reply to a request from him to "try your hand at a draft (for discussion only) of an Executive Order offering to buy newly mined gold for 30 days at a fixed price say $28 an ounce and an offer to sell gold to the arts and dentists etc at the same price." The reply, perhaps, was too negative in telling him first, and at length, what he could not legally do instead of stressing what he could do. It produced his querulous but interesting comment that lawyers were supposed to do the latter not the former. I did, however, send him through Secretary Woodin on August 18 a draft of an order by which the Secretary of the Treasury was authorized to receive gold newly mined in the United States on consignment for sale to licensees in the arts, industries, and professions or for export "at the best price obtainable in the free gold markets of the world," as determined by the Secretary. This draft became Executive Order No. 6261 of August 29, 1933.

At this time my wife and our close friends, the Canadian Minister William Duncan Herridge and his wife Mildred, the sister of Prime Minister Richard Bennett (later Lord Bennett), renewed their urgings that I get out of Washington for a rest. They urged a fishing trip on the Nipisiguit River in New Brunswick, which flows into the Bay of Chaleur. The combination of the company and the plan made the temptation irresistible. An illusion of a lull in the monetary debate was created by the fact that we were in the eye of the hurricane. On September 11 we started off for a two weeks' holiday.

Bill Herridge was one of the ablest diplomats this country has received and in the early nineteen-thirties one of the best-known and liked men in official Washington. The first, central, and all important fact about Herridge was his vitality. It poured out of him, sometimes as ideas tumbling over one another, sometimes as gaiety, or as physical activity — he was a great fisherman and camper — or as host and conversationalist, or pretty wild political schemer. Whatever he did was done with verve and often with a good deal of noise. To be with him was to be alive, to be moving, and to be breathless. It was also to be with a man who gave and inspired affection.

The function of a diplomatic envoy is to observe and report to his government all that may concern it and to affect in favor of his own country the course of events, so far as he is able to do so. No one has understood or performed these duties in Washington, within my experience, better than William Herridge.

As the New Deal began its improvisations, Canada was deeply concerned with the effect upon its economy of the controls exercised over agriculture by the Agricultural Adjustment Administration, over manufacture and commerce by the National Industrial Recovery Administration, and over the gold value of the dollar by the United States Treasury and the Reconstruction Finance Corporation. While government management of the economy was decreed from the highest quarters, the controls were operated by the able young academicians and lawyers brought into the new bureaucracy of the multifarious alphabetical agencies. Access to Cabinet officers is easy for a diplomat of Herridge's ability and charm. His special achievement was to establish easy and friendly relations with the bureaucracy. His methods were so simple and intelligent in their understanding of his problem as to be unique.

The first was the luncheon for men. His luncheons were small, six or eight; his guests, of Little Cabinet rank and never more than one from the same department or agency. He sat down promptly at one o'clock, not waiting for later arrivals, and ended the lunch as promptly at two. There were no cocktails, but an excellent white wine with the meal, which, in turn, was light, well chosen, well cooked, and served with flair by Horsely, the butler — as much of a character as the Minister.

Herridge's part was to stimulate conversation. At this he was a past master. He would poke fun at himself, in a delightfully slow, clowning manner, for his inability to grasp the current crop of rumors and leaks, and make such gay nonsense of them and of the rivalries between the Cabinet prima donnas, that his guests would take over the talk and vie with one another to make all clear. Dawning understanding from Herridge and wholly erroneous guesses as to the future would bring forth further enlightenment. Sometimes he would speak hopelessly of some predicament which Canadian interests faced, stimulating helpful suggestions.

Another occasion that much tempted Herridge was the departmental or agency outing, more common in the days when everything was smaller in this city. The Canadian Minister was a sought-after guest. He was particularly successful as a softball relief pitcher for the civil servants against the political officers. Today, I suppose, he would be said to be "projecting an image in depth." But in those days he was getting to know more people, picking up more information, and dropping seeds in friendly minds.

After two glorious and reviving weeks at the best time of year, in beautiful country and with congenial friends, we were back again in Washington. Any illusion of a lull was soon dissipated. In seven weeks to the day from our return I was out of the Treasury and a private citizen. In that time, I had been through a searing row with the President, directed the largest Treasury refinancing since the war (the retirement of $1,875,-000,000 of the Fourth Liberty Loan), participated in the release of $1,000,000,000 to depositors in closed banks, and conducted a discussion with the British on their war-debt problem. A rest before beginning this experience proved a considerable asset.

On the day we returned, Henry Morgenthau, as I learned later, told the President that the lawyers in the Farm Credit Administration believed, contrary to my views, that the government had legal authority to buy gold at any price it might fix. The Department of Justice had agreed with my opinion and drafted Executive Order 6261 of August 29, 1933, on that basis. This had seemed to close the issue, unless the President should ask for new legislation.

But within a week a good friend, Harold Stephens, then an

Assistant Attorney General, brought to me an unaddressed, unsigned memorandum given to him by the Attorney General for study and opinion. It disturbed Stephens because it ran counter to our earlier views, on which he had drafted Order 6261. Could I throw light on the document? I could. Both the paper on which it was written and the style were familiar and pointed to Herman Oliphant, Morgenthau's General Counsel.

At my request Henry Morgenthau came to see me and, learning that I knew about the memorandum, quite frankly told me of its origin in his talks with the President. He believed that the President was determined to go ahead with the plan. I did not argue or quarrel with Morgenthau. He was devoted to the President and wanted only to serve him. In later years we worked closely together and remain friends today.

Troubled, I sought advice from Justice Brandeis on one aspect of the problem opening before me: assuming that the Attorney General should rule as the President wanted him to on the legality of the plan, should I, as a matter of sound governmental practice, forget that I was a lawyer and be governed by the opinion of the highest law officer of the Executive Branch?

The Justice's reply was Delphic, but clear enough to me. I can hear him now saying, "Dean, if I wanted a legal opinion, I would prefer to get it from you than from Homer Cummings." This faced me squarely with the legal problem which was my principal difficulty. Then and since, the plan seemed to me futile, though then it looked more harmful than it proved to be. Not that it ever seemed to me as horrendous as its opponents claimed. What bothered me was the fraud it might perpetrate on those people who at our urging were about to exchange Liberty Bonds for a new issue at lower interest. But even so, I might well have hung back from conflict with so formidable an adversary on the merits of an economic issue where my opinions were so derivative.

The battle over gold-buying soon moved underground, while

other events were taking place on the public stage. There events had confusing and opposite effects. Some of them reassured those who wanted reassurance that no inflationary scheme was imminent. This strengthened the dollar. At the same time, prices fell again, which stimulated the President and his more intimate advisers to inflationary action.

The call by the Treasury on October 11 of 30 per cent of the Fourth Liberty Loan, offering twelve-year bonds, paying 1 per cent less interest in exchange, was described by the *New York Times* as a "Reply to Inflationists" and "distinctly a surprise move, believed to be the forerunner of an early definition by the government of monetary policy." The refinancing was a great success, heavily oversubscribed. The dollar rose on the exchanges, wheat prices broke the permissible limit, five cents a bushel; and Governor Langer of North Dakota declared an embargo tying up fifty-million bushels. The whole refinancing had been carefully cleared with the President himself — by me.

The same article announcing the refinancing contained another reassuring item: the preparation of a plan to release a billion dollars to depositors of closed banks. The *New York Times* commented: "This latest step in the administration program aimed to stave off unsound currency inflation will, the President thinks, release about $1,000,000,000 and greatly extend credit and purchasing power." When the plan was announced on October 15, I was named as the Treasury representative on the administering board.

Another dubious present awaiting me on my return from Canada was to undertake the "conversation," as it was delicately put, with a British group about their war debt. Wily old Cordell Hull announced that this had been "unanimously agreed" (the only negative vote being absent in Canada), and that the conversations would be conducted by the Treasury at the Treasury. To underline the complete detachment of the State Department from my kamikaze mission, he added that this "was in accord with custom and was a logical procedure." He concluded with the ironically true and gloriously ambiguous statement that I "would be as competent as anyone in the Government to conduct the conversations. . . ." Thus garlanded for sacrifice, I approached the altar.

The First World War inter-Allied debt and German reparations have generated an immense literature. College debating teams flourished on the subjects. It is enough to say here of the war debts that nothing could have been more naïve and ignorant than to believe it desirable or possible for one Ally to pay another immense sums in cash through the medium of international monetary arrangements, designed for a wholly different purpose, for military equipment and food furnished and destroyed or eaten to carry on a common cause. The Lend-Lease arrangements of the Second World War showed that President Roosevelt came to understand this as well as anyone. But in 1933 he suffered from the same illusions that politicians had about prohibition — that it was "politically dangerous" to educate the electorate to take an intelligent and necessary step. We are in the grip of the same paralyzing inhibition about birth control today.

The British had been induced not to raise the subject of war debts at the London Conference by the assurance of a discussion later. The time came when the British delegation arrived on October 3. The details and substance of our talks on the British war debts are not important to this story, only its denouement. They did give me the opportunity to make warm friendships with two of my British colleagues, Sir Ronald Lindsay, the British Ambassador in Washington, and Sir Frederick Leith-Ross, financial adviser to the Cabinet. Sir Ronald, a large man, genial and relaxed, an able old-school diplomatist, commanded a wealth of anecdote, from which I have often pirated one treasure. As a young man, Sir Ronald was a gentleman-in-waiting to the Prince of Wales, later King George V. The Prince had a passion for punctuality. One evening Sir Ronald, unusually prudent, dressed for dinner well ahead of time, then set an alarm clock before picking up a book. Alas, he trusted too much in modern inventions and arrived late for dinner. The Prince glowered. "I suppose you have an excuse ready?" "No excuse, Your Royal Highness," replied Sir Ronald, "but an explanation." The Prince was amused, and the evening saved.

Leith-Ross, known as "Leithers," a Treasury civil servant and thoroughly orthodox economist, managed to give the erroneous impression of a wise owl. Not that he lacked wisdom, but that he was not owlish and solemn, as his horn-rimmed glasses, beaklike nose, small mouth, and sepulchral voice made him appear. He could be good company.

My instructions from the President held out no hope that our talks could be useful. I was to listen sympathetically, agree that the settlement with the British had been much harsher than with the French or Italians, but I was to make no drastic sacrifices. The British had in mind a cut to one tenth of the formerly agreed total payments. In our first formal meeting on October 10 Sir Frederick put forward the British case for a revision of the settlement. It was agreed that I should brief the press. The *Times* of London reported:

> The brief and scrupulously fair résumé made yesterday evening by Mr. Acheson, Under Secretary of the Treasury, of Sir Frederick Leith-Ross's exposition of the British argument as to the debt is faithfully reproduced in all the newspapers today. The thing was done with such grace and feeling for justice as to make an extremely happy impression everywhere, and particularly upon newspapers whose complaint for years past has been that they are left in a fog of uncertainty as to all that affects these intergovernmental obligations . . .

This happy impression was not, however, created in the editorial rooms of the Hearst press. A front page editorial on October 14, excoriating the British for "pulling a poor mouth and trying to trade on our needs . . . to put through a bankrupt's composition," concluded:

> But we rely on the Administration's spokesmen in Washington to convey to the British commissioners, and through them to the British public, how thoroughly England's attitude is understood in this country, how profound is the disillusionment throughout the United States as to English faith, and how transparent it is to American eyes that England is building prosperity upon her defaults as a debtor, and is willing to become strong by disabling a competitor with the burden of her own callously disavowed obligations.

Nor was the President much more sympathetic with my urgings to seize the opportunity to get this problem behind us while there was time before an election to reeducate the electorate away from Cal Coolidge's simple analysis — "Well, they hired the money, didn't they?" The President was irritated with me as it was, and my importunity over this unpopular and, to him, unnecessary complication only added to it. I increased it further by the unwise decision to enlist allies in the Cabinet to make one more try to persuade him. Secretary Hull and Miss Frances Perkins, the Secretary of Labor, agreed to help at the next Cabinet meeting. The Cabinet is usually a poor place in which to take up an important and complicated matter with the President. Too many uninformed people are likely to get involved and confuse matters. But on this occasion there was no alternative.

Memory of that meeting is painfully clear. The President opened briefly and called on Mr. Hull, who went to work on the need for reciprocal tariff reductions. As a horrible example of something, he talked about our tariff on rag rugs (which came out as "wag wugs"). The President fiddled nervously with his long cigarette holder and harried him. Mr. Hull, rattled, straggled to his end. It was my turn.

I hurried through our talks, which had turned up nothing new. The conclusion was inevitable. It was time to face the facts. The President cut in neatly.

"Nothing new," he said. "I was afraid so. I must go into it with you later. It's not a matter of general interest here."

"But, Mr. President," I began, just as Secretary Hull cleared his throat.

"Did you say something, Cordell?" asked the President. Mr. Hull shook his head. "Well, Bill," the President went on, turning to William Dern, Secretary of War, "What's on your mind?" The Secretary began his report. After the meeting, as I approached Mr. Hull with a sad and accusing mien, he anticipated me. "He didn't give me a chance to begin maneuvewing," he said.

Our talks staggered on for a while and then collapsed. The *Times* of London was probably right that "neither the British nor any other debt agreement can be revised or finally settled until American financial policy has been determined." After the Fireside Chat of October 22 the British Government knew that final determination was some time off. At the end of the month the British delegation folded their tents and departed.

After the middle of October and while the British talks were going on, the guerrilla fighting over Oliphant's gold-buying plan turned into swift-moving open warfare. The President had lost patience with my objections and told the Attorney General to rule (and what to rule) on the legal question. We were summoned to the latter's office, then on the corner of K Street and Vermont Avenue. Those present included Homer Cummings, Harold Stephens (perhaps other Justice Department lawyers), Herman Oliphant, Stanley Reed (later Mr. Justice Reed), then General Counsel for the Reconstruction Finance Corporation. The Attorney General opened by telling us that upon his informal assurance that the Oliphant plan was within the authorization of existing law, the President had decided to go forward with it. The time for argument was over. He had called us together to work out with him his formal opinion and the necessary papers to put the plan into action.

The battle was on. I said that the time for argument was not over; it had only just begun, for the plan had not been subjected to any real examination. Furthermore, I was the official who under the plan would have to authorize the payment of government funds without, as I believed, legal authority. If any existed, someone could surely point it out. If they could not, I would not violate the law. This produced the debate which the Attorney General had tried to avoid. Oliphant and Reed supported the plan; Stephens and I opposed it. The Attorney General fumed in impotent fury, doubtless congratulating himself that he had kept me out of his department.

Briefly the issue was this: under the August 29 Order, the Treasury accepted domestic newly mined gold for sale abroad in free markets and gave the miners the proceeds less expenses. This was currently about $29.80. It was conceded that the Treasury itself was required by law to pay $20.67 per ounce. No more, no less. Oliphant proposed that the RFC pay steadily increasing prices fixed by the President (at first for domestic newly mined gold) until the desired gold-dollar ratio of $35 to $40 per ounce should be reached. Since the RFC could not pay cash beyond the market price (without giving away public funds), it would pay in its own debentures which the Treasury would then buy from the seller of gold at face value. The proponents of the scheme said that the RFC in turning over its debentures for gold at a fictitious price was "selling" them at a discount. I said that the sale was a sham and a violation of law which, since the Treasury must redeem them at face value, contemplated a sale at full market value.

On November 28, after Stanley Reed's views and mine had been made public, Ralph Robey commented:

> I do not see how any reasonable person can question that between these two lines of thought Acheson is correct. We all

know that it was not the expectation of Congress in passing the Reconstruction Finance Corporation act that the right to discount obligations would be used as legal authority for this organization to enter commodity markets and pay any price it likes for anything. Yet that is the burden of the Reed argument.

Our meeting with the Attorney General ended in his reaffirming his views and saying that he would write an opinion to that effect. After the meeting Stanley Reed came to see me and told me how foolish I was being, ending the possibility of a distinguished career. He himself went on to be Solicitor General and a Justice of the Supreme Court.

Then events moved fast. The President sent for me and laid down the law. He wanted my opposition to stop. I told him how much I regretted the situation, that I would gladly step aside; that, whatever the Attorney General said, he had not written an opinion. The responsibility, I added, was being put squarely on me to do something contrary to the law. This responsibility I could not accept. If ordered in writing by superior authority to take the action required of the Secretary of the Treasury, I would do so; but I could not do so otherwise. The President flushed and ended the interview.

At a meeting of the RFC Board to adopt the necessary resolutions I made the same statement and gave my reasons, which some of the directors did not know. I would not oppose or approve the resolutions.

The President announced his decision and the action to be taken in his Fourth Fireside Chat on the evening of October 22. The reception here and abroad might be described as one of calm bewilderment. Senator Thomas thought it forecast "controlled inflation"; Senator Fletcher, Chairman of the Banking and Currency Committee, that it put too much emphasis on gold. Europe waited. So did I. Somebody was going to have to take some action. On October 24 I received this telegram, followed by an identical letter:

NEW YORK NY 647PM 24TH

HON DEAN ACHESON
    TREASURY

I HEREBY DIRECT AND INSTRUCT YOU IN MY BEHALF AND IN MY
NAME TO APPROVE THE ISSUANCE OF NINETY DAY DEBENTURES BY
THE RECONSTRUCTION FINANCE CORPORATION TO BE SOLD AT A DIS-
COUNT BASIS IN ACCORDANCE WITH ITS RESOLUTION OF OCTOBER
20TH AND FURTHER TO APPROVE SUCH PRICES OF SAID DEBENTURES
TO BE PAYABLE AS STATED IN THE SAID RESOLUTION IN GOLD AS THE
CORPORATION MAY DETERMINE AFTER CONSULTATION WITH THE
PRESIDENT I FURTHER DIRECT AND INSTRUCT YOU IN THE SAME
MANNER TO AUTHORIZE THAT THE GUARANTEE OF THE UNITED
STATES BE EXPRESSED ON THE FACE OF SUCH DEBENTURES AND TO
ISSUE SUCH ORDERS AS MAY BE NECESSARY TO EFFECT THE PAY-
MENT OF SUCH DEBENTURES IF AND WHEN THE SAME ARE PRE-
SENTED TO THE TREASURY FOR PAYMENT IN ACCORDANCE WITH THE
TERMS OF THE GUARANTEE

WM H WOODIN SECRETARY OF THE TREASURY
745PM

The first day of RFC buying was October 25. The President
fixed the buying price at $31.36 an ounce, twenty-seven cents
above the London price. The instructions were given on a chit
in longhand. They raised the price each day and soon had the
U.S. price above the world price. Then Morgenthau and the
President decided to move into the world market and on
November 1 did so. Meanwhile prices generally moved slightly
downward and farm prices remained unaffected. I left the
alchemists alone to turn gold into rising prices if they could.
Skepticism in the press was attributed to me.

On October 29 I was summoned to the White House. There
I found the higher officials of the Federal Reserve Bank of New
York, the Reconstruction Finance Corporation, Governor Eu-
gene Black of the Federal Reserve Board, and the Attorney
General, and perhaps others.

We were collected downstairs and shown up in a body to the Oval Room. The President, seated at his desk, greeted us affably enough, but when we were seated his manner changed. He had called us together, he said, to make clear that he was the head of the Executive Branch and intended to act as such. Since March 4 he had put into effect measures on which opinions could and did differ. The gold-buying plan was such a measure. He was glad to have everyone's suggestions and help. But, when the decision was made, that was to be the end of the matter within the government. Anyone who could not accept his decisions could get out but he could not stay on and oppose them. And so on. Nothing specific was said; no incident or names mentioned.

It was a magnificent and intimidating performance. So intimidating that it survived an accident which might have destroyed a lesser one. Fred Kent of the Federal Reserve Bank, who was very deaf, had put a small chair in front of the President's desk and the microphone of his hearing aid on the desk. As the tension mounted, he leaned back; the chair collapsed depositing him and the microphone on the floor. Not a sound came from the group as the President paused while Kent collected himself and withdrew to a stronger base.

When this proclamation of primacy ended, we were dismissed without further word. Not since schooldays have I seen a group so filled with a sense of individual guilt. Except for those in the inner circle of the recent episode — and, indeed, even including some of those tainted with sympathy, if not complicity, with me — each believed that the warning was directed to him. Undoubtedly the President wished it so. But I and a few others knew that the end for me was near; and I was content to let it take its own form.

Looking back over thirty years my thoughts about this whole episode have in some respects changed from what they were at the time. On its merits the Warren gold-buying policy was an ill-conceived adventure. The summary of Mr. G. Griffith Johnson, Jr., seems to me fair:

> While the gold-buying program failed in its primary purpose of producing an immediate price rise, it did succeed in depreciating the dollar and thus in preparing the way for revaluation at a lower level than might otherwise have been possible. And the latter in turn permitted a further considerable internal rise in prices without generating further disequilibrium with the sterling countries. It was on the whole, however, a dearly bought gain. . . . More serious, possibly, than the uncertainty at home were the fears and resentments generated abroad, where United States policy was considered injurious to both sterling and the Gold Bloc, causing speculations to arise over the possibility of a currency war.
>
> Most significant of all, however, may have been the precedent created by the gold-buying policy in that manipulation of the gold value of the currency to achieve an artificial exchange level became openly and admittedly an instrument of political policy.

The President's action in replacing me seems to me now, as it did at the time, quite right and proper. My own actions also still seem to me right, although tinged with stubbornness and lack of imaginative understanding of my own proper role and of the President's perplexities and needs. The action I was asked to take was without legal authorization. Was it so horrendous as to require, in the current phrase, making a federal case out of it? Today I am not at all sure. Perhaps the trouble sprang from lack of sympathy between the President and me. A few occasions arose in later years which could have developed into serious differences between President Truman and me. I had then had long training in my duty to the President, however, and he had no trace of imperiousness about him. With these assets to draw on, and as devoted friends, we worked out the difficulties together. The final conclusion is, I think, that whatever mistakes made in 1933 might have been avoided, it was best for me to leave when I did. It made possible a return under better circumstances. No such relaxed and hopeful thoughts occurred to me at the time.

Toward the middle of November a message from Mr. Woodin told me that he would soon be in Washington. When he arrived, looking very frail, he told me that the President had been in a high temper, insisting on summarily removing me from office *pour encourager les autres*. Will had refused to hear of it, saying that I had carried the load during his illness, that I wanted to resign quite as much as the President wanted me to; that Will, himself, would have to resign at the President's earliest convenience, and that he would do it then and there if the President persisted in his intention to remove me. This had done the trick. Will asked me to give him a letter of resignation in longhand. Henry Morgenthau was to be appointed to succeed me.

The letter was a short one:

My dear Mr. President,

In view of the leave of absence which Secretary Woodin's health requires him to take, I am sure that you will wish, and you, of course, should have, complete freedom of choice as to whom you will place in charge at the Treasury. In order to facilitate this I am tendering my resignation as Under Secretary of the Treasury to take effect when my successor is appointed, or at an earlier date should you so desire.

I am most appreciative of the opportunity which you and the Secretary have given me to have had some part in your administration during these stirring times, and also of the many marks of kindness which you and he have shown me. In leaving the Treasury may I also leave with you my most sincere good wishes for the success of your administration in the years that lie ahead.

Respectfully,
DEAN ACHESON

Henry Morgenthau's induction was to take place in the Oval
Room of the White House on November 17. All the high
officers of the Department had been instructed to attend this —
all, that is, except me. When the Secretary heard about this, he
put his foot down again. Overruling my protests that I did not
want to go where clearly I was not wanted, he said that we
were not going to slink out of office, but march out with colors
flying and insisting on a salute as well. He even refused to telephone the White House about it. If Henry Morgenthau, his
Under Secretary and probable successor, could have guests,
he damn well could too. He was taking me as his guest.

Our entrance sent a ripple across the room, but the President
only waved a greeting. Fortunately no one knew in those days
how tenuously the White House was held together, or the addition of two more guests might have turned the ripple into a
panic, so large was the company. Three generations of Mor-
genthaus furnished the core, to which friends and the Treasury
staff were added. Henry was sworn in, thereby gently edging
me off the federal payroll. The President made a speech, prais-
ing Henry's ability and loyalty and the loyalty of Secretary
Woodin and all the assistant secretaries, naming them. Henry
replied, paying tribute to the same qualities of the same people.

The ceremony ended but no one moved to congratulate the
initiate. I thought it time to remove the ghost at the banquet,
so, crossing the room, said goodbye to the President and thanked
him for the opportunity to work with him. He motioned me to
come around the desk, then taking my hand pulled me down to
him. "I have been awfully angry with you," he said in a low
voice. "But you are a real sportsman. You will get a good letter
from me in answer to yours."

Alas, I never did. Our relations in that year seemed destined
to be star-crossed. As I went out of the White House, reporters
asked me whether I had resigned and had received a letter from
the President. I replied that I had resigned, but had not as yet

received the President's reply. This was given an unfortunate twist; but more was to come. To escape the telephone, we left town on a visit to kind friends. One morning, a few days later, the press carried my memorandum and Stanley Reed's on the legality of executive devaluation of the dollar. (Reproduced here in the Notes.) Some overenthusiastic partisan, probably of mine, had leaked them both, a thoroughly inexcusable but unhappily common practice at the time. Apparently it was officially laid at my door, as Chief Moran of the Secret Service explained to me when he interviewed me later in futile search of the culprit. This suspicion happily was dispelled, but I received no letter. The whole episode was not, however, wholly barren of fruit. I have been told on credible authority that some years later one of my many successors in office resigned in a letter bristling with cogent criticism of President Roosevelt's policies. The President read it through, handed it back to Steve Early, and said, "Return it to him and tell him to ask Dean Acheson how a gentleman resigns." I like to believe the story, and treasure it more than any smooth letter accepting my resignation.

10

THE ROAD BACK

BACK AT MY OLD DESK in the law firm, among familiar faces, engaged in accustomed work not likely to booby-trap one, the past six months appeared as someone else's experience. My ties with the Treasury and my friends in the government were cut completely. But seven years of enjoyable and profitable law practice opened for me. Considerations of law, propriety, and good taste ruled out departmental practice. This left — in Washington — practice before the courts and administrative tribunals where one's conduct was a matter of public record. Trials and appellate arguments soon spread to other jurisdictions and to the Supreme Court of the United States. My short venture from private practice into government service did not hurt; on the contrary, it improved my practice. I had become known, and known throughout the business community, as a "sound" man. It was very different later on when I disappeared from this desirable practice for more than a decade of a man's supposedly most fruitful years, and returned to the bar known not as a lawyer but as a Cabinet officer upon whom politicians and sections of the press had been trying out novel forms of mayhem. A "sound" man is a more desirable lawyer than a "controversial" one. In 1933 I was very "sound."

One echo of the recent past came from my employment by the Federal Reserve Bank of New York to defend a suit by the British-American Tobacco Company to recover for gold which had been held by the bank earmarked for the company. When private gold holdings were forbidden in April 1933, the bank had taken over this gold and credited the company with the then legal dollar equivalent. The company demanded the gold's value in a free market. The bank's action was upheld. An added dividend was the friendship made during the proceedings with my opponent, Colonel Hartfield, one of the senior partners of White & Case in New York, an able and pleasant gentleman.

Our firm was soon engaged in a litigation which went on for some years and gave one an interesting insight into the point of view of public utility magnates of the day, an attitude leading to the famous "death sentence" which Congress later pronounced on public utility holding companies. The Public Works Administration, under Secretary of the Interior Harold L. Ickes, had embarked upon extensive rural electrification. Government aid in doing this was an innovation in the United States, though not, for instance, in Scandinavia, and was hailed as galloping socialism. We were employed by a utility holding company to enjoin Ickes from financing a cooperative enterprise in Oklahoma which would compete for business with a subsidiary of the company. By unusual skill and good luck my partner, Edward B. Burling, had obtained an injunction pending an appeal from a lower court order dismissing our case. The injunction stopped Secretary Ickes in his tracks. Soon a flood of similar cases came to us from all over the country, some forty or more, as I remember, each resulting in an injunction pending a decision of the constitutional question stated on the face of our pleading. Furthermore, that decision would be made, as the pleadings stood, on the assumption that the facts we had stated were true. In our statements we had understandably put our best foot forward.

Before the time for argument was reached, that excellent lawyer, and later voluble judge and author, Jerome Frank, took over the government's case. With good judgment he changed tactics. Instead of accepting the facts as we stated them, he decided to make us prove them. The pilot case was sent back for trial; but all the injunctions remained in force until the decision below should be reviewed on appeal.

In this situation, Ned Burling gave our clients sound advice. The course of litigation which the government had chosen, he said, would take some time — in fact, some years — before the final judgment of the Supreme Court. Considering the trend of the times, it required a good deal of hope and faith to believe that we had an even chance of its being in our favor. The question was, therefore, how to use the time the litigation provided. If it were used to extend electric lines to rural areas and send rates down, the cooperatives would find getting started much tougher than if the companies held an umbrella over rates.

This wisdom was not appreciated and so shook confidence in our constitutional orthodoxy that we found Mr. Newton D. Baker's firm added to us in the litigation. The conduct of this fell to me on returning to practice. After I participated in the trial and argument in the Court of Appeals, it was a relief to have Mr. Baker's firm assume major responsibility for presentation in the Supreme Court, where the result was defeat. Left to our own devices, however, we were able to enjoin Mr. Tugwell from financing a housing development in New Jersey.

Not all my efforts were devoted to representing the forces of reaction in opposition to the children of light. An old interest was revived when the International Ladies' Garment Workers' Union employed me to argue their appeal in the United States Court of Appeals in Kansas City from an injunction against a strike to unionize the Donnelly Garment Company. This argument produced one of the most bizarre incidents of my professional experience. Nelly Don (as she was known in the trade) not only had built up a large and successful business manufacturing women's dresses at popular prices, but contributed mightily to furthering the classless society in America. Any woman with a passable figure and the basic aids could look like her more affluent sisters in Nelly Donnelly's well-styled and low-priced dresses. Her company's labor policies, however, were authoritarian. When she came in conflict, as she inevitably did, with David Dubinsky's union the war was sure to be long and bitter. The record abounded in evidence of clashes between female pickets and female strikebreakers in which hair was pulled and blouses torn. Legal hyperbole translated these incidents into "violence."

The Court of Appeals had given over the whole day to the argument of this case which, because the factory was located in Kansas City, was well-known locally. Not only that, but Nelly Donnelly had married James A. Reed, the vitriolic former Senator from Missouri. Jim Reed was representing his wife's company, and the show promised to be a good one. As in Lincoln's day, the courtroom was a prime source of entertainment in the Middle West. My performance must have been a disappointment, cast as it was in the lower key of Eastern appellate arguments.

Jim Reed's opening sentence, however, suffered from no such pallid anemia. Well into old age, he rose slowly from the counsel table and, leaning on his cane, hobbled to the lectern in a hushed courtroom. Then he seemed to shake off his age. Starting in a growl which rose to a leonine roar, he began his argument.

"If the devil scraped the caldrons of hell, and out of the scum created a sensate being, he would not be as vile as this man" (pointing his cane at me) "who comes here to defend stripping women naked in the streets of our city!" From this start he turned on my clients with no less colorful invective. The public got what it came for. When the argument ended and the Court had withdrawn, I said to my colleague Frank P. Walsh, Jr., whose father until his death had conducted the union's case, that I was going to shake hands with my opponent. He strongly advised against it, insisting that the old gentleman would as likely as not break his cane over my head.

But I walked across the room, held out my hand and said, "Brilliant argument, Senator. Probably successful, too. You gave me a new idea of myself." He glowered for a moment, then relaxed and took my hand.

"You're worthy of a better cause," he muttered, and turned away. It seemed, at least, a draw.

In 1936 two friends who had been in the New Deal at its beginning, approached me with the idea of joining them in a "Democrats for Landon" movement, as did Senator Reed. Nothing, so it seemed to me, could be more foolish. Whatever differences we had had with FDR were as nothing compared to the gap between, at least, my ideas of desirable public policy and the Republican platform even as interpreted by the rather sensible Mr. Landon. It seemed to me that our fellow citizens could work out their decision without help from the three of us. But if they were publicly changing sides I would publicly stick to mine. In the event, this is what we did. I wrote a letter from our place in Maryland to the Baltimore *Sun*. That estimable newspaper was somewhat startled to receive it through the mail unannounced and telephoned to inquire into its authenticity. I was told that both Mr. Hull and the President were surprised and pleased when it was printed by the *Sun* and reprinted as a political pamphlet.

October 17, 1936

To the Editor of the Baltimore Sun,
Baltimore, Maryland

Sir:

Since returning to private life I have refrained from any public statement regarding the policies of the present Administration and had hoped to do so through this campaign. Recently, however, I have received invitations to speak and reports of what my position was supposed to be which require a choice between assuming a false position through continuing a desired silence and assuming a false idea that the matter is of any importance. I ask your courtesy to avoid the former.

When your editorial stating your position in the campaign appeared, I found myself in substantial agreement with it. As the campaign has progressed, however, I have become convinced that I should vote for the reelection of the President and, barring some unexpected development, I shall do so.

Prior to his Minneapolis speech, Mr. Landon had removed from the campaign any issue of responsible fiscal management. His advocacy in general terms of sound money and a balanced budget had been interspersed with more specific proposals which negatived both.

Nor has Mr. Landon given proof of any realistic comprehension of the direction which the regulatory functions of government must take in a crowded and complicated world to achieve the ends which he, as well as the President, avows.

But Mr. Landon in his Minneapolis speech and Mr. Hamilton in his challenge to the President to engage in a Red hunt have decided my vote. You have stated far better than I can the admiration and respect which the country has unreservedly given to the sanity, courage and determination of the Secretary of State. I believe so strongly that his efforts to revive international trade are among the most constructive acts of any government in the post war period that when they are attacked I must be on his side.

To this is added my intense hostility to the attitude of intolerance which Mr. Hamilton's speech discloses. It seems to me utterly fantastic to suggest that Communism is in any manner involved in this campaign. It serves only to arouse a spirit of bigotry which we have experienced before and which always results in violation of constitutional guarantees of liberty and makes impossible sane consideration of public questions. I am against any party which inflames this spirit.

This year, more than in most, one's vote whatever it may be, must be cast more in hope than in faith. The hope which accompanies mine is that Mr. Hull's liberalism, sanity and patience may increasingly shape the policies of the government.

Very truly yours,
DEAN ACHESON

Sandy Spring, Maryland.

In 1939 other duties began to infringe upon law practice. On January 5, 1939, President Roosevelt nominated Professor Felix Frankfurter of the Harvard Law School to be an Associate Justice of the Supreme Court of the United States, an appointment described the next day by the *New York Times* as "one of the most popular ever made by the President." We had been close friends for many years. A day or two after the nomination he asked me to be his adviser and representative in Washington, attending the hearings before the Senate Judiciary Committee and responding to such requests as they might wish to make. I readily agreed. Some of his friends had suggested, he said, that the hearings might bring out anti-Semites and witch hunters of the Palmer days and that by obtaining the right of cross-examination as his counsel I could show up the fanatical intolerance of these people. This I vetoed emphatically. These were not adversary proceedings in which he was seeking anything. Fools and bigots would show themselves up, and friends on the Committee, with help where necessary, could correct downright falsehood. My mission was to aid his unanimous confirmation. Such proved to be the case.

The witnesses were an odd lot. A Seneca Indian woman, tall, expressionless, with long black braids and voice in deep monotone, opposed the nomination because the nominee was a member of the American Civil Liberties Union which had supported the Administration's Wheeler-Howard Act for the protection of the American Indians, of which the witness disapproved. Mrs. Elizabeth Dilling, with her Red Network chart, also found the nominee's association with the Civil Liberties Union and its activities subversive. She held the same views, so she said, of the President and of several members of the Senate Committee.

Then I was asked to prove that FF was a citizen. This hinged upon his father's naturalization and upon his being a minor at the time. The first fact was easy, but the proof of age required the immigration record which seemed to have been destroyed when the old customhouse in New York burned down years ago. Finally, Judge Learned Hand of the Court of Appeals in New York, being appealed to, was able to run down some surviving record which satisfied the Committee.

Then we came to the crux of the hearings. Its members informed me in private session that they wanted the nominee to appear before them and testify. This, I said, he would gladly do, provided the Committee gave me some written evidence of its desire, and provided it understood that FF would not discuss any questions relating to how he would decide matters which might come before the Court. Furthermore, since he had meticulously refrained from expressing any views on the President's effort in 1937 to amend the law relating to the tenure of the Justices, their retirement for age, and the composition of the Court, he would not do so then.

At no time did he tell me what his views were on that issue. Knowing his profound convictions on the place of the courts in the American system, and his reverence for the judicial function, I would make a guess that he was dead against it, yet, understanding the exasperation with the "Nine Old Men" which drove the President to this grave mistake, his loyalty and devotion to the President made him unwilling to join the chorus of opposition.

I did not ask the Committee to agree to this self-imposed silence, but simply wanted them to know the fact of it. A long wrangle ensued; I did not budge. Frankfurter would not appear as a seeker after office, but would comply with a request by the Committee to appear. At length the Committee agreed and a morning or so later Frankfurter breakfasted with us.

We went together to the jam-packed, large Caucus Room of the Senate Office Building, so packed that police had to precede us like icebreakers to open a path to the witness table. The subcommittee in charge of the hearings, under the chairmanship of Senator Matthew M. Neely of West Virginia, were already at the long table before us — beside the Chairman, Senators King of Utah, McCarran of Nevada, Connally of Texas, Hughes of Delaware, Borah of Idaho, Norris of Nebraska, Austin of Vermont, and Danaher of Connecticut. The Chairman, calling the subcommittee to order and admonishing the audience against demonstrations of approval or disapproval, continued:

Dr. Frankfurter, the subcommittee of the Committee on the Judiciary of the United States Senate, before which your nomination is pending, has invited you here in order that the members of the subcommittee may become acquainted with you. We now welcome you and assure you that we shall be glad to hear any statement that you may care to make. . . .

Dr. FRANKFURTER. I am very glad to accede to this committee's desire to have me appear before it. I, of course, do not wish to testify in support of my own nomination. Except only in one instance, involving a charge against a nominee concerning his official act as Attorney General, the entire history of this Committee and of the Court does not disclose that a nominee to the Supreme Court has appeared and testified before the Judiciary Committee. While I believe that a nominee's record should be thoroughly scrutinized by this committee, I hope you will not think it presumptuous on my part to suggest that neither such examination nor the best interests of the Supreme Court will be helped by the personal participation of the nominee himself. I should think it improper for a nominee no less than for a member of the Court to express his personal views on controversial political issues affecting the Court. My attitude and outlook on relevant matters have been fully expressed over a period of years and are easily accessible. I should think it not only bad taste but inconsistent with the duties of the office for which I have been nominated for me to attempt to supplement my past record by present declarations.

That is all I have to say.

The Chairman then invited questions from members of the Committee, an invitation accepted first by Senator Borah, who took the witness through a series of matters brought to the Committee's attention by the hearings or privately — the origin of and his connection with the American Civil Liberties Union, his work as Secretary and Counsel of the President's Mediation Commission to settle wartime strikes in the copper mines of Arizona and the spruce forests of Washington and to report on the Bisbee deportations and the Mooney murder trial, which were both the result and cause of labor unrest in the West and Southwest. These questions produced as fascinating a social history of the United States in the first quarter of this century as one could wish to hear.

Senator McCarran, taking up the questioning, established that FF was born abroad, that Mr. William Z. Foster, of the Communist Party had once been a member of the sponsoring committee of the Civil Liberties Union, that FF had not read the reports of the Dies (Un-American Activities) Committee, or of the Fish, Lusk, or American Legion committees on that organization, and that he did know Harold Laski.

SENATOR McCARRAN. Was he one of your students?

DR. FRANKFURTER. No; he is an Englishman who graduated from Oxford University. He was disqualified for service in the war for physical reasons. He was a teacher in McGill University in Montreal when I first heard of him through my friend, Mr. Norman Hapgood, who is, perhaps, known to members of the committee. Having been a Harvard man, he spoke to me about this young man, and eventually Mr. Laski became a teacher at Harvard University. He later returned to England, and became professor of political science at the University of London, and has been there ever since.

SENATOR MCCARRAN. Have you ever read any of his publications?

DR. FRANKFURTER. Oh, certainly.

SENATOR MCCARRAN. Do you agree with his doctrine?

DR. FRANKFURTER. I trust you will not deem me boastful, if I say I have many friends who have written many books, and I shouldn't want to be charged with all the views in books by all my friends.

SENATOR MCCARRAN. You can answer that question simply.

DR. FRANKFURTER. No; I cannot answer it simply. If you have a recent book of his, you will find the list of books he has written, some 12 or 15 or 20. He is an extraordinarily prolific writer. How can I say I agree with his doctrine? That implies that he has a doctrine.

SENATOR MCCARRAN. Do you know whether or not he has a doctrine?

DR. FRANKFURTER. I assume he has more than one. All people have.

SENATOR MCCARRAN. I refer now to a publication entitled "Communism," and ask you whether you have read that?

DR. FRANKFURTER. I have read it.

SENATOR MCCARRAN. Do you subscribe to his doctrine as expressed in that volume?

DR. FRANKFURTER. Senator McCarran, how can I answer that question without making a speech about my views on government and the relations of the various branches of government to one another?

SENATOR MCCARRAN. You say you have read it and know the author, and you know the sentiment prevailing in this country now in regard to socialism and communism. If you have read this small volume, you can surely answer whether you subscribe to the doctrine?

DR. FRANKFURTER. Have you read the book?

SENATOR MCCARRAN. I have just casually glanced at it.

DR. FRANKFURTER. What would you say is its doctrine?

SENATOR McCARRAN. The doctrine is the advocacy of communism.

DR. FRANKFURTER. You see, we could debate all day on whether that is in fact the doctrine of that book.

SENATOR McCARRAN. Do you believe in the doctrine set forth in this book?

DR. FRANKFURTER. I cannot answer, because I do not know what you regard as the doctrine. You have never read it. I understand that it is a study of certain beliefs, of a theory called communism. So far as I know, it would be impossible for me to say whether I agree with the doctrine in that book or not, because I think it is impossible to define what the doctrine is.

SENATOR McCARRAN. If it advocates the doctrine of Marxism, would you agree with it?

DR. FRANKFURTER. Senator, I do not believe you have ever taken an oath to support the Constitution of the United States with fewer reservations than I have or would now, nor do I believe you are more attached to the theories and practices of Americanism than I am. I rest my answer on that statement.

SENATOR McCARRAN. Is that all the answer you want to make? Do you prefer to let your answer to the question I propounded rest in that form?

DR. FRANKFURTER. I do, sir.

SENATOR KING. Do you believe in what might be called the ideology of Marx or Trotsky?

DR. FRANKFURTER. It would be terribly easy for me to answer that question, Senator King. I withhold any further discussion, not because there is any secret about my views or feelings, but because I am in a position in which I cannot help it. It may be that I shall be called to a position that might be very embarrassing. If I were before this committee for any political office, nothing would give me more pleasure than to pursue the line of inquiry of Senator McCarran and Senator King. I think I can appeal to the common understanding of lawyers that this is not a situation in which one can speak freely. I prefer to rest it on the general statement I made to Senator McCarran. You will have to decide, in the light of my whole life, what devotion I have to the American system of government.

After some desultory questions from others, proceedings languished while Senator Neely motioned me to come to him. Senator McCarran, he said, was building the impression that FF was a dangerous radical, if not a Communist, and that Frankfurter was falling into the trap. The Chairman believed that it was best to bring the matter into the open and ask the witness the direct question whether he was or had ever been a Communist. I agreed, and, returning, repeated the Chairman's statement to FF and urged him to be sensible and not reply by asking the Chairman what he meant by "Communist."

Senator McCarran broke in again. "May I ask another question, Mr. Chairman?"

SENATOR NEELY. Certainly.

SENATOR McCARRAN. Doctor, going a little further into your explanations of these matters, do you believe in the Constitution of the United States?

DR. FRANKFURTER. Most assuredly.

SENATOR McCARRAN. I am very glad to get that positive answer from you.

DR. FRANKFURTER. I infer that your question does not imply that you had any doubt about it.

SENATOR NEELY. Gentlemen of the committee, do you desire to ask Dr. Frankfurter any other questions?

If not, Dr. Frankfurter, the chairman, with great reluctance, propounds one inquiry which he thinks ought to be answered as a matter of justice to you. Some of those who have testified before the committee have, in a very hazy, indefinite way, attempted to create the impression that you are a Communist. Therefore, the Chair asks you the direct question: Are you a Communist, or have you ever been one?

DR. FRANKFURTER. I have never been and I am not now.

SENATOR McCARRAN. By that do you mean that you have never been enrolled as a member of the Communist Party?

DR. FRANKFURTER. I mean much more than that. I mean that I have never been enrolled, and have never been qualified to be enrolled, because that does not represent my view of life, nor my view of government.

A great roar came from that crowded room. People shouted, cheered, stood on chairs, and waved. The Chairman, banging his gavel, was inaudible. Every time the uproar would begin to quiet, someone would start it up again. At last, able to be heard:

SENATOR NEELY. Dr. Frankfurter, the subcommittee appreciates your appearance and the opportunity which you have afforded the members to become acquainted with you. I am personally very much obliged to you.

DR. FRANKFURTER. Senator, I am very much obliged to you and to the subcommittee.

SENATOR NEELY. The hearing on the nomination of Dr. Frankfurter is concluded, and the subcommittee now adjourns, but will convene in executive session before the end of the day to vote on the confirmation of Dr. Frankfurter.

(Whereupon, at 12 noon the hearing was closed, and the subcommittee adjourned.)

The audience made a rush for Frankfurter and nearly submerged him in the effort to shake his hand. The police cleared a breathing space around him and gradually got the crowd moving out. But the end was not yet. The newsreel men had missed the dramatic moment. It had to be repeated several times for their benefit by Chairman and witness.

By this time we were due for luncheon with the Chairman of the full Committee on the Judiciary, Senator Henry Ashurst of Arizona, one of the most colorful and able of the men combining those qualities who have adorned the Senate. He looked and could act like a stage senator; but the look was deceptive. Throughout the fight over the "Court-Packing Plan" he never once appeared to oppose the President, yet he engineered his defeat. We made our way to his office in the Senate wing of the

Capitol, a treasured perquisite of chairmen of major committees. The Senator, tall, handsome, with the long hair, flowing black bow tie, and coat halfway between morning coat and Prince Albert, then *de rigueur* for Southern senators of a passing generation, greeted us warmly. He had already heard of the triumph and had prepared for a celebration. Though a strict abstainer himself, he was no bigot and knew that after the morning's ordeal we would like a "cocktail." His messenger was asked to produce it. Out of a small refrigerator he produced a chilled bottle of brandy. The Senator had established his title as abstainer. But even though Mr. Churchill was yet to make *fine à l'eau* notorious, *fine glacée* held out even greater prospects of effectiveness. It lived up to all of them with surprising speed.

We plunged into talk about the hearings. "Tell me about McCarran," asked FF. "He seems a hardheaded, shrewd sort of man, but obsessed about communism. Explain it. Are there Communists in Nevada?"

"No, no," said Ashurst, "he's never seen one. How can one explain obsessions. If you probe deep enough you will find that everyone is a little cracked on some subject. I know I am." Felix protested. "Yes, I am," the Senator insisted. "I go quite off my top on the subject of Roscoe Conkling."

My client froze, amazed, glass in hand; then burst out, "Good Lord, I'm crazy too! Only I'm crazy at the mention of Katie Chase." At this they both let out a shout and, to the amazement of the messenger and myself, who were ready to believe them both crazy as loons, rushed into a true Latin *abrazo*. In a moment Senator Ashurst caught sight of my stupefied expression.

"Look at him," he cried, pointing at me, "it can't be true; but it is true. He doesn't know what we're talking about, and he's been to college, too." Felix explained that it was only to Yale. They were half right — I knew about Roscoe Conkling, the powerful and striking Senator from New York in the post-Civil War period. I knew of his great head with golden Byronic curls and finely chiseled face, his prominence in Republican politics and as an orator in the Senate, and his death, which came as the result of the great blizzard of 1888, when, angrily refusing a hansom cab because the cabby sought to profiteer, he walked home through the snow. My ignorance of Kate Chase was complete. Two highly articulate instructors rapidly remedied that deficiency.

Catherine Chase, the daughter of Lincoln's Secretary of Treasury, who was later Chief Justice and continuous rival for the Presidency, was her widowed father's hostess and strong partisan. Understandably, with the addition of wit and beauty, she stood at the pinnacle of Washington's society. Her marriage to Senator (and former Governor) Sprague of Rhode Island was unfortunate. Rich, uncouth under the surface, and violent, the Senator was not received by Rhode Island society or welcomed in the far less demanding social circles of Washington. Kate Chase Sprague's position declined. Soon gossips were connecting her name scandalously with that of Senator Conkling's. The climax came when Senator Sprague returning unexpectedly to their home near Newport, found Senator Conkling in residence. After high words, the Senator from New York withdrew, followed by the Senator from Rhode Island armed, so his son said, with a pistol loaded with three balls but no caps. Then followed a dramatic incarceration of Kate and her children in the Newport house, an even more dramatic escape and pursuit, and a much publicized divorce. To top the tragedy the lovers' passion cooled, as each thought the other too self-regardful, and each contemplated a career ruined by their relationship. They died far apart, lonely and embittered.

Through an excellent lunch and well into the afternoon with *fine glacée* to ward off fatigue, we pursued our joint obsession. In the course of it the Senator, taking a proper oratorical stance and using all the stops of his magnificent voice, recited for us the best passages of Conkling's speeches. At length, after reluctant farewells and assurances of speedy confirmation for a nominee so eminently qualified (it was unanimous in both Committee and Senate), we issued from the Capitol to find an utterly mystified group of newspapermen. What on earth had been going on? Nothing, we answered, but a pleasant luncheon and, pleading an urgent train departure, took to a taxi, with the press in hot pursuit.

When elusive circling of the station plaza had put us in the clear, FF put forward a startling proposal: "Let's see the President before going home. He'll love this story." Undoubtedly he would. But I had not seen him for nearly six years and thought Felix had better go alone. This he refused to do. We drove to the police box at the north gate and, to my surprise, the officer let us through despite our absence from his authorized appointment list, since FF was a constant caller. Similarly the head usher let us in on our assurance that "Missy," as Miss Marguerite Le-Hand, the President's secretary, was known in the White House, would take care of us. When she appeared, she was greeted in the future Justice's buoyant style and heard part of the story.

"Why, oh why, did this have to happen today?" she complained mournfully. "We're an hour behind schedule; and more coming every minute. I'll tell him and try to keep you out, but this isn't my lucky day. Remember, fifteen minutes and not a second more." She took us into the President's office the back way, through the Cabinet Room. This meeting, I knew, would be an interesting one. That the President would carry it off with aplomb, I had no doubt; and, of course, he did, greeting me with genial ease as though we had parted only yesterday on the best of terms.

The story poured noisily out of FF — the McCarran inquisition, the crisis, the triumph, the luncheon. The President roared with delighted laughter. "Tell him about Roscoe Conkling,

Dean," Felix commanded, and I obliged. More laughter. After half an hour Missy LeHand came in.

"You two have got to get out," she ordered. "There's such an uproar going on in here that the customers know he isn't working."

"Five minutes more, Missy," pleaded the President. After ten, she drove us out the way we had come in and sent us home in a White House car.

Several weeks passed. Then one Sunday afternoon, coming home from a day in the country, I was given a message awaiting me to call the White House operator. This meant little since many of the staff used that unequaled method of locating their friends. I called and gave my name. "Just a moment," the operator said; and then, "The President." Before I could say a word, the unmistakable voice said, "Hello, Judge!"

"I'm afraid there's some mistake, Mr. President," I said. "This is Dean Acheson."

"Not at all," came back over the wire. "Judge Acheson of the Court of Appeals for the District of Columbia. Your nomination goes to the Senate tomorrow morning."

"But I don't want to be judge," I burst out. "Would you?"

"No," he answered cheerfully, "but I'm not going to be one and you are — that's the great difference." The President then explained to me that he was in a row with the Senate about a judicial nomination in Virginia which he had submitted without prior consultation with the Virginia senators. To make his point he wanted to submit three nominations without consultations which the Senate would have to confirm. They were to be: Robert Patterson, afterward Under Secretary and Secretary of War, for the United States Court of Appeals in New York; Francis Biddle, afterward Attorney General and Judge of the Nuremberg Court, for the Court in Philadelphia; and myself for the one in Washington. I could not, he urged, break the symmetry of this plan. After much argument I got him to hold off until I could see him the first thing in the morning.

The President received me early the next morning. Knowing his method of seizing the initiative in conversation when he did not want to listen to his caller and holding it until the dazed victim was led out, I had written a letter:

February 6, 1939

My dear Mr. President:

I expressed most inadequately, when you spoke with me over the telephone, how deeply I was touched and honored by the suggestion you made to me. The honor of the confidence you expressed in me is plain enough, but that you should feel and express it seems to me so fine an act of sportsmanship that I shall never forget it. I wish with all my heart that I could feel fitted for the life which you offered to me, but I know that my instinct is right and that I could not be successful or happy in it. I would be less than fair to you or myself to go into something which would not have my whole heart and head and soul.

I think my gratitude to you is even greater than if I could accept the nomination. It certainly is greater than I can ever express.

Most respectfully,
DEAN ACHESON

Handing it to him before he had a chance to speak, and thanking him again, I said that I would not take more of his busy morning and started out.

"That," he said, "was a good try. Come here, sit down, and tell me why you don't want to be a judge." I quoted the Latin proverb *de gustibus non est disputandum* and Mr. John G. Johnson's less elegant remark when he was offered an appointment to the Supreme Court — "I would rather talk to the damned fools than listen to them." The heart of the matter was that I was too young for a life sentence to such sedentary confinement.

The President understood and did not press the point. Rather, he switched to another. He had been thinking of establishing a new Assistant Attorney General to be charged with protection of civil rights of all sorts (what a farsighted conception that

was!). Would I take on that unsedentary assignment? Again I
begged to be excused. I could serve the government in many
ways (and would soon be doing so on the Attorney General's
Committee on Administrative Procedure). The time had not yet
come to go back to public office. Neither of us foresaw the
forces which would soon precipitate that time for so many.
With good grace and in a thoroughly friendly manner the President let me go. In my stead on the Court of Appeals, he appointed Wiley Blount Rutledge, Dean of the University of Iowa
Law School, who later became an Associate Justice of the Supreme Court of the United States.

The Attorney General's Committee on Administrative Procedure grew out of criticism of one of the tenets of liberal faith
discussed in Chapter 6 — that the expertise involved in the decisions of administrative agencies could not be attained by review-
ing courts; hence these decisions should be well nigh final. Not
only was the premise denied, but the charge was made that many
of these agencies had become prosecutor, judge, and executioner
in their own causes. The remedy suggested was to turn them
into little more than makers of records for court consideration
and decision.

A committee to investigate and report was appointed by Attorney General Murphy on February 23, 1939, and soon after, I
succeeded Judge James W. Morris as its Chairman. The Committee's method and result were unique among such bodies.
Instead of taking volumes of testimony and producing a dust-
gathering report, it made its own investigation and produced legislation. A small but outstanding staff, assembled under the able
direction of Professor Walter Gellhorn of the Columbia University Law School, conducted studies and wrote a series of defini-
tive monographs on each of the administrative agencies, setting
out how each actually operated, the reality as opposed to the
theory. These became classics, widely read and used in both
government and education. From this solid foundation, and

after long and strenuous debate, the Committee evolved by no means unanimous recommendations for legislation. The Administrative Procedure Act, which became law on June 11, 1946, has for nineteen years and with minor amendments been accepted by regulators and regulated as providing workable and fair procedures. For once we in the United States were ahead of our British brethren in turning our attention to this troublesome field. It was not until November 1955 that the Royal Commission on Administrative Tribunals under the chairmanship of Sir Oliver (now Lord) Franks took up the same work. Those of us who labored hard and obscurely on this then unknown and now forgotten task take our satisfaction from Justice Holmes's observation that "legal progress is often secreted in the interstices of legal procedure."

While I was immersed in these minor activities our world for the second time in my lifetime was blown apart. It is curious how vividly the trivial settings of these shattering events stand out in memory. I can still feel the hot sun and smell the acrid dust in front of the small post office in Norfolk, Connecticut, where we waited for our morning mail and newspapers, during the month after Archduke Franz Ferdinand was murdered at Sarajevo. The newspapers reassured us each day that war was impossible in the twentieth century. If the silly word had then been in vogue, it would have been called "unthinkable." As it was, Mr. Walter Lippmann of the *New York World* told us, "The stakes are too enormous, the issue of the game too uncertain, for civilized Europe, if it is in possession of its senses, to risk its future well-being at the caprice of military gamblers."

And the *New York Times* played the same refrain: "That [war] is too dreadful for imagining, and because it is too dreadful it cannot happen."

Then came the news of August 4, 1914. In that month, there was no "phony war." The fate of Europe hung by a thread — one dared not breathe.

September 1939 was very different. In the year since Munich either war or the hegemony of Hitler in Europe had to me become inevitable. We had taken a house in Murray Bay on the St. Lawrence. A friend, Maude Atherton, whose husband, Ray Atherton, was at his post as our Ambassador in Copenhagen, was visiting us. As the tension mounted, hers did, too, since we all expected the cataclysm, if one occurred, to break again on Western Europe. When the British and French declared war in support of Poland, she left us to try to rejoin her husband. But the cataclysm did not break on Western Europe. It broke from both sides on unhappy Poland and the Baltic states. We set about closing the house. Then my son and I started off, ahead of the female contingent, to get him installed at Yale. On the drive south we talked of what the future held for him. It seemed to me certain that in some way the United States would be drawn into the war. The best way for him to carry his education as far as possible and at the same time qualify for a commission in one of the services was to enroll in a Reserve Officers' Training Corps. He agreed, on the way south chose the Navy, and three years later had both a Yale degree and ensign's commission. Soon a destroyer escort carried him off for three years' duty in the Pacific War.

A debate soon raged throughout the country on the significance of the war to the United States, one side led by an organization called "America First," which supported the traditional isolationist line; the other, by the Committee to Defend America by Aiding the Allies. Having strong opinions on the subject, I was soon caught up in the controversy. Passages from two speeches at the time, one at Yale, where I was then a member of the governing body, and the other at the national convention of the International Ladies' Garment Workers' Union give my current thought.

At New Haven I tried to get away from the day-to-day preoccupation with the immediate situation of a war in Europe and the division at home over our best course, and "take a longer swing to get on our target." The speech is reproduced in the Notes. As a forecast in autumn 1939 of the realities and requirements of both immediate and later postwar United States policy, in both of which I was to play a part, it is of some interest. It made these points:

The economic and political world system of the nineteenth century, which had had such vast consequences, was breaking up.

A large part of Europe and Asia was setting up a competitive economic and political structure.

We should immediately raise and equip a military and naval force capable of making us secure in both oceans.

Meanwhile, the outcome of the present war in Europe and Asia would vitally affect our security. We must see that the "conscripts of necessity" fighting the Germans and Japanese had the necessary weapons and supplies. The neutrality acts must go. We should take further positive steps to help them, though this might involve us in war.

We should begin work on a new postwar world system in which
  (a) arrangements were made for the flow of adequate development capital; and
  (b) impediments to trade were removed and orderly methods of marketing raw materials established; and
  (c) a stable international monetary system was provided.

In New York City, talking to a truly inspiring assemblage of a great union's members, I hoped to rouse in these people the conviction and energies of which I knew they were capable. At the opening session of the convention I had seen the auditorium of Carnegie Hall filled with thousands of workers, meeting under a huge banner which read "Dictatorship Dooms Labor; Labor Dooms Dictatorship." Brave words, indeed; but did they mean them in all their portent? So I put the question: "Do you mean those words?"

Clearly, it is not hard to believe that "Dictatorship Dooms Labor." That is a plain statement of what all have seen. To say it requires no act of will. But do you mean the rest of that sentence, proclaimed so boldly across the balcony — "Labor Dooms Dictatorship"? . . . If you mean it at all, you mean it as a proclamation of your fighting faith.

For, if it is not a fighting faith, it has no meaning. It is only words, painted on cotton, hanging from a balcony. You do not doom with paint on cotton. Those who would doom you paint with blood upon half the earth. Theirs is a fighting faith, to which they bring unswerving purpose and competence, courage and cruelty, ruthlessness and power. They can be met only with greater power and steadfastness.

. . . I saw and heard and felt you respond to your President when he said in his address that you could not be and were not neutral; that your every hope and prayer was with the free peoples who are fighting so desperately against the thing which you would doom; that you were heart and soul behind the program of national defense.

But the question whether you mean the words upon your banner was not wholly answered by this response. It is only answered if you put behind those words the same iron will which has brought your industry out of the chaos and agony of 1910 to where you are to-day. . . .

. . . I do not come to you to argue about the meaning of words used, or about the form of resolutions, or about the details of policies, or the merits of leaders. . . . But I ask you to search your hearts and know that you must mean that labor dooms dictatorship and that behind that faith you are ready to put yourselves, your souls and bodies to be the full, perfect and sufficient sacrifice.

For all that the enemy asks is the smallest shadow of irresolution and doubt upon which to work, the slightest suspicion of those with whom we must stand shoulder to shoulder, in order to foment discord and confusion. . . . We shall be told that the Dictators have no quarrel with America; that they could not reach us if they would; that under an Axis peace and free of Great Britain's so-called yoke, Europe will be for the first time united for peace and will be a great market for our goods. They will go on to say that after the war the Axis powers, for a time, must remain armed to prevent the return of chaos, but that no danger threatens or can threaten the Americas and that expenditure on armaments is a useless waste which undermines our solvency and benefits only the profiteers and communists. We shall be warned that those who point to danger are creating danger and preventing peace and reconciliation, or are hysterical, or ambitious to overthrow our institutions and seize power themselves.

. . . The same subtle and poisonous talk has deceived men as highly placed in Austria, in Czecho-Slovakia, in Scandinavia, in Belgium and Holland, in England and France. We are seeing now the terrible penalty that the guilty and innocent alike must pay for this error. This is no decision where good intentions or clever arguments are enough. Here we cannot afford to say magnanimously that reasonable men may differ. We are faced with elemental, unmoral, and ruthless power. In dealing with it, we can be wrong only once. Remember, I beseech you, that the judgment of nature upon error is death.

. . . [T]he defeat of those who are holding the last fringes of Europe would be a reverse to us of incalculable and perhaps irreparable effect. Its vital consequences to our national safety do not rest upon any debate as to whether we could then successfully defend this continent, but upon the grim reality that for the first time in a hundred years we should be faced with the imminent necessity of doing so — and of doing so under conditions which could hardly be more adverse. The decision which we must make is whether we shall put forth the greatest national effort in our history to meet the danger now, or whether we shall let it come to us and gamble upon our unaided power to fight the world.

If anyone doubts that error in our decision here carries with it the judgment of death, he has only to consider a few of the plain possibilities of German victory. . . . What would happen to the remnant of these [British and French] fleets which might be afloat after a

German victory, no one can say. Nor can one certainly say what has happened or may happen to the Dutch and Swedish and Italian naval vessels. But only the blind or foolish can ignore the possibility that enough of these vessels may fall into German hands or control to confront us with the unhappy dilemma of deciding in which ocean our navy should be stationed. If either ocean is abandoned, it becomes an open avenue of attack upon us. . . .

But loss of the battle fleets is only a portion of the danger. The British merchant fleet comprises three-quarters of the world's tonnage. In the last war it carried two million men to Europe and supplied them. Is it fantastic to suppose that in other hands that movement could be reversed. . . .

And what of our own hemisphere? . . .

Every time a German ship entered a South or Central American harbor it would be a gamble whether troops and machine guns or cargo would pour out of the hold.

It is hardly necessary to remind you of the immense military and diplomatic problem of preventing the establishment of bases of operation by all the devious ways of the modern Machiavelli on coasts which would extend from Greenland to the River Plate, from Alaska to Valparaiso. . . .

But the danger is not wholly a foreign one. I have already mentioned the admiring echoes of Nazi conduct and efficiency which we have heard already. These, in the event of German victory would increase. We would hear again from those whose prototypes reported with admiration that Mussolini made the trains run on time and that Hitler solved the problem of Jewish encroachment. . . . The very framework of labor legislation could be turned against the labor movement. The rest of the technique of Nazification you know only too well; and knowing, you rightly say that "Dictatorship Dooms Labor."

So I say again that the defeat of the western democracies would be a disaster striking at the very foundation of American security and the freedom of the American people. That defeat can and must be prevented. The tide can be turned to victory if we here in America will unite in turning all our energy and determination and resources to the task of help and preparation.

To do this our leaders must lead, courageously and frankly. Our people must demand that leadership, putting aside old shibboleths and political folk lore, insisting upon the truth, and having the steadfastness and self-discipline to follow those who will tell the truth and lead honestly in hard paths.

For the paths will be hard. In the first place, and immediately, we must undo much that has been said and much that has been written into the statute books. The first necessity is to enable those who are holding the battle line to continue to hold it until the essential fighting equipment can come and dogged resistance can be turned into victory. Here we can act at once. We can and should send to Britain and France food from our surplus for the millions who have sought refuge there or who have had to leave their homes and work. . . .

Equally pressing is their need for planes and the smaller fighting ships — even those which we class as obsolete. A plane or a ship now at the front is worth more to us than it ever can be again. We should go to the limit of prudence in making available all that can be of use.

But our greatest effort must be to turn the vast energy and resources of this country to the production of instruments of war, both for ourselves and others, to train hundreds of thousands of men to use these instruments expertly and resourcefully, and to temper our wills to act wherever and whenever the national safety can best be served.

The effort called for is a gigantic one. It means not only a transformation of our industry but a transformation of our thought. We are a people organized for peace and absorbed with the thoughts and activities of peace. The danger which confronts us is from peoples who are organized for war, whose whole effort and best and most inventive brains are devoted to war, whose wills are disciplined for war. . . .

. . . .

We are far behind; the time is short. The danger is immediate and great. There can be no holding back, no fumbling, no maneuvering for position among our public men, no reliance upon mere appropriations and committees. . . .

This effort will cost billions of dollars. It will mean sacrifice for all of us. It will mean that we must discipline ourselves and accept discipline, and for hundreds of thousands of us a wholly new and, perhaps, distasteful life. It will mean that our best men, our best brains, our most ingenious inventors must give up everything to this race with disaster, to the building of new and better instruments of war and to mastery of their use.

To shrink from this decision, to be satisfied with anything short of it, is to risk the error upon which the judgment is death, the death of hundreds of thousands of our men, the death of everything which life in America holds for us.

In the late spring of 1940 the "phony" war ended with a vengeance as Hitler's panzer divisions and dive bombers broke the Allied front, turned the Maginot Line, and rolled the British army north to its hairsbreadth escape from Dunkirk and the French south to surrender in the railway carriage at Compiègne. With the Battle of Britain joined in the air, and awaiting invasion from across the Channel, the British were desperately in need of more destroyers to meet it. Our navy had in "mothballs" a large number of old "four stackers" from the First World War. Cautious of political repercussions, the Administration seemed to doubt its legal authority to transfer these old ships. Congressional authority, it was thought, was needed; yet Congress was not called upon to act.

At this point my friend Benjamin V. Cohen gave me his analysis of the legal problem and his conclusion that the necessary authority existed under the law as it stood. He stressed the urgent necessity of action and proposed that together we write a legal opinion setting forth the authority and if possible get some eminent lawyers to join in publishing it. I agreed. We gathered the necessary material and, to escape interruption, wrote the opinion in Ben's apartment in New York. I took it to several men well known at the New York bar. Messrs. John W. Davis and John Foster Dulles, after consideration, declined to sign the document because of professional connections which they said made doing so inappropriate. But Mr. Charles C. Burlingham, who then might properly have been called the patriarch of the bar of the City of New York, Mr. Thomas D. Thacher, formerly United States District Judge in New York and Solicitor General of the United States under President Hoover, and my partner George Rublee, whom I have described at length in Chapter 7, did sign it.

Charles Merz, a classmate at Yale, then Editor of the *New York Times*, published the letter-opinion in full on the editorial page of the *Times* for Sunday, August 11, 1940. It attracted a good deal of attention, most of it favorable. But that was not the purpose of the exercise. What we were after was the favorable attention of two men in particular. The first of these was the Attorney General of the United States, Mr. Robert H. Jackson. His office reported that he was on a camping trip in the mountains of Pennsylvania with his daughter. A persistent telephone operator added that the camp had no telephone connections (wise man), but that, if the matter was urgent, a messenger could be sent in a few miles to call him to a telephone. The matter, I said, was urgent.

Somewhat to my surprise, in a few hours Bob Jackson was on the telephone. To say that he was in a happy state of mind would not be truthful, but friendship helped him control annoyance and listen. I pleaded the dreadful urgency of the President's knowing that he had the power, and with it the responsibility, to act; and outlined the legal justification. Bob would promise nothing more than consideration; but from a man of high intelligence and character, as he was, that was enough. He did cut short his vacation and he did write an opinion reaching the same conclusion as ours, though by a somewhat different route.

The next man to persuade was the President. Despite his friendliness to me, the course demanded a more potent mediator and advocate. A forthcoming meeting at Ogdensburg,

New York, between the President and the Prime Minister of
Canada, Mr. William Lyon Mackenzie King, pointed to the
man. Unsuccessfully I tackled Mr. Loring Christie, then Canadian Minister to the United States. Something of a Canadian
nationalist, he would not intervene. Standing discouraged and
baffled in front of the Canadian Embassy on Massachusetts Avenue, I wondered what next; then, on an inspiration, took a taxi to
the British Embassy. There, at least, one would not have to argue the need for action.

Lord Lothian, formerly Philip Kerr, the Ambassador, had
long been a frequent visitor to Washington on his duties for the
Rhodes Trust, famous for its scholarships to Oxford. As a man
of wide experience and a wartime private secretary to Lloyd
George, governmental processes held neither mystery nor awe
for him. But my proposal that he approach Mackenzie King
stumped him. He did not know the Prime Minister well enough
to have confident judgment about his reaction. Then there was
the British bureaucracy. His staff would send any communication to the Foreign Office to be passed to the Dominions Office
for transmission, with minutes passing back and forth. He knew
the Governor General, the Earl of Athlone, much better; but
there remained the bureaucracy. I had another inspiration. On
the Ambassador's desk were pen, writing paper, and stamps. A
post box stood outside; I could post the letter.

Lord Lothian was delighted with the conspiracy. What the
law calls "the overt acts" were soon accomplished, and in due
course Mackenzie King presented to the President the renewed
British plea for the "overage destroyers." The phrase always reminds me of a friend to whom we are deeply devoted, Mrs. Alice
Roosevelt Longworth, who says that it is an apt description of
herself.

The Battle of Britain and the Presidential election of 1940
were each approaching its crisis. I was far more concerned over
the outcome of the former than the latter. The President's easy

confidence in his speech to the Teamsters Union had communicated itself to me. (Would a candidate choose that organization as a forum today?) But when, in response to a summons from the White House in the latter half of October, I joined a meeting in the upstairs study, I found a worried company. The President, a cocktail tray on his desk before him, was surrounded by a large company including Frank Walker, then Postmaster General, Harry Hopkins, and Judge Rosenman. I sipped my cocktail and listened to an unrelieved tale of woe. Wendell Willkie was catching on. His cohorts had the zeal and enthusiasm of crusaders. The main issues seemed to be the third term, and which of the candidates could better keep us out of war. The pessimism seemed overdrawn and unreal; but they were the experts, not I.

The President, looking for relief from this repetitious refrain, remarked that I had been strangely silent and asked me to recite. I pleaded shyness in disagreeing with such impressive political experts and for the courage to be expected from another cocktail. Fortified by this, I suggested that the situation was not really so bad, that the Democratic campaign had not been pulled together and was becoming too defensive. Danger lay in the campaign turning into a mere horse race, and nothing else. If, rounding the clubhouse-turn into the stretch, Willkie seemed to be coming up, the crowd could become hysterical and anything might happen. What was needed was to relate the past eight years of the New Deal and the great horizons it had opened for the common man to the dangers threatening freedom everywhere, including our own land. Did anyone seriously think that what was happening to the ordinary citizens watching Hitler's and Mussolini's divisions goosestepping into their countries would stop there? Was this a time to trust the party which had let us drift to the very brink of disaster with assurances that recovery was just around the corner? Some of the same people thought that nazism, the wave of the future, was just around the corner. Perhaps if they were running things it would be. And so on.

The President listened carefully. "Could you put that on paper for Harry by tomorrow morning?" he asked. I agreed; the meeting ended; and I worked most of the night. In the morning Harry Hopkins had the memorandum, which can be found in the Notes to this chapter. In the outcome, the election did not justify the discouragement of that October meeting.

My days of freedom were coming to an end, a time which was, in a way, as happy as any I remember. If all my powers were not used to the full in an environment giving them scope, they were healthily exercised with a minimum of frustration. Later they would be stretched to their limit; my highest efforts would be demanded; the greatest difficulties interposed; frustration would be a common experience. So would discouragement, exhaustion, exhilaration, and achievement. The days of which I write here, though milder, were happy and satisfying ones. They brought me to the last decade of middle age.

Just as 1940 ended, Mr. Hull asked me to call on him. He had been watching me, he said, my growing involvement in foreign affairs, my speeches, and my work on the fringes of responsibility. Why not take the plunge, come into the Department, and go to work full time? I waited for more. Henry Grady, he went on, was leaving to go back to the University of California. Would I take over his place as Assistant Secretary of State for Economic Affairs? I asked for time to think it over, to consult my wife and partners.

How futile these exercises in thought and consultation are! Mere rationalization of decisions already made. Forces stronger than reason determined the result, and the right one, as my life turned out. It was an insane decision for a supposedly responsible professional man, dependent on his earnings, with a wife and three children at their most expensive age. And I knew nothing of the Department of State, its internal and interdepartmental feuds and frustrations. My own field of future work was almost as unfamiliar as the Treasury had been. The world was moving toward a cataclysm, however, sweeping me with it. I was too conscious of this, too restless even to want to escape the current.

So the die was cast.

I accepted Secretary Hull's offer and on February 1, 1941, went with my wife, Mr. and Mrs. Archibald MacLeish, Attorney General and Mrs. Francis Biddle, and Justice and Mrs. Felix Frankfurter to Justice Brandeis's apartment, where he administered the oath of office. At the time, this decision did not seem as crucial as it has since in retrospect. I see now that the Fates took a new and zestful interest in their work. Clotho found new yarns of life to spin, and Lachesis, She of the Lot, drew her chances from greater odds. Only Atropos hung back and, happily, withheld her shears, as the thread lengthened.

NOTES

NOTES

INTRODUCTION

"The first covers childhood": Duff Cooper, *Old Men Forget* (London: Rupert Hart-Davis, 1953), p. 11.

CHAPTER 2
"I'VE BEEN WORKIN' ON THE RAILROAD"

"Putting to myself your question": *Correspondence of John Adams and Thomas Jefferson, 1812–1826,* Paul Wilstach, ed. (Indianapolis: Bobbs-Merrill Company, 1925), pp. 134–137.

CHAPTER 3 THE OLD ORDER CHANGETH

"packed with men who are avowed socialists": *Washington Post,* October 21, 1919.

50 "fair ship, *Mary Miller*": *Letters of Franklin K. Lane* (Boston: Houghton Mifflin Company, 1922), p. 197.

CHAPTER 4 "OUR COURT"

"our associate in duties": Mr. Justice McKenna, in tribute to Chief Justice White, May 31, 1921, 256 U.S. v, vi.

60 Elihu Root's argument: The National Prohibition Cases, 253 U.S. 350 (1920), pp. 361–367.

60   "will undoubtedly decrease": *Ibid.*, p. 393.

61   " 'the Constitution' ": *Ibid.*, pp. 366–367.

62   *Standard Oil* case: Standard Oil Co. v. United States, 221 U.S. 1 (1911), p. 62.

65   "He was, of course, one of the towering figures": Alexander M. Bickel, *The Unpublished Opinions of Mr. Justice Brandeis* (Cambridge: Harvard University Press, 1957), p. 241; hereafter cited as Bickel.

66   "A little, bearded, birdlike man": Bickel, p. 244.

66   "a hot little gent": Bickel, p. 66.

67   "came, more and more": Bickel, p. 244.

67   "as Brandeis always said": Bickel, p. 66, quoting from *Holmes-Pollock Letters . . . 1874–1932*, Mark DeWolfe Howe, ed. (Cambridge: Harvard University Press, 1941), Vol. II, pp. 113, 150.

67   *Arizona* cases: Arizona Employers' Liability Cases, 250 U.S. 400 (1919).

68   "But for Pitney": Bickel, p. 74.

68   Arizona labor statute: Truax v. Corrigan, 257 U.S. 312 (1921).

68   Justice Frankfurter's paper: Felix Frankfurter, "The Supreme Court in the Mirror of Justices," *University of Pennsylvania Law Review*, Vol. 105 (April 1957), p. 781.

70   "a man of numerous and abrasive personal idiosyncrasies": Bickel, p. 245.

73　"an amorphous dummy": Proceedings in Memory of Mr. Justice McReynolds, March 31, 1948, 334 U.S. v, xi.

73　*Gold Clause* cases: Norman v. Baltimore & Ohio R. Co. and United States v. Bankers Trust Co., 294 U.S. 240; Nortz v. United States, 294 U.S. 317; Perry v. United States, 294 U.S. 330 (1935).

73　"He completely departed": Proceedings cited above in 334 U.S. v, pp. ix–xi.

74　"Those who were present": *Ibid.*, p. xvii.
In an address in 1922: Delivered at the Annual Dinner of New York University Law Alumni, February 4, 1922. *Virginia Law Register*, Vol. 8, No. 4 (August 1922), pp. 241, 243.

Page
CHAPTER 5 WORKING WITH BRANDEIS

79　Jacob Ruppert v. Caffey, 251 U.S. 264 (1920).

81　Sutton v. United States, 256 U.S. 575 (1921).

82　This rested on the law of conspiracy: W. S. Holdsworth, *A History of English Law* (Boston: Little, Brown, 1926), Vol. VIII, pp. 378–381.

83　"general propositions": Lochner v. New York, 198 U.S. 45 (1905), p. 76.

84　"The change in the law": Duplex Printing Press Co. v. Deering, 254 U.S. 443 (1921), p. 481.

84　"judgment or intuition": Lochner v. New York, cited above, p. 76.

86   "All rights are derived": Duplex Printing Press Co. v. Deering, cited above, p. 488.

86   Truax v. Corrigan, 257 U.S. 312 (1921).

88   Mr. Taft with others: Simeon E. Baldwin, Francis Rawle, Joseph H. Choate, Elihu Root, Moorfield Story, Peter W. Meldrim. *New York Times*, March 15, 1916.

88   United Mine Workers of America v. Coronado Coal Co., 259 U.S. 344 (1922).

89   "The facts," I wrote: Bickel, pp. 92–95.

89   "In the mountains of western Arkansas": Bickel, pp. 85–88.

92   "Toward the end of May": Bickel, p. 97.

93   Strathearn Steamship Co. v. Dillon, 252 U.S. 348 (1920).

93   "This opinion was prepared": Bickel, p. 54.

95   Lochner v. New York, 198 U.S. 45 (1905); Adair v. United States, 208 U.S. 161 (1908); Coppage v. Kansas, 236 U.S. 1 (1915).

103 "The other strand in these memories": *Harvard Law Review*, Vol. 55 (December 1941), pp. 191–192.

CHAPTER 6
LITMUS FOR LIBERALS IN THE TWENTIES

Page
108 Crichel Down furore: For a full and readable account of this historic battle between a stubborn Briton and the bureaucracy, see R. Douglas Brown, *The Battle of Crichel Down* (London: The Bodley Head, 1955).

109   "The Fourteenth Amendment": Lochner v. New York, 198
       U.S. 45 (1905), p. 75.

112   "poor and puny anonymities": Abrams v. United States, 250
       U.S. 616 (1919), p. 629.

113   United States v. Darby, 312 U.S. 100 (1941).

114   the *Adkins* case: Adkins v. Children's Hospital, 261 U.S. 525
       (1923).

114   two other cases: Murphy v. Sardell, 269 U.S. 530 (1925);
       Donham v. West-Nelson Mfg. Co., 273 U.S. 657 (1927).

115   Morehead v. New York *ex rel.* Tipaldo, 298 U.S. 587 (1936).

115   Justice Roberts switched his vote: West Coast Hotel Co. v.
       Parrish, 300 U.S. 379 (1937).

115   "There is a condition": Quoted in a flyer, entitled *Tory
       England and Democratic America,* edited by Judson King,
       Executive Secretary, National Popular Government League,
       Washington, D.C.

116   "If the [steel] strike succeeds"; "Judge Gary is fighting";
       "What we need": *Ibid.*

117   "The Bill of Rights is a born rebel": Reprinted by George
       Foster Peabody, with a headnote: "I have received Mr. Cobb's
       permission to print and circulate this because of my confi-
       dence that it is of the greatest value that the younger minds
       of the country should have the advantage of reading these
       very wise words." (A banker, Mr. Peabody's directorships
       of educational institutions included the General Education
       Board, the Southern Educational Board, the Hampton Nor-
       mal and Agricultural Institute, the Tuskegee Normal and
       Industrial Institute, the University of Georgia, the Skidmore
       School of Arts.)

118   Signers of "An Appeal to the People of the Churches of
       America" were:
       George Alexander, pastor, First Presbyterian Church, New
           York.
       Charles H. Brent, Bishop of Western New York.
       Benjamin Brewster, Bishop of Maine.
       Chauncey B. Brewster, Bishop of Connecticut.
       Arthur J. Brown, corresponding secretary, Board of For-
           eign Missions, Presbyterian Church.
       William Adams Brown, professor, Union Theological
           Seminary, New York; secretary, General Wartime Com-
           mission of Churches.
       Henry Sloane Coffin, pastor, Madison Avenue Presbyterian
           Church, New York.
       Harry Emerson Fosdick, pastor, First Presbyterian Church,
           New York.
       Charles E. Jefferson, pastor, Broadway Tabernacle, New
           York.
       William Lawrence, Bishop of Massachusetts.
       Frederick Lynch, editor of Christian Work, New York.
       Charles S. Macfarland, general secretary, Federal Council
           of Churches of Christ in America.
       John A. Marquis, general secretary, Board of Home Mis-
           sions, Presbyterian Church.
       Francis J. McConnell, Bishop of Methodist Episcopal
           Church, Denver.
       John McDowell, department head, Social Service Depart-
           ment, New Era Movement, Presbyterian Church.
       Arthur McGiffert, president, Union Theological Seminary,
           New York.
       William Pierson Merrill, pastor, Brick Presbyterian
           Church, New York.
       Frank Mason North, secretary, Board of Foreign Mis-
           sions, Methodist Episcopal Church.
       Charles Lewis Slattery, rector, Grace Church, New York.
       William Austin Smith, editor of The Churchman, New
           York.

Ethelbert Talbor, Bishop of Bethlehem.
Worth M. Tippy, executive secretary, Commission on the Church and Social Service.

118   "We the undersigned ministers": *The Churchman*, January 24, 1920.

119   "In this case": Abrams v. United States, 250 U.S. 616 (1919), pp. 629–630.

121   neutrality legislation: Act of Aug. 31, 1935, ch. 837, 49 Stat. 1081; Act of May 1, 1937, ch. 146, 50 Stat. 121.

CHAPTER 7 STARTING AT THE TOP

Page.

124   case to be argued at The Hague: Permanent Court of Arbitration at The Hague, United States–Norway Arbitration under the Special Agreement of June 30, 1921. U.N. Rep. Int'l Arb. Awards 309 (1922).

135   "(a) That the 'taint' of Hannevig": *Ibid.*, Argument of the United States of America (Washington: Govt. Printing Office, 1922), pp. 270–271.

140   "In the Argument of the United States": United States–Norway Arbitration, Stenographer's Transcript, pp. 1538–1539.

141   a letter from Secretary Hughes: *See* "United States–Norway Arbitration Award," Editorial Comment, *American Journal of International Law*, Vol. 17 (1923), pp. 287–289.

142   Omnia Commercial Co. v. United States, 261 U.S. 502 (1923).

CHAPTER 8 AND WORKING DOWN

Page.
145 "a kind of instinctive regard": Alexis de Tocqueville, *Democracy in America* (New York: Alfred A. Knopf, 1945), p. 273.

147 Mr. George Kennan complains: George F. Kennan, *Realities of American Foreign Policy* (Princeton: Princeton University Press, 1954), pp. 18–19.

148 Swedish claim against the United States: *The Kronprins Gustaf Adolf* (Sweden–United States), 2 U.N. Rep. Int'l Arb. Awards 1239 (1932).

154 Arizona case: Arizona v. California, 283 U.S. 423 (1931).

155 "Mr. Justice McReynolds": *Ibid.*, p. 464.

157 decisions of the Supreme Court: *See* Leisy & Co. v. Hardin, 135 U.S. 100 (1889); Lyng v. Michigan, 135 U.S. 161 (1890); Thurlow v. Massachusetts, 5 How. 504 (1847); Heyman v. Southern Ry. Co., 203 U.S. 270 (1906); Louisville & Nashville R. Co. v. F. W. Cook Brewing Co., 223 U.S. 70 (1912).

158 "Mr. Dwight Morrow's speech": *New York Times*, May 16, 1930.

158 "Dwight Morrow is the first major figure": Baltimore *Sun*, May 16, 1930.

CHAPTER 9 BRIEF ENCOUNTER — WITH FDR

Page.
162 "Fresh Point of View": Baltimore *Sun*, May 5, 1933.

164 Saint-Simon tells us: *Saint-Simon at Versailles*, Lucy Norton, ed. (London: Hamish Hamilton, 1958), pp. 191–192.

167   "to get the world as a whole back": *The Public Papers and Addresses of Franklin D. Roosevelt*, Samuel I. Rosenman, comp. (New York: Random House, 1938), Vol. II, pp. 138, 140; hereafter cited as *Public Papers*.

167   Joint Resolution: H.J. Res. 192, 73rd Cong., 1st Sess., 48 Stat. ch. 48, p. 112.

168   "four great objectives": *Public Papers*, Vol. II, pp. 160, 167.

168   Secretary Woodin at once denied: *Public Papers*, Vol. II, p. 245.

168   "we must retain full freedom"; "far too much importance": Arthur M. Schlesinger, Jr., *The Coming of the New Deal* (Boston: Houghton Mifflin Company, 1959), p. 215.

169   reaffirmed as lately as May 16: *Public Papers*, Vol. II, pp. 185–186.

169   "The American Government at Washington": *New York Times*, June 23, 1933.

170   "naturally puzzle[d] the other nations": *New York Times*, June 19, 1933.

171   "the wild gyrations of the dollar": *New York Times*, June 30, 1933.

171   Rejected Monetary Declaration: Quoted from the *New York Times* for July 2, 1933.

REJECTED MONETARY DECLARATION

London, July 1. — The text of the proposed declaration of the leading nations at the World Economic Conference as to the gold standard and international monetary stabilization, which has been rejected by President Roosevelt, is as follows:

DECLARATION, in which nations on the gold standard and those not on that standard join:

It is agreed that stability in the international monetary field should be obtained as quickly as practicable, and the common interest of all concerned is recognized;

That re-establishment of gold as a measure of international exchange value should be accomplished with recognition that the time at which each of the countries off gold could undertake stabilization and the time at which parity is established must be determined by the respective governments.

It is reasserted by governments, the currencies of which are on the gold standard, that it is their intent to maintain the free working of that standard at current gold parities and in conformity to their respective monetary laws, believing that maintenance of existing gold parities is in the interest of world recovery.

Governments subscribing to this declaration whose currencies are not on the gold standard take note of the above declaration and recognize its importance without in any way prejudicing their own future ratios to gold, and reiterate that the ultimate objective of their currency policy is to bring back an international standard based on gold under proper conditions.

Each government whose currency is not on the gold standard agrees to adopt such measures as it may deem most effective to limit exchange speculations, and other signatory governments undertake cooperation to the same end.

Each of the governments signatory hereto agrees to ask its central bank to work together with the central banks of other governments which sign this declaration in limiting speculation and, at the proper time, reinaugurating an international gold standard.

On July 1 the President: *New York Times*, July 2, 1933.

Secretary Hull's statement: *New York Times*, July 4, 1933.

173   The President's Statement [of July 3, 1933]: Quoted from
       Public Papers, Vol. II, pp. 264–265.

I would regard it as a catastrophe amounting to a world
tragedy if the great Conference of Nations, called to bring
about a more real and permanent financial stability and a
greater prosperity to the masses of all Nations, should, in
advance of any serious effort to consider these broader
problems, allow itself to be diverted by the proposal of a
purely artificial and temporary experiment affecting the
monetary exchange of a few Nations only. Such action,
such diversion, shows a singular lack of proportion and
a failure to remember the larger purposes for which the
Economic Conference originally was called together.

I do not relish the thought that insistence on such action
should be made an excuse for the continuance of the basic
economic errors that underlie so much of the present
world-wide depression.

The world will not long be lulled by the specious fallacy
of achieving a temporary and probably an artificial stability in foreign exchange on the part of a few large countries only.

The sound internal economic system of a Nation is a
greater factor in its well-being than the price of its currency in changing terms of the currencies of other Nations.

It is for this reason that reduced costs of Government,
adequate Government income, and ability to service Government debts are all so important to ultimate stability.
So too, old fetishes of so-called international bankers are
being replaced by efforts to plan national currencies with
the objective of giving to those currencies a continuing
purchasing power which does not greatly vary in terms
of the commodities and need of modern civilization. Let
me be frank in saying that the United States seeks the kind

of dollar which a generation hence will have the same purchasing and debt-paying power as the dollar value we hope to attain in the near future. That objective means more to the good of other Nations than a fixed ratio for a month or two in terms of the pound or franc.

Our broad purpose is the permanent stabilization of every Nation's currency. Gold or gold and silver can well continue to be a metallic reserve behind currencies, but this is not the time to dissipate gold reserves. When the world works out concerted policies in the majority of Nations to produce balanced budgets and living within their means, then we can properly discuss a better distribution of the world's gold and silver supply to act as a reserve base of national currencies. Restoration of world trade is an important factor both in the means and in the result. Here also temporary exchange fixing is not the true answer. We must rather mitigate existing embargoes to make easier the exchange of products which one Nation has and the other Nation has not.

The conference was called to better and perhaps to cure fundamental economic ills. It must not be diverted from that effort.

173   "Tonight the delegations": *New York Times*, July 4, 1933.

175   "I believe that the following": Memorandum of August 7, 1933, from G. F. Warren.

176   "the assumption that the price level"; "A general revival of business activity": "Memorandum on Changing the Price of Gold" by O. M. W. Sprague.

176   "I should hope": "Memorandum for Mr. Acheson on Monetary Policy" by Dr. Sprague.

177   Reports of the New York Group:

INTERIM MONETARY REPORT

I. SUMMARY STATEMENT

The monetary program, which the group recommends for adoption, falls into two divisions; first, the immediate program based upon immediate needs, and, second, the ultimate program designed to reestablish a sound international monetary standard, and to approximate "a dollar of constant purchasing power and debt-paying power." The group has been at work only a little more than a week. It has had to cover a tremendous range of problems. And it presents its first conclusions fully realizing that they require further study and elaboration.

The conclusions of the group may be summarized as follows:

Monetary action alone cannot bring about national recovery. It can, however, create an environment favorable to the success of action along other lines, or an environment which will impede or frustrate such action. The monetary policy which for the immediate future is adapted to bring about conditions in which the policy of the Administration can succeed should, first, prevent at the present time the strengthening of the dollar, and induce, for the next few weeks only and in the absence of unforeseen developments in the foreign exchange market, some slight tendency toward weakness; second, bring about an expansion of credit which will synchronize with the anticipated program of the N. R. A. to stimulate the purchases of manufactured goods and agricultural commodities, without inducing such fear among business men as to render them unwilling to undertake the normal risks of trade.

The policy which, it is believed, will for the next two months most nearly create these conditions is a fairly vigorous program of open market purchases by the Federal Reserve Banks, preparatory to the N. R. A. purchasing campaign, and, if desirable, increased purchases beginning with the opening of that campaign. Should this policy result in sudden or pronounced weakness of the dollar or in a dangerously rapid rise in prices, it may be necessary to modify it.

This immediate monetary program will consistently merge into the longer-term program recommended. For the longer-term program following the achievement of trade recovery, the group recommends the establishment of an improved gold standard as the best means of approximating a money unit of "constant purchasing and debt-paying power." The method recommended for transition from the immediate to the longer program is the initiation of conversations with the British coincident with the war debt discussions, designed to secure, if possible, the adoption of a common policy with regard to a trade recovery, prices, and currency revaluation.

II. THE IMMEDIATE PROBLEM

(a) *The Value of the Dollar in Terms of Gold and Other Currencies.*

A general improvement in business conditions has undoubtedly been obtained since last March. The departure from gold and the depreciation which followed exerted an energizing influence, particularly evident in the prices of sensitive basic commodities sold in organized markets. To what extent raw material prices vary in direct relation to the fluctuation of the dollar, either in gold or in foreign exchange, is not entirely clear, but it is probably reasonable to assume that a pronounced strengthening of the dollar would at this time, when farmers are selling their crops, have unfavorable consequences.

There is danger that, if nothing is done, the dollar will be strengthened, because the dollar is inherently strong in terms of foreign exchange by reason of the balance of payments being in our favor, and because prices have not yet risen to a point which corresponds to the present depreciation. In other words, the present quotation of the dollar contains a strong element of anticipated further depreciation. If this anticipation were removed, the dollar might rise sharply.

It follows that some action is required to off-set this inherent tendency on the part of the dollar to rise, and, in the absence of unforeseen developments in the foreign exchange market, to induce, for the next few weeks only, some slight tendency toward weakness.

(b) *The Need for Credit Expansion to Supplement Action Being Taken Along Other Lines.*

We seem to have reached a stage in which other than monetary influences are becoming of primary importance as a means of bringing about a general trade recovery. The depreciation of the dollar has not influenced prices universally, and not even all agricultural prices. Prices of livestock, butter, eggs, and milk, for example, have been largely impervious to the influences of a depreciated dollar. Moreover, a further advance in the prices of basic materials, — as well as of other prices, — if it is to hold, requires a general broadening of industrial activity, with its attendant lessening of unemployment. To bring that about, the National Recovery Administration has been actively engaged in the establishment of industrial codes, designed, among other things, to increase the purchasing power of wage earners. Public works expenditures are also designed to accomplish the same purpose.

If these efforts are to succeed they must be carried forward in a medium of expanding credit, but expanding so as to induce such general confidence in the future that business will employ additional capital and labor, and market an enlarged output. It follows, therefore, that credit must be made freely and abundantly available to flow into the channels of commerce and trade without causing apprehension.

In connection with this thought the group points out that more than fifty per cent of the unemployment is concentrated in the heavy goods or producers goods industries and that in large measure the activities of these industries depend upon ability to obtain long time credit in the securities market. If, therefore, the unemployment in these industries is to be substantially diminished it is important that there be created sufficient confidence in our monetary policy to encourage long time investments.

III. THE MONETARY POLICY RECOMMENDED TO MEET THE IMMEDIATE PROBLEMS

The group believes that open market operations in substantial amounts have had in the past and may be expected to have in the future some effect upon the exchange value of the dollar. The group is advised that within a few weeks the N. R. A. intends to start a vigorous campaign to stimulate buying by wholesalers, retailers and the consuming public as a means of disposing of the increased production which the operation of the codes is designed to stimulate. This campaign will be aided by the expansion of credit which open market purchases are designed to bring about.

To achieve both these immediate aims of monetary policy and to avoid the undesirable results of fear by the business public the following recommendations are made. During the weeks prior to the initiation of the N. R. A. buying campaign a fairly vigorous program of open market purchases by the Federal Reserve Banks, in the absence of pronounced weakness of the dollar or of a dangerously rapid rise in prices, should be pursued. With the initiation of that campaign it may be desirable to increase the purchases and maintain them at substantial figures until the results of the campaign are apparent. Such a program should occupy from eight to twelve weeks and furnishes, in the view of the group, the most hopeful monetary environment in which to test out the various forms of direct action now being employed to stimulate industry and agriculture.

IV. CONSIDERATIONS RELATIVE TO OTHER
MONETARY POLICIES

(a) *Devaluation*

It is essential that if and when this action is taken it should be final and constitute the first step towards the ultimate program recommended.

In the opinion of the group the present is not the expedient moment to devalue the dollar; first, because the trend and velocity of price movement and purchasing power are not yet clearly enough established to permit of finality in devaluation; and second, because the possibility of cooperation with the British to minimize repercussions abroad should be explored before the step of devaluation is taken.

The first of these considerations — uncertainty as to the trend and velocity of price movement and purchasing power — requires further observation of the following factors:

1. To what extent the operations of the N. R. A. will increase the cost of living in advance of creating additional consumer purchasing power, and to what extent industry will be able to support increased costs by reason of greater volume.

2. The effectiveness of government expenditure in building up consumer purchasing power, and how soon its effectiveness will be felt.

3. To what extent capital issues will be impeded by recent legislation, which, though necessary in principle, may prove to have been too stringent in some of its provisions.

4. How freely the banking system will function in aiding the rehabilitation of business, particularly in view of the going into effect of the Glass Steagall Bill at this particular time.

The second consideration — exploration of possible co-operation with the British — will be possible in October when, as recommended below, discussions can be had coincidental with the war debt conversations. An effort toward cooperation with the British is necessary because:

1. Devaluation undertaken by us without cooperation with other nations would probably result in retaliatory action in the nature of gold and trade embargoes, the effect of which on trade and price movements would be injurious.

2. The effect of our fixing the amount of devaluation without British cooperation might be to remove fear of further depreciation and, therefore, to start a return flow of expatriated capital and a covering of short positions in the dollar which would tend so to strengthen the dollar as to render the effect of devaluation void.

The group does not believe that all uncertainties in the domestic field must be removed before revaluation is possible, but it does believe that a strong upward trend in the factors mentioned should be discernible. It, therefore, believes that the subject of revaluation — including the important question of how best to use the gold freed by this action — is one pressing for consideration and study, so that the possibility of full discussions with the British may not be lost and so that we may be prepared to act at the earliest possible moment.

The group is prepared to undertake this further study if so desired.

(b) *Equalization Fund*

To attempt to manipulate the dollar with an equalization fund would require Congressional action to protect the Federal Reserve Banks against loss, and this method is therefore not immediately available. Furthermore, it is almost certain to prove a very expensive and not necessarily effective procedure, because it would probably produce retaliatory action abroad.

(c) *Free Import and Export of Gold*

To attempt to regulate the dollar by freely importing and exporting gold would result in our draining gold from abroad so rapidly that a gold embargo against us would almost inevitably result.

(d) *Thomas Amendment Notes*

It is the opinion of the group that the issuance of Thomas Amendment Notes at the present time would be harmful to the whole Recovery program, because:

1. Given the attitude which the great mass of business men hold, it may obstruct the free lending of funds without which trade recovery is unlikely.
2. While it is theoretically possible to control the printing press, once it is started, it is practically and politically exceedingly difficult to do so. To embark upon printing money, therefore, involves a grave danger of uncontrolled inflation.
3. Public opinion, which is now solidly behind the Administration, will undoubtedly be divided if Thomas Amendment Notes are now resorted to.
4. If we embark upon this course we shall almost certainly precipitate offsetting action in Europe. This, in turn, will not only largely offset the advantage gained, but may cause a "race for depreciation" and political upheavals abroad, or the equally undesirable erection of trade embargoes against this country. Whether or not these consequences are inevitable, on which opinions may differ, there is no doubt that they constitute at least a very strong possibility.

(A more detailed study of Thomas Amendment Notes will be made.)

V. THE TRANSITIONAL PROGRAM RECOMMENDED

Supplemental to the Immediate Program and Preliminary to any Long View Program.

It is clear from the foregoing that it would greatly add to the chances of success of both the immediate and the ultimate programs recommended, if there were some assurance that we were moving towards, rather than away from international cooperation. The aims of the British Dominions and of the British Government are fundamentally much the same as ours, though not as clearly defined at the present time. If these governments would agree with us on a program of cooperation most of the so-called Sterling Countries would likewise fall into line. The bloc so formed would be strong enough to pull the world out of its present disorder, even without the cooperation of the so-called Gold Bloc. It is by no means to be assumed, however, that the Gold Bloc would not also cooperate at a later stage.

It is, therefore, recommended that conversations be initiated with the British Government coincidental with war debt discussions, such conversations having as their object:

1. A clear mutual understanding that the aim to be pursued is a further rise of prices. This probably means the British breaking away from the Franc, and joining us in a gradual movement toward revaluation which will take place when each of us has reached a point of satisfactory equilibrium. The ultimate sterling-dollar rate of the future would then be determined of itself. In the meantime, while approaching this goal, arrangements could be made to avoid exaggerated fluctuations of the two currencies in terms of each other.

2. An understanding of each other's procedural plans. We would set forth the N. R. A. aims, our public works program, and our open market policy, showing how we hoped to bring about business revival and reemployment by the two former, and to adjust temporary accelerations or retardations as much as

possible by increasing or decreasing our open market purchases. We should expect that the British would want to take measures to produce a like effect in their country.

3. The development of trade agreements to further our mutual interests. This might ultimately involve a revision of the Ottawa Agreements.

4. A settlement of the British debt to us. This is one of our strongest weapons, but unless used very soon it is likely to be destroyed by default. We should bear in mind that a settlement will tend to strengthen sterling in terms of the dollar.

5. An understanding as to the eventual monetary standard to be adopted, when conditions are such that an international standard can be reestablished. (The group's recommendations in regard to this standard are separately treated in a later section hereof.)

If these conversations turned out to be successful, the problem would be vastly simplified. The chances for obtaining the desired result do not seem unfavorable, if both we and the British understand what the alternative might be, — namely, drastic inflation here, further chaos abroad, default of debts, increased restrictions on trade, and very likely competitive devaluation with social and political upheaval.

Assuming that we do reach an agreement with the British, we could then jointly study ways and means of preventing as much as possible the disorder which might result in the gold countries as a result of our combined action.

VI. THE ULTIMATE PROGRAM RECOMMENDED

As to the ultimate monetary standard to be adopted, the group believes that the ideal of a "Dollar with constant purchasing power and debt-paying power" can best be approximated by the adoption of a revised and more flexible gold standard. The group does not believe that under this or any other monetary standard price and business

stability can be attained in the absence of far-reaching reform in the conduct of banking and investment business.
On the other hand, the group is convinced that an international gold standard promises far more in this direction
than any other monetary standard that has been brought to
its attention. In this memorandum we have not discussed
other monetary standards in detail, but are prepared, if
desired, to analyse them, and contrast their merits with
the proposal herein recommended.

1. In so far as it is possible to make specific recommendations without knowing what will happen between
the present time and the time when it will be possible
to reestablish an international monetary standard, the
group recommends that, when such a standard is reestablished,

   (a) gold coin should be entirely withdrawn from
       circulation,

   (b) the holding of monetary gold should be confined
       to Central Banks, who would use it for the settle-
       ment of international balances of payment result-
       ing from temporary disequilibria in the foreign
       account, and who would likewise hold it as cover
       for their note issues,

   (c) note issues should be redeemable in gold bullion
       for export only, and shipments should be made
       only between Central Banks,

   (d) gold miners should be compelled to offer their
       output to their respective Central Banks, and
       should only sell to others for use in the indus-
       tries, arts, and professions, when permitted to do
       so by their respective central banks, and when
       the purchasers are duly licensed to buy.

2. It would seem further that under such a system

   (a) the legal minimum ratio of metal cover against
       note circulation should be reduced to about 25%,

   (b) the required metal cover should consist prepon-
       derantly of gold, say to the extent of four-fifths,

    (c) some part of it, say one-fifth, should optionally consist of gold or silver, provided that prior steps are taken, such as those contemplated by the London agreement, to stabilize the world price of silver.

3. The above ideas have already been discussed in a preliminary way at the London Conference. They are designed to free the world from the danger of gold scarcity, and to free the Central Banks from the disturbing influence of a loss of gold due to hoarding. As soon as we are clearly decided that this is the sort of monetary standard we want established eventually, we could profitably take up the discussion thereof with some of the other major nations, notably with Great Britain. The chances are that if the U. S. and the British Empire can agree on such a standard the rest of the world, except the silver countries, will fall into line as well.

4. Most important of all from the point of view of avoiding a repetition of past occurrences, we should study with British experts what method could be adopted to make such a standard more adaptable to changing conditions.

    (a) For short-run control the familiar methods of contraction and expansion through central bank discount rates and open market operations are the most satisfactory devices with which the world has had any experience. For this purpose they and they alone of the various devices proposed give promise of being amply effective. It should be realized that these methods have in the past perhaps not been as fully or effectively used as they might have been. The statistical material and indices used by central banks should be made more complete and more uniform so as to afford the basis for more effective and, when appropriate, cooperative action. Furthermore, it is of the utmost importance that central banks should use their powers of contraction in times of inordinate business expansion as well as their powers of expansion in times of depression.

(b) For long-run control, on the other hand, the group recommends that study be directed along the line of whether provision should be made for periodic but infrequent changes in the price of gold. Such changes should not be automatic. Nor should they be based solely on the movement of commodity prices. There have been periods, like that from 1923 to 1929 for example, when a money and banking policy which sustained a virtually constant price level, nevertheless, was influential in building up much future finanical trouble. When in the future, however, either a shortage or an overabundance of gold shall make its appearance by restraining otherwise effective credit policies, its world price might be changed. All changes however should be under a highly intelligent authority, and whenever possible should be made by international agreement.

5. Another problem relating to the ultimate standard, which should be studied, is that of treating holdings of foreign exchange by Central Banks as gold. The lowering of the legal minimum reserve adds to the flexibility. It would further add if holdings of foreign exchange in currencies which are unconditionally redeemable into gold for export were to be treated as part of the gold reserve. This practice should probably be limited in countries with primary currencies, such as Great Britain and the United States, and more freely permitted in countries whose major trade is in other currencies than their own, such as Latin America.

REPORT OF SEPTEMBER 27, 1933 TO THE PRESIDENT
FROM THE NEW YORK GROUP.

The group unanimously and unqualifiedly recommends that —

1. The Treasury Department be immediately instructed to prepare itself for discussions with Great Britain, having as their objective the stabilization of the dollar in terms of sterling and looking toward the eventual return of both currencies to some such modernized gold standard of the type suggested in the group's interim report.

2. In the meantime the Federal Reserve Bank of New York be authorized to take such steps including the export of gold as may be necessary to prevent the dollar from depreciating below 4.86 sterling rate and the present gold rate.

3. Open market operations, which were recommended in the interim report as a method of preventing the strengthening of the dollar, would under the present circumstances seem unnecessary, both from the point of view of the exchange situation and from the point of view of the banking and credit position. This recommendation is made without consideration for any factors other than the purely economic ones.

177 "The President listened patiently": James P. Warburg, *The Money Muddle* (New York: Alfred A. Knopf, 1934), p. 147.

177 "try your hand at a draft": Penciled, handwritten, undated note from FDR.

178 The reply:

MEMORANDUM FOR THE PRESIDENT:

Re: Price paid for gold by the United States.

There is no express statutory authorization for any officer or agency of the United States to purchase gold on behalf of the United States. Section 3519 of the Revised Statutes (U. S. C., Title 31, Sec. 327) provides that:

> "Any owner of gold bullion may deposit the same at any mint, to be formed into coin or bars for his benefit. It shall be lawful, however, to refuse any deposit of less value than $100, or any bullion so base as to be unsuitable for the operations of the Mint. In cases where gold and silver are combined, if either metal be in such small proportion that it can not be separated advantageously, no allowance shall be made to the depositor for its value."

This provision contemplates the delivery to the owner of the bullion of coin or bars formed therefrom. If bars are delivered no question of value arises, the owner simply receives bars the equivalent in weight of the gold procured from the bullion deposited by him. If coin is delivered the face value of such coin equals the value of the gold procured from the bullion deposited. The standard unit of value of coins issued under such statute, must conform to the standard prescribed for the dollar by Section 3511 of the Revised Statutes, as amended, (U. S. C., Title 31, Sec. 314) as follows:

> "The dollar consisting of twenty-five and eight-tenths grains of gold nine-tenths fine shall be the standard unit of value, and all forms of money issued or coined by the United States shall be maintained at a parity of value with this standard, and it shall be the duty of the Secretary of the Treasury to maintain such parity."

This standard is equivalent to $20.67 an ounce for pure gold, arrived at by the following calculation:

There are 480 grains in one ounce. 25.8 grains of gold .9 fine is equivalent to 23.22 grains of pure gold. Dividing 480 by 23.22 will give the value at $20.67 an ounce.

As a matter of practice the owner of gold bullion is paid by check drawn on the Treasurer of the United States, which check in turn is paid in legal tender. No appropriation is actually involved, the transaction being merely an exchange. The Government can give in legal tender no more than the value of the coin derived from the bullion.

Under the Executive Order of April 5, 1933, the owner of a gold mine may export ores, concentrates, precipitates, and unretorted amalgams. But if he turns his product into gold bullion, he is required to turn in the bars to the Government. Upon turning in the bars payment is made at the rate of $20.67 per ounce of pure gold.

Congress could, of course, provide an appropriation out of which the President could purchase this gold at any price which it or he may fix. But in the absence of such an appropriation, the only method by which the gold miner may obtain the going world price for his commodity is by opening a market to him.

A domestic market cannot be provided without reversing the entire policy of the Administration on gold, since this would involve the purchase and holding of gold by our people. However, governmental agencies may be authorized, as in Canada, to take over the new gold produced and dispose of it for the miner in foreign markets. This would not involve the general policy of the Administration, and later on, if it were desired, an appropriation could be obtained to be used for acquiring this gold for the Government.

(Signed) DEAN ACHESON
Under Secretary of the Treasury.

178   draft, of an order, August 18, 1933:

The Secretary of the Treasury is hereby authorized to receive on consignment for sale, subject to such rules and regulations and upon such conditions as he shall prescribe, gold recovered from natural deposits in the United States or any place subject to the jurisdiction thereof. Sales may be made,

    (a) to persons licensed to acquire gold in the arts, industries or professions, or

    (b) by export to foreign purchasers.

Such sales shall be made at a price which the Secretary

in his sole discretion shall determine to be equal to the best price obtainable in the free gold markets of the world after taking into consideration any incidental expenses such as shipping costs and insurance.

Such sales may be made through the Federal Reserve Banks or such other agents as the Secretary may from time to time designate and shall be subject to such charges as the Secretary may from time to time in his judgment determine.

Every person depositing gold for sale as provided herein shall be deemed to have agreed to accept as conclusive without any right of recourse or review the determination of the Secretary or his duly authorized agent as to the amount due such person as a result of any sale.

Consignments shall be sold as nearly as may be in the order of their receipt.

Executive Order No. 6261:

EXECUTIVE ORDER

RELATING TO THE SALE AND EXPORT OF GOLD RECOVERED FROM NATURAL DEPOSITS

By virtue of the authority vested in me by section 5(b) of the act of October 6, 1917, as amended by section 2 of the act of March 9, 1933, entitled "An act to provide relief in the existing national emergency in banking and for other purposes", I, FRANKLIN D. ROOSEVELT, PRESIDENT of the UNITED STATES OF AMERICA, do declare that a period of national emergency exists, and by virtue of said authority and of all other authority vested in me, do hereby issue the following Executive order:

The Secretary of the Treasury is hereby authorized to receive on consignment for sale, subject to such rules and regulations and upon such conditions as he shall prescribe, gold recovered from natural deposits in the United States or any place subject to the jurisdiction thereof. Sales may be made:

(a) To persons licensed to acquire gold for use in the arts, industries, or professions, or

(b) By export to foreign purchasers.

Such sales shall be made at a price which the Secretary shall determine to be equal to the best price obtainable in the free gold markets of the world after taking into consideration any incidental expenses such as shipping costs and insurance.

Such sales may be made through the Federal Reserve banks or such other agents as the Secretary may from time to time designate and shall be subject to such charges as the Secretary may from time to time in his judgment determine.

Every person depositing gold for sale as provided herein shall be deemed to have agreed to accept as conclusive without any right of recourse or review, the determination of the Secretary or his duly authorized agent as to the amount due such person as a result of any sale.

Consignments shall be sold as nearly as may be in the order of their receipt.

The Secretary of the Treasury, in his discretion and subject to such regulations as he may prescribe, is hereby authorized to issue licenses permitting the export of articles fabricated from gold sold pursuant to this Executive order.

———

This Executive order may be modified or revoked at any time.

FRANKLIN D. ROOSEVELT.

The White House,
August 29, 1933.

[No. 6261]

182   "Reply to Inflationists": *New York Times*, October 12, 1933.

182   Cordell Hull quotation: *New York Sun*, September 28, 1933.

184 "The brief and scrupulously fair résumé": London *Times*, October 12, 1933.

184 "pulling a poor mouth": *Washington Herald*, October 14, 1933.

185 "Well, they hired the money": "His [President Coolidge's] biographer Claude Fuess could not discover a source for this remark. Mrs. Coolidge could not remember it, although she said it sounded like her husband. Lyle Wilson, a member of Coolidge's presidential press conference, believes the President made the remark to the reporters, although it appears nowhere in the transcripts." *The Talkative President: The Off-the-Record Press Conferences of Calvin Coolidge*, Howard H. Quint and Robert H. Ferrell, eds. (Amherst: University of Massachusetts Press, 1964), p. 176.

186 "neither the British": London *Times*, October 12, 1933.

187 "I do not see how": *Washington Post*, November 28, 1933.

188 "controlled inflation": *Washington Star*, October 23, 1933.

188 too much emphasis on gold: *Loc. cit.*

191 "While the gold-buying program": G. Griffith Johnson, Jr., *The Treasury and Monetary Policy* (Cambridge: Harvard University Press, 1939), pp. 26–27.

194 my memorandum and Stanley Reed's on the legality of executive devaluation of the dollar: Quoted from the *Washington Post* for November 27, 1933:

THE CLASHING OPINIONS

Following are parallel opinions, in which, on behalf of the Treasury, former Acting Secretary Dean G. Acheson challenged the legality of R. F. C. gold buying transactions, and

Stanley Reed, general counsel of the R. F. C., upheld the legality of the operations which have precipitated the issue over monetary policy:

THE TREASURY OPINION:

It would seem that the proposal that Reconstruction Finance Corporation purchase gold with its own debentures under section 9 of the Reconstruction Finance Corporation act is one of doubtful legality.

Under section 9 the Reconstruction Finance Corporation is empowered, with the approval of the Secretary of the Treasury, to issue notes, debentures, bonds and other obligations either interest-bearing or noninterest-bearing on a discount basis. The pertinent words with reference to the disposal of these obligations are:

"Such obligations may be issued in payment of any loan authorized by this act or may be offered for sale at such price, or prices, as the corporation may determine with the approval of the Secretary of the Treasury."

In the first place, it must be frankly admitted that the issuance of obligations by the Reconstruction Finance Corporation was contemplated by Congress only as a revenue measure for the purpose of putting the Reconstruction Finance Corporation funds for use in connection with its authorized lending functions.

THE R. F. C. OPINION:

(After stating that he had been requested for an opinion "as to the legality" of the R. F. C. issue of $50,000,000 of its short-term notes now being exchanged for gold, and quoting Section 9 of the R. F. C. act, Mr. Reed rendered the following opinion. The text herewith presented omits a number of case citations.)

It is desired to ascertain whether a transaction so carried out would be a "sale" within the terms of Section 9 of the Reconstruction Finance Corporation act:

"Such obligations may be issued in payment of any loan authorized by this act or may be offered for sale at such price or prices as the corporation may determine with the approval of the Secretary of the Treasury."

Argument: The above transaction is a sale within the terms of Section 9 of the Reconstruction Finance Corporation act because:

The word "sale" does not necessarily import an exchange for money only.

The word "sale" has a variety of definitions. In Section 5 of Meecham on sales, it is pointed out that:

"It seems impossible * * *

The power to issue such obligations "in payment of any loan
authorized by this act" does not
in any way qualify this assumption. Congress realized that in
the case of loans to financial institutions the highest degree of
liquidity in connection with
sound banking practice often
dictated an immediate reinvest-
ment by the borrowing institution of the proceeds of the loan
in income producing Government guaranteed obligations,
and this provision was inserted
to accomplish this result, while
at the same time eliminating
useless Treasury financing.

In the second place, it seems
difficult to construe an exchange of Reconstruction Finance Corporation obligations
for gold as a sale of such obligations. It would be remembered that the emphasis in the
exchange is on the sale of the
debentures and not on the purchase of the gold, since the Reconstruction Finance Corporation has no separate power to
purchase gold. The question,
therefore, is, is the exchange of
Reconstruction Finance Corporation obligations for gold
on the basis of a price in excess
of parity a sale? The Reconstruction Finance Corporation
act states that the obligations
may be offered for sale "at
such price or prices" as the
corporation may determine.
The use of the word "price"
indicates a money transaction
and does not mean an exchange

for courts and text-writers to
agree as to the meaning of the
word ("sale") or as to the essential elements of the idea
which it represents."

Holds Sale Is "Exchange."

But its definition is rarely
limited to an exchange for
money only. Thus, while a sale
is sometimes defined as a "transfer of property from one to
another in consideration of a
price named or agreed to be
paid in current money," it is
more usual to find a sale is "the
exchange of an interest in real
or personal property for money
or its equivalent," or "a parting
with one's interest in anything
for a valuable consideration,"
or "held to include barter and
any transfer of personal property for any valuable consideration," or "a delivery of an
article at a fixed price."

The issue has never been
presented to the Federal courts
and their dictum has not been
clear. A recent case, Ferguson
v. Commissioner of Internal
Revenue, 45 Federal second,
573 1930 lists several definitions, including "a transfer for
any consideration," "a money,"
"a certain price in current
money," "a fixed price in
money or its equivalent," but
never chooses among them,
since this part of the definition
is not pertinent to the issue. It
is worthy of note, however,
that the Supreme court in the
5 per cent cases defined a sale

of commodities. If the obligations are to be exchanged for gold, the gold must, therefore, be considered not as a commodity, but as money. Gold as money has a definite statutory value, namely, the legally established parity price. At any other price it could not be money, since to denominate it as such would result in the creation of moneys of different values, i. e., a dollar of one kind of money would not buy a dollar of another kind of money.

Argues on language.

It should be further noted that the act by its specific words does not authorize the Reconstruction Finance Corporation to sell its obligations at such price, or prices, as it may determine, but rather says that its obligations "may be offered for sale at such price, or prices, as the corporation may determine." Couching the issuing power in terms of an offer for sale, rather than of a sale, would seem to argue that the obligations must be sold more or less in the open market. An offer to exchange such obligations only for gold could hardly, even in normal times, be considered as offering them in the open market.

Under present conditions with the only free gold in the country being newly mined gold, an offer to exchange for gold only is even more remote from an open market

as "a transfer of property for a fixed price in money or its equivalent." It would seem that the "equivalent" must be some personal property, the value of which is measured and stipulated in money.

The application these definitions have received is likewise pertinent, for it reveals that a broad definition of the word "sale" is not limited to a transaction of a particular class.

Quotes authorities.

Williston, in his treatise on sales, identifies contracts of sale and contracts of exchange for all purposes, saying that the term "sale" in a statute is often interpreted to include "barter and any transfer of personal property;" that is, Williston suggests the word sale as used in a statute may have even a broader definition than would be necessary to term as a sale the type of transaction under consideration.

Section 9 of the R. F. C. act is no limitation upon a broad construction of the word "sale."

The R. F. C. act merely provides that a price or prices must be determined, but it does not provide that the exchange must be for money at that price. Nor is such an implication considered necessary. In this connection the uniform sales act is persuasive. Section 1 (2) of the uniform sales act provides that the sale of goods is an agreement whereby the

operation. The only other authorized means of issuing such obligations is, of course, for payment of an authorized loan as above mentioned, since gold producers are not eligible borrowers and no form of loan to them is authorized by the Reconstruction Finance Corporation act, this method of issuance is, of course, clearly out of the picture.

Open market impossible.

That provision of the Reconstruction Finance Corporation act which empowers the corporation, with the approval of the Secretary of the Treasury, to sell on a discount basis its short-term obligations payable at maturity without interest merits consideration. It might be contended that the Reconstruction Finance Corporation could exchange its short-term, noninterest-bearing obligations for gold at such a discount that the gold could be considered as accepted at the parity price as cash. In other words, Reconstruction Finance Corporation could exchange its short-term, noninterest-bearing obligations to pay $100 for $66 worth of gold at the present mint parity price. This, of course, could not be done on the open market, but would have to be restricted to exchange for gold only. But even if the necessity of offering for sale in the open market was not considered essential, it is difficult

seller transfers the property in goods to the buyer for a consideration called the "price," and section 9 (2), defining "price," says, "the price may be made payable in any personal property."

Meecham, in his book on sales, although not referring specifically to this quotation, nevertheless contributes to its clarification by emphasizing price in distinguishing sale from barter, and makes clear that money is important only as a measure of value and is not the thing that must be exchanged for the article.

Following several citations the opinion continued:

The sale of the obligations of the Reconstruction Finance Corporation, in the manner provided for in Section 1, does not conflict with Congressional intent, as revealed in the debates of Congress.

Restrictions denied.

In answer to the objection that the R. F. C. has power to issue its obligations only for the purpose of using the proceeds for its normal functions (i. e., making loans, purchasing preferred stock, &c.), it may be said that there is nothing in the legislative history or in the congressional debates which tend to show that Congress desired to so restrict the language of Section 9. In fact, Senator Copeland several times emphasized the hope that the sale of Re-

cult to construe such a spread between the sale price and the maturity value as a discount. Quite clearly it would not be a discount justifiable for revenue purposes, and to consider it as a discount at all within the meaning of that term as used by legislators would be to open wide the door for any and every kind of a manipulation for ulterior purposes where a statute provides revenue-obtaining machinery on a discount basis. The effect of such an interpretation upon the discount provisions of Federal Reserve legislation is interesting to contemplate.

construction Finance Corporation obligations "will bring back much hoarded money" (75 Congressional Record, 1421). Again at page 1431, Senator Copeland remarked "There are certain features in connection with these bonds (Reconstruction Finance Corporation obligations) making them less desirable as a piece of security than a Government bond. Therefore, to bring out the hoarded money and to find sales for the bonds, there will have to be a rate of interest attractive enough to cause their sale * * *" Similar remarks may be found by Senator Walcott at page 1421 of 75 Congressional Record.

In view of such statements as these, it can not be said with any degree of finality that it was the intention of Congress to prevent the Reconstruction Finance Corporation from selling its obligations for any purpose other than the financing of its usual business.

Summarizes case.

Application of argument: It will be noted that the eighth paragraph (of the R. F. C. proposal to offer notes) provides that the obligations shall be offered for sale "at such price or prices as the corporation may determine, payable in such gold as the Secretary of the Treasury may offer for sale under the Executive order of August 29, 1933, or in gold imported from abroad after the date of this resolution, at the option of the corporation, at such rate as may be from time to time fixed." I assume that the obligations will be offered at a price in money from day to day adjusted to produce the discount from par believed to be sufficient to sell the obligations, payable in gold "at such rate as may be from time to time fixed," which will mean that a certain value in money will be attributed to the gold delivered on any particular day. Conducted in this way, the transaction would comply with the requirements of the statute that the obligations would be sold at a price fixed by the corporation and that the price, while paid in gold, would be measured in terms of money. This brings it clearly within the definitions of a sale given in the preceding section headed "argument."

Conclusion! It is therefore to be concluded that section 9 of the Reconstruction Finance Corporation act permits the sale of the obligations at a price to be measured in gold at a value per ounce fixed by the seller from time to time.

CHAPTER 10 THE ROAD BACK

Page.
195 British-American Tobacco Co. v. Federal Reserve Bank of New York, 104 F.2d 652 (1939); *aff'd,* 105 F.2d 935, *cert. denied,* 308 U.S. 600 (1939).

196   litigation which went on for some years: Alabama Power Co.
       v. Ickes, Federal Emergency Administrator of Public Works,
       et al., 302 U.S. 464 (1938).

197   Case enjoining Tugwell: Township of Franklin, N.J. v.
       Tugwell, Administrator, 85 F.2d 208 (1936).

197   International Ladies' Garment Workers' Union v. Donnelly
       Garment Co., 119 F.2d 892; 121 F.2d 561 (1941).

201   Details of the hearings are taken from: *Hearings before a
       Subcommittee of the Committee on the Judiciary, United
       States Senate* [76th Cong., 1st Sess.], *on the Nomination of
       Felix Frankfurter to be an Associate Justice of the Supreme
       Court,* January 10, 11, 12, 1939 (Washington: U.S. Gov't
       Printing Office, 1939).

215   "The stakes are too enormous": *New York World,* July 13,
       1914.

215   "That [war] is too dreadful": *New York Times,* July 28,
       1914.

216   two speeches . . . one at Yale: The following is the address
       given at the annual dinner of Davenport College of Yale Uni-
       versity on November 28, 1939:

           AN AMERICAN ATTITUDE TOWARD FOREIGN AFFAIRS

       The article "an" in the title of this address, is important.
       What is said here is merely my own imperfect and fallible
       view. It makes no exclusive claim to the patriotic adjec-
       tive.
           Whenever a matter takes on the character of an issue,
       we tend to develop antithetical attitudes toward it. We
       have done so here. One is the hard-boiled or cynical atti-
       tude. Its advocates, it has been said, are desperately ab-
       sorbed in the attempt to keep out of the *last* war. Opposed

to this is the Pilgrims Progress attitude in which some nation, often our own, is cast as Valiant struggling with a
myriad national embodiments of original sin. To both of
these attitudes we may say with Justice Holmes,

"I confess that altruistic and cynically selfish talk seem
to me about equally unreal. With all humility, I think
'whatsoever thy hand findeth to do, do it with thy might'
infinitely more important than the vain attempt to love thy
neighbor as thyself. If you want to hit a bird on the wing,
you must have all your will in a focus, you must not be
thinking about yourself, and, equally, you must not be
thinking about your neighbor; you must be living in your
eye on that bird."

If there ever was a bird on the wing, it is the multifarious
life beyond our shores, which we call foreign affairs. The
first step is to live in our eye on that bird.

It is all too easy to take an episodic view of the world —
to think in terms of pre-war and post-war Europe, or the
Far East before and after 1931, or of Ethiopia or Munich as
turning points, or of New Deal America. We must take a
longer swing to get on our target.

What is the world situation toward which we must take
an attitude? It would certainly be fortuitous if it were the
same today as it was fifty or a hundred or a hundred and
fifty years ago. Yet much of our thinking assumes that
there has been no change. May I suggest the outline of
things present and to come as I see them.

The economic and political system of the Nineteenth
Century, which throughout the world produced an amazing increase in the production of wealth and population,
has been for many years in the obvious process of decline.
The system is deeply impaired. It probably cannot be reestablished in anything approaching its old form, if at all.
The desperate struggles of populations to maintain themselves in the numbers and on something approaching the
standards permitted in the recent past, without vital parts
of the mechanism which made it possible, has made pos-

sible the breeding of disorganization, hatred, war, and tyranny which we are seeing, as bacteria, present but harmless in a healthy organism, may increase to destroy it when it weakens. Not that the old Adam in man has no share of responsibility. I am not saying that morals are a matter of economics, but, rather, that there is high authority for the belief that if we are not led into temptation we may better be delivered from evil.

This Nineteenth Century world economy was far from perfect. It contained within it injustices which demanded correction. Nevertheless, it brought about an enormous increase of the human population of this earth and at the same time a standard of living never before thought possible. In terms of our own country it made possible its material development and the evolution of a social order recognizing (however imperfectly) both the worth of the individual and the unity of society — the freedom of the human spirit and the interdependence of human life.

It is beyond my capacity to trace the causes which have brought about the impairment of this world system. But we can see that certain important factors in its operation are no longer in existence or functioning as they did. We can see that the credits which were once extended by the financial center of London no longer provide the means for the production of wealth in other countries. We can see that the free trade areas, which once furnished both a market of vast importance and a commodities exchange, no longer exist. We can see that British naval power no longer can guarantee security of life and investment in distant parts of the earth and a localization of conflict nearer home. We can see, too, that immigration to the United States is no longer a solution for surplus populations elsewhere.

With credits unavailable, markets gone, and with them the means of obtaining the price of needed new materials, with populations pressing upon restricted resources, the stage was set for the appearance of the totalitarian military state. To some extent it can create the means of production by sweating its people. It can obtain markets and natural resources by successful war. In this program there is no surplus population. But to achieve it, the state must have not only unquestioning obedience, but fanatical adherence. It is not necessary to describe the means by which it achieves both.

This system is the response of Asia and a large part of Europe to the failure of some of the vital mechanisms of the Nineteenth Century world economy. Both the failure and the response constitute those "foreign affairs" toward which we are asked to frame an American attitude.

If this is, in reality, the world condition we face, it seems to me that one conclusion stands clear and inevitable at the outset. We must make ourselves so strong that we shall not be caught defenseless or dangerously exposed in any even possible eventuality. The future is unpredictable. Only one thing — the unexpected — can reasonably be anticipated. In a situation as confused and dangerous as this, the part of wisdom is to be prepared for what may happen, rather than to base our course upon faith in what should happen, or to waste time debating as to what will happen. Here you can be wrong only once. If I may quote Justice Holmes again, "The judgment of nature upon error is death."

I waste no time arguing the metaphysics of defensive as against offensive weapons. Nothing seems to me more foolish than a policy designed to assure that if we must fight, the fighting shall be upon our own territory. I think it clear that with a nation, as with a boxer, one of the greatest assurances of safety is to add reach to power. To do this we need a navy and air force adequate to secure us in both oceans simultaneously and with striking power sufficient to reach to the other side of one of them. We need this force both to secure ourselves, if the disintegration of the world order cannot be checked and the system revised and revived, and also to take an effective part in the attempt to recreate it.

But the providing of the means to support a policy does not provide the policy. A realistic American policy should have two aspects — one we may call the prophylactic side; the other, the therapeutic. One should attempt to check the disintegration of the world, in which our national life and individual lives are rooted, by strengthening the forces opposing disintegration; the other should attempt a cure.

As the President of this University has said, our vital interests do not permit us to be indifferent to the outcome of the present war in Europe — and, may I add, to the present war in Asia. This to my mind is not because of emotional or even moral or ideological sympathy with one side in both of these wars. It is because the consequences of Russo-German and Japanese victories in terms of our own lives are too serious to permit indifference. What we can do is another matter to which I shall come in a moment. I am here saying that we are not indifferent. We are not indifferent because the consequence is — to greater or less degree dependent on the extent of any victory — our internment on this continent and such portion of the one to the south as we can physically control. Here, surrounded by armed and hostile camps, we will have to conduct our economy as best we can and attempt to preserve the security and dignity of human life and the freedom of the human spirit.

This break-up of the world into exclusive areas of armed exploitation administered along oriental lines, would have clear implications in terms of the defense of the great resources of our part of it. One does not have to be a crystal gazer to see complications arising with our neighbors in this hemisphere. It is hardly conceivable that a prudent defense policy would contemplate Canada, Mexico, Central America, the northern part of South America, and the islands of the Caribbean being left open as avenues of attack upon us.

Furthermore, if anything is plain it is that the new technique of attack contemplates the creation of a disaffected element in the population of the country about to receive attention, which will weaken or destroy its will or power to resist. If such an attempt should be made in this country — and indications of the possibility have not been lacking — the destructive consequences to our constitutional guarantees of individual liberty cannot be over-estimated. It is a narrow step from the suppression of activities and speech which constitute a present danger of immediate evil to sweeping away all opposition to the results we want with all our hearts. It is expecting too much to believe that an angry or frightened people would not take it. Once that has been done in a thoroughgoing way and without shame, we have come to the end of the American experiment.

So, I say we are not and cannot be indifferent. What then can we do? We can realize, I think, that we are in the most enviable position of having other people who must of necessity fight the forces which are hostile to us. They must do this to save themselves. We can see to it that those conscripts of necessity have the weapons and supplies with which to fight. Insofar as they weaken those whom we want weakened, we gain. Insofar as they are able to defeat them we gain even more.

If I am told that what I suggest is unneutral and amounts to acts of war, I answer that I am not interested in the words or epithets applied to it. I am interested in the balance sheet of gain and risk to the people of this country. The gain seems plain. The risk, I think, negligible. It would still be negligible if, should it be necessary to the end in view, we furnished more direct aid in the form of naval and air units. On the other hand, the risk would be far too great if it involved sending an army to Europe. Here we would give a real hostage to fortune which would leave us weak and exposed in case the French cannot stay on the Maginot Line and the British on the seas. With our fleet necessarily in the Pacific, we cannot risk another army in Europe.

In the Far East the prophylactic measures take the form

of hindering and creating deterrent hazards to the Japanese domination of Asia and the elimination of the white populations from the South Seas. To state the means by which this can be done requires technical knowledge to which I cannot pretend. One obvious objective is to strengthen resistance to the Japanese and weaken their striking power. Whether it is practicable to get necessary material to the Chinese through cooperation with powers upon their borders and to cut off supplies from the Japanese, I do not know. Neither do I know the risks involved. But practicality and risk are the factors which should govern. Another objective is to create a menace to imperialistic adventure in the South Seas. Naval men can enlighten us as to whether strong bases in the Philippines and Guam are practicable means to this end.

But a mere attitude of negation is not enough. The world order, which is so vital to us, will continue to disintegrate, even without the bludgeoning of revolutionary attack, unless vigorous reconstruction is undertaken. We cannot stand aloof from this effort if we are alive to our own interest. The first step is to awake from the autohypnotic trance induced by repeating that we can take no part in the affairs of a world in which we are one of the most important factors, because our fellow citizens are not willing to do so. We should stop analyzing ourselves — stop Gallup polling ourselves — and start analyzing the needs of our situation and the potentialities of our power. We shall find, I think, that we can make a great and essential contribution to reestablishing the foundations of peace within tolerable costs to ourselves.

If I am right that the progressive deterioration of their conditions of life has been a potent breeder of war among some, at least, of the peoples who are now engaged in it, the problem is to make possible a better life through the ways of peace. We can do much to make this possible. We can, for instance, join with other financially strong nations in making available capital in those parts of Europe which need productive equipment upon condition that Europe does its part to remove obstructions to trade within itself and provide, so far as it can, scope for commerce. We can join in offering a broader market for goods made under decent standards and, in this way, a means of purchasing essential raw materials. We can join in providing a stable international monetary system under which credits can be made and repaid and goods purchased and sold. We can join in removing exclusive or preferential trade arrangements with other areas created by military or financial conquest, agreement, or political connection. We can cease exporting more than we import and spend abroad, and so remove a disturbing influence upon the world economy. We can see to it, and insist as a condition of our help that others do, that the supply of raw materials needed in other parts of the world is not restricted and their price not enhanced through the device of holding undeveloped resources out of production to maintain prices and not for necessary conservation.

It is of course far easier to state these generalities than to give them specific application and to devise the processes for making them effective. This requires far more knowledge and wisdom than I can summon. But man is an ingenious creature once he possesses understanding and the will to act. At present, the lack of understanding and will is our greatest obstacle. Any action, of course, requires a limitation upon our power to act at any time in any way we please on any conception, however erroneous, of our immediate and local interest. It is this so-called impairment of our sovereignty which frightens many of us from the idea of accepting responsibilities in the world essential to make our own position more secure. This, I think, overlooks the fact that no limitations on our freedom of action which we might be willing to accept would equal those which internment on this continent would impose. There is no wisdom in refusing to choose between these alternatives, when, if we do not do so, events will do it for us.

So I offer these three points for the triangulation of an American attitude toward foreign affairs. Make ourselves strong to meet a future which is dark and obscure. Recognize that the further destruction of world order threatens our most vital interests and use and support the peoples who must fight those from whom the offense cometh. Be willing to accept the minor limitations which come from assuming some responsibility for making possible a world of order, to avoid having forced upon us the limitations of a world collapsing about our ears.

"Do you mean those words?": Address before the Annual Convention of the International Ladies' Garment Workers' Union, New York City, June 4, 1940.

Memorandum for Harry Hopkins:
[The first part of this speech is to deal with defense; the second with the social program. The following suggestions are for a transition.]

And so we move swiftly toward marshalling the might of America to guard the New World from the tragic horror which has engulfed the Old World. But let no man tell you that might alone can do this. We must and shall thrust out into the seas bases from which our ships on the water and under the water and in the air will watch day and night to give a warm reception to any ugly customer who may prowl toward this hemisphere. Behind them shall be forts and planes, guns and tanks and men hardened and trained to fight them. But it is not enough to forge the sword. We must have the stout heart and the will to wield it. And to have these we must have a fighting faith in ourselves, in our America, in the future of our democracy.

We are not arming here today, as more than once our fathers armed, against some side show of a dynastic war in Europe. Today we face a violent and fanatical challenge to every article of our democratic faith, to every hope of decent and free life in the hearts of plain men and women to the very conception of human liberty. Those who fling this challenge back it to the limit with every device of military force. But they are armed too with fanatical faith in themselves and in their destiny. And they strike not first with arms but with the very violence of their belief wherever they see the feebleness of doubt.

"Citizens," cried John Milton, whose blind eyes were not darkened to truth, "it is of no small concern what manner of men ye are whether to acquire or to keep possession of your liberty." And, may I add, it is of no small concern what manner of men you choose for the sacred trust of authority.

You have seen great nations go down in ruin and come to the very brink of ruin, because the men who led them could not see the danger that threatened. And they could not see because they were so afraid of the forward surge of common men to stake out new homesteads of freedom in a new age that the dictator did not seem so bad. He made the train run on time. He made industry hum. He broke up the labor movement. He put radicals and dissenters in jail. Above all he was a practical man. You could come to an understanding with him. The people who followed those men are lucky now, if in their misery, they can even mutter their curses above their breath.

But these leaders, who were so blind, had first chosen something worse. They had destroyed the faith of the people in themselves and in their future. They had made democracy a mere word shouted from platforms. They had made it a cloak for things as they were, an excuse to evade stark realities and the bold march forward to meet new problems. They had forgotten — if they ever knew — that democracy as a fighting faith can only live by attack — attack on every front against those burdens and oppressions of the body and spirit which some complacent people believe are the inevitable lot of the common man.

When a hundred and thirty million people answer with

one voice that there is no inevitable lot but a free and good life for every man and woman, and no stopping place upon the road, and no effort too great to make, and no power strong enough to stop them, then democracy lives and there then is no power strong enough to stop its faith. For it is the faith of the common people in their own capacity and will to make their life more decent and more just than any man on earth or any group of men can make it for them. Negatives are not enough; not even those great negatives for which we would give our lives. No impairment of freedom to think and to speak and print our thoughts, to worship, and to be secure in our homes. Without these, freedom cannot live, but without more democracy can never come to birth. And it must be born in each generation anew from the travail of a people bringing forth, not words or generalities, but the living forms which deal with the problems of their time.

That faith has been born again with us. For eight years our people, with a people's government, have gone on from task to task, and no man dares say today that he would undo one thing that you have wrought. The start had to be made with the bare necessities of life: food, shelter, clothing. You have not forgotten those who said that these things were no concern of this nation but only of local charity and poor house. Then together we faced the folly of idle men and idle tools with houses to be built and roads to be laid and streams to be dammed and power to be made, and carried from farm to home. And all these things were fought by men whom you remember — and all these things were done and are being done.

And then you found that the top soil of America, which was here before Columbus and should be here for our children and our children's children, was being exported at starvation prices for wheat and cotton and corn or being washed down every river valley, along which farm mortgages were foreclosed. And you stopped that and gave the farmer the first chance he has had in two decades.

You wrote into our law the right of working men and

women to bargain collectively and you set up machinery
to enforce that right. You turned to the problems of youth
and age. Our youth you and your government took out of
the factory and shop and gave the chance to prepare themselves in body and spirit and mind to take up from you
the moulding of a fuller and brighter day. And for age
you provided security and rest.

You made safe the banks which held your savings. You
stopped once and for all gambling on the stock market
with the lives of people and looting under the name of
finance.

The men who fought you every step of the way still
do not understand what they have seen. They think that
what is only a start in the transition of the democratic
faith into action is an end. Their very words betray them.
They speak of these first steps as objectives. We approve
the objectives, they say, but if you will let us administer
we shall achieve them so much better. These things which
you have done are not objectives; they are only positions
which have been stormed, consolidated, and passed. The
objective which these men can never understand, and on
which they would put the kiss of death, is the ordering
by the common man of his own world.

Once again a generation has begun the forward march.
The outposts have been taken. We are still in the dawn
of the new day. We who believe in democracy have only
begun to fight.

INDEX